THIS WAS HOME

This Was Home

BY

HOPE SUMMERELL CHAMBERLAIN

CHAPEL HILL
THE UNIVERSITY
OF NORTH CAROLINA
PRESS

Copyright, 1938, by
The University of North Carolina Press

Dedicated to the memory of
my friend
William Kenneth Boyd, Historian,
This book about the State he loved

CONTENTS

Part One

I.	The Yadkin River	1
II.	"Gold is Chancy Stuff"	10
III.	A Young Doctor from Eastern Carolina	20
IV.	And the Doctor's Wife from Chapel Hill	30
V.	A New Home in Salisbury	39
VI.	A Small-town Neighborhood	49
VII.	Doctors and Patients in the Forties	60
VIII.	About Railroads and Taxes	70
IX.	"Her Own Bright Spirit"	83
X.	Changing Weather	95
XI.	"Time of the War"	107
XII.	After the Surrender	122

Part Two

XIII.	I Come to Live in Salisbury	137
XIV.	I Find Things Interesting	147
XV.	On Home Levels	156
XVI.	Going Places and Learning Things	168
XVII.	Bread and Butter (with Imagination)	184
XVIII.	Two More Years in Old Salisbury	198
XIX.	Mountain Trails of Blowing Rock	211

CONTENTS

XX.	An Old-time Girl's School in Hillsboro	221
XXI.	A Year at "Miss Baldwin's"	231
XXII.	No Thoroughfare	248
XXIII.	Doing the Next Thing	261
XXIV.	Varieties in Salisbury	270
XXV.	The Seamy Side of the Home Town	281
XXVI.	A Yankee Courtship	291
XXVII.	New York State Honeymoon	307
XXVIII.	Southwards, Toward Home	327

PART ONE

"And the gold of that land is good."—Genesis 2:12

I

THE YADKIN RIVER

REGARDING HISTORY, I steadfastly believe that it should be constructed as much as possible out of chronicles of everyday life, and that, if too much depersonalized, it will lose all its color of reality and become dry and faded, like that arid historical paragraph criticized by the Duck, in *Alice in Wonderland*. And I, too, enjoy finding that an abstract "it" refers to something living, even if my interest, like the Duck's, is concerned with small things. No "drum and trumpet" history for me. Few parades, and fewer shoutings. Who can tell what is of final importance, and what is unessential? As one of the older American authors wrote long ago, "The axis of the earth sticks out visibly through the center of each town or city," and, I should like to add, out of the heart of every smallest community as well.

Several writers have been moved of late to symbolize the ever-flowing, ever-changing story of the past under the figure of a river, a simile as true as it is trite. Speaking quite literally, this chronicle will begin with a river and will tell of a region, a town, a people, as they appeared to the mind of an eager child. And when the child grows older and sees more of the world, the seeing eyes and the mind will be the same.

We always called it "The River," as if in all the world there was but one. When first I began to know it, the same low-lying channel restrained its tawny current as when, more than a hundred years before I was born, the wagons of the first settlers came plunging down its northern bank with locked wheels. The river was always colored reddish-yellow by the soil of its bed, and sometimes it ran thick as soup when heavy rains swelled its volume. Always it has been a stream capable of staging magnificent freshets, with muddy waters that hurled and plucked at the arches of the highway bridge. From the height of this bridge may still be seen the ruined piers of two former bridges destroyed in years past by the angry stream. But in moderate seasons it is commonplace enough. When I was a child it looked much the same, but in the century passing before I saw it the country all along its course had been tamed and settled, and remains today a fertile, pleasantly rolling farming country, which must once have been thick with woods of oak and hickory. The substance of the soil, deeply tinctured by the iron which is one of the elemental ingredients of it, varies in intensity of color from a warm red to a luminous orange or to the somber russet of dried blood. This soil, although stubborn and tough in texture, yields good crops and affords the rootage preferred by a dozen varieties of oak trees. In wet weather it will melt into a morass of sticky mud which stains like red paint.

Our Yadkin River in North Carolina, makes a slow curve from northwest to southeast, holding the county of Rowan in its embrace. From the southeastern corner, the stream flows on, broadening as it goes, until it enters South Carolina, where the name is changed to the "Great Pee Dee." Not always has there been a bridge by which the river could be crossed near town. Long ago there was only a ferry. In horse-and-buggy days, when I used to ride with my father out to the river and down the sloping bank to the level of the water, we would always wait a moment, the horses' feet sunk in the damp, oozy sand of the margin, to listen to the lapping current. On the far side of the stream a pigmy ferryman could be seen moving about his cabin, his flatboat tied ready at the landing.

With hands cupped around the mouth, Father must call, "Coo-e-e!" long and loud like a trumpet. Even then, if the wind blew from the wrong quarter, our man might not hear,

THE YADKIN RIVER

but he would be certain to see us at last. Then, shoving the ferryboat leisurely over, setting his pole against the river bottom and walking backward to push, he would cross to us. "Old Frank," our steady horse, would understandingly step on board, although had he been a skittish animal he would have been taken out of the shafts and held firmly by the bridle.

The crossing of the river was smooth and silent, the best part being the place equidistant from either bank, where you might look upstream to a wide curve and downstream to another. The river there resembled a lake—a good big one if you had not seen many lakes. Father would chat with the ferryman, first about the river. Was it rising or falling?—and then about his fishing—did he catch any "red horses" in his snatch-net this morning? And, if he had, we should like some on the return trip to take home to Mother. Naturally, I must once have asked him, "What are red horses?" and Father explained, "Big fishes, to cook for dinner." And on one especial day the ferryman replied, "Ain't got no red hosses today, but if the little gal wants ter see that big ole gar-pike I found in the net this mornin', thar he is!"

So he showed me, in a little pond where he kept his fish walled in with stones at the river's brim, a long, slender, villainous-looking fellow flapping about, having a mouth split well back to divide his long snout and make room for a double row of vicious teeth. There used to be a proverb in Rowan, "Mean as gar-broth." Some hungry man must once have cooked a gar-pike to find out.

From the Yadkin it is six miles southward to Salisbury, the town where was our home. Nobody knows now how it came to be named for a cathedral town in Old England—perhaps by some homesick immigrant; or as has been plausibly suggested, because our high rolling lands with open spaces resemble somewhat the region of Salisbury in the old country.

While there are many Salisburys set here and there about the United States, ours, here in North Carolina, is one of the first named.

"Did any Indians ever live 'round here, before the white people came?" I asked Father on one of those long jogging rides which allowed time for so many questionings. And he replied, "They tell that long ago, before people settled in here, there used to be an Indian village of the Saponas by the Trading Ford of Yadkin River, but to be certain, you had better ask Mother."

Now Mother invariably knew things, and she liked to tell you, but with Father you discussed them, and had the pleasure of piecing his bits of knowledge together with your own. Mother, being asked, repeated to me the musical names of the Tuscaroras and Cherokees, tribes who once hunted over our hills but who had gone northward before the middle of the eighteenth century when settlers began to come thickest. An Indian trail there surely had been, by which the first traders were guided south, for the Indians had known how to establish the most practicable route. This road crossed the Yadkin at the Trading Ford, where the great river spread out and lay so shallow that at most times it could be easily passed on stepping-stones.

In my childhood there were two separate sides to the County, outside the town. To the east and south there were settlements composed solely of Germans from Pennsylvania, the "Dutch" as we inaccurately called them. Over to the north and west of Salisbury, almost everyone had a Scotch-Irish name and was a Presbyterian. Besides these stocks, there were a few English, who drifted in singly and became the more influential citizens of the town. Among the Pennsylvanians who were not Germans came young Daniel Boone with his parents, about 1750, and in Rowan County he married his wife. It was in Salisbury that Boone met Richard Henderson, and together they became interested in land schemes. Boone moved westward after the ending of the French and Indian War. He explored Tennessee with a view to its settlement, and for years he and Henderson were associated in such undertakings.

From the Main Street of Salisbury, there can be seen a blue lump or hillock on the horizon to the southeast, which is called "Dunn's Mountain." This has been for me all my life a fascinating landmark, although it is but a dwarfish mountain after all. It is a sudden granite knoll, which must have emerged like a gigantic bubble from the primordial rock-substance while all was still plastic. Soil has gathered on its stony head, roots of trees have found anchorage in seams of the rock, but it remains one solid mass of excellent building stone, which in later days has been much quarried. This mountain is well out in the "Dutch" side of the County. I remember the striking geology of the locality, with flat surfaces of bare rock and boulders in the fields; and I also remember the excellent peaches the Dutch farmers who lived "out in the rocks" had for sale every summer.

I cannot recall anything of intimate acquaintance concerning the German side of town. These people liked to keep to themselves. I knew the early and excellent granite buildings here and there, the "Old Stone House," dated 1755, the "Organ Church," so called from the organ built in colonial times by a man named Steigerwalt, and the "Lower Stone Church."

Where there were Germans there were Lutherans. The first church ever built in Salisbury, only twelve years or so after the town was named, was Lutheran. It was no longer standing when I knew "The Old Lutheran Graveyard" as a lovely place in a dreary part of town. This had a high brick wall, shutting out the cindery disorder of the railroad yards outside, but within, all was mossy marbles, brick-laid paths, trees, grass, and peacefulness. That was more than half a century ago.

In the Scotch-Irish neighborhood we had personal friends, and often I have been to their homes. They had always been fighters, these Scotch-Irish; almost all had forbears concerned in the Revolution. They liked to tell of King's Mountain, and of that memorable 2nd of February when General Greene went through Salisbury on his way to the Battle of Guilford Courthouse, giving Cornwallis the slip—the time the rivers took part in the campaign, our river and the Catawba, next south of us. Both had gone rampaging into a freshet just in the nick of time to protect Greene and retard Cornwallis. Over and over I have heard the story of the scout overtaken by the British at Dunn's Mountain, who rode his horse straight through Michael Braun's great stone house, leaping it from the rear doorway down to the "branch" at the bottom, escaping along the creek. The gashes of the British broadsword, so they said, were long to be seen on the sturdy doorjamb.

The dormer-windowed house where Cornwallis had lodged when in Salisbury was torn down forty years before my time, but still Miss Christine Beard could tell how he and the cruel Tarleton cursed and swore because the Yadkin was up, with Greene safe on the far side. And along with these tales would be told, with a snicker, how the beaver hat of the last of the royal governors was fished out of the river after all was over. The royal governor must have been there, or thereabouts, to lose it off his head, with his name and entitlements plainly written inside; but nobody had paid him any mind!

By no means was it forgotten, in my childhood, whose folks had been Tories and whose had fought with General Davie. Memories are long in such quiet places.

A short distance out of Salisbury to the northwest, there used to be a very large millpond, covering a full square mile of land. This had been made by, and belonged to one John Frohock, county clerk and wealthiest man of the frontier county. His money was gained by milling, and by seeing and taking the first chance to buy in all the very best farm land. He was an old man at the time of the Revolution and, of course, a Tory. Tradition tells of his entertaining distinguished guests, Lord Rawdon, for instance. Cornwallis was fabled to have caught the chills at Frohock's.

It is certain that malaria, always a curse of new-cleared land, hung about this great pond and was said to produce "yellow chills," sometimes called "Frohock's chills." Every summer one or two of the Frohock Negroes died of "the fever," and people chose to consider this a judgment on Frohock, the wicked, grasping official. In the present tender-minded epoch, the feelings of the Negroes might be considered, and so spoil the moral of the story. The miasma must have been due to the mosquitoes which swarmed and sang over the shallow water in August drouth; it continued long after the Revolution to be a scourge to the surrounding territory. I can remember seeing how tall and dark grew the corn on the site of Frohock's old pond, just after it had been drained.

Then there were stories of the Hessians. Some thousands of them, left to shift for themselves, settled here and there throughout the colonies after the surrender at Yorktown. In Rowan it was still customary, when I was a child, to shout at your stubborn cow or unruly pig, "You old Hessian!"

An old lady told me of one of these unwanted men. Once a Hessian deserter wandered forlorn by a cabin at the edge of a clearing. He saw a girl alone, spinning at her flax wheel. This stirred the memory of home in him. Grinning amiably, the fellow gently lifted the band from her wheel with his stick, and as they knew no word of each other's language, they could only laugh aloud together. This was repeated time after time, until it ended finally in an elopement, the couple slipping away into the "back settlements" to avoid the girl's angry father. And when the story had gone thus far, my aged friend would say, "And that man was my great-grandfather, and he made a good husband, too!"

During my father's earlier experience as a medical man in Salisbury, there came a fine, thrifty old German named Fischer to settle his bill. Leafing over the ledger to find the account, the Doctor saw several headed by the name "Fischer," and finally asked, "Gottlieb, what kin to you is John Fischer down on south fork of Yadkin River?"

"Ach, py Gott, *no* kin at all to *me!* He's—he's a nichts— He's a Hesse-Fischer!" And Gottlieb stamped out, his round face as red and angry as the sun in a fog.

There were stories current of a few "people you could read of in books," who had passed through our little world. Washington was in town for one night in his tour of the South. Moreover, as he came into town, he stopped his carriage at a farmhouse and asked Betsy Brandon for hoecake and buttermilk. I believed this story, because I played with Betsy Brandon's great-granddaughter, and she assured me it really happened. Andrew Jackson, after whom so many men were named, had studied law in Salisbury. The old office building where he lived was standing in the corner of the front yard where Mrs. Boyden lived. Mother said that when he was here he had been a wild, mischievous young scamp, the sort of boy of whom nobody would be apt to prophesy anything good.

It is a question how soon the idea of a world outside, different from our own, comes of itself into a child's mind. To me, of course, domestic ways which seemed later to be quaint, and which seem now to be interesting because they belong to real antiquity, were unquestioned—the only way life could possibly be carried on. Mother's housewifery was better than most. She had a big cooking-stove, and did not use an open fireplace, as many did. She did not have a whole week's baking done at once out under a tree in the yard, as the country women did, in great outdoor brick bake-ovens. But to the end of her life she preferred to bake her fruitcakes in the hearth-ovens, and wonderful cakes they were. She knew how to cure meat, how to make sausage and liverwurst; she put up great crocks of sun-preserves. She was interested in the making of quilts for bed-covering. She must have owned a dozen of those home-woven wool-and-cotton bedspreads with traditional names: patterns with such pretty names as "Whig-rose," "Butterfly," and "Blazing-star," made by weavers' cards brought in the first place from Ireland. Mother could spin, for I have seen her do it. One of the neighbors taught her when all handicrafts were revived during the Civil War. The use of vegetable dye-stuffs did not entirely disappear until commercial dyes grew very cheap.

My personal memory begins in the middle seventies. It was the usual practice to lay to the undeniable poverty of after-the-war, all such customs as we knew to be behind the times. But it comes to me how much all domestic affairs were still conducted like the model established in the beginning of the century. A child could not know how far the sap had gone down in the tree by that time, nor how truly it was a time of exhaustion, a time of waiting, of inner transition. It will be better to account for this condition, which begins at length to be not so much of a misfortune as we used to think. How did North Carolina fall so far behind the procession that nothing could be done about it?

II

"GOLD IS CHANCY STUFF"

My habitual reading of all the printed records available has convinced me how inevitably a narrowing process had been going on in my home county for several generations before my time. At the close of the Revolutionary period, North Carolina was as safe a wager for prosperity as any one of half a dozen frontiers. Colonizers had poured in to take up her cheap Piedmont lands. But after the beginning of the new century the best settlers began to go west instead of south. Loose-footed moving, a frontier habit, received a mighty impetus in the time of Jefferson's presidency, when Louisiana was purchased, and it did not afterwards slacken. The opening of the Cherokee lands in Georgia and of the state of Florida tempted away many of our native-born adventurers, while the Erie Canal was the conduit by which, a few years later, the eager pioneers of the whole nation began to drain away across the North.

From North Carolina it was not easy to move west in a direct line. The Blue Ridge had but three practicable gaps in the state, and these admitted only to hundreds of miles more of the same kind of broken mountain country. Manifestly, the easiest way was the best way and the North Carolina born, in quest of a path westward, scattered up and down from Missouri to the Gulf, while people born in any other state were conspicuously lacking in North Carolina.

Thomas Jefferson's idea of a republic of independent farmers might be hard to surpass in promise of true happiness, but overnight all the development of our nation had changed, had grown in volume and had been commercialized. In the first third of the nineteenth century all our come-outers and adventurers drifted away from the state because there was no prospect of thriving there by trade, or manufacture, or land schemes. The long-settled western counties could only grow more reposeful and sink into drowsy inactivity as the century grew older.

Not that our citizens thought they were permanently out of the stream of progress. The more thoughtful of them were concerned, but not hopeless. Our most distinguished townsman, Charles Fisher, who owned and edited the *Western Carolinian*, who was our representative in Congress, who was a personal intimate of the great John C. Calhoun and favored his policies, especially as they recommended internal improvements all over the South. At Fisher's invitation, Calhoun visited Salisbury and enlisted the support of Western North Carolina in his campaign for presidential nomination on a ticket of internal improvement. Andrew Jackson decided to run for a second term himself, was elected, and his new term was vexed with one of those nation-wide panics so recurrent in the United States. Calhoun broke with the administration. Party alignment changed. Van Buren succeeded Jackson. Then in 1840 the Whigs came shouting into power, with the picturesque "Tippecanoe and Tyler Too" presidential campaign. This was an orgy of sentiment and cheering, without one idea behind it save that there must be a change. For months, log cabins on wheels went trundling about, distributing free hard cider to the thirsty populace, because, forsooth, Harrison had once lived in a log cabin and was said to prefer the frontier beverage. This was one of the first of those naïve attempts to turn back the flight of time, which so regularly come about. Impressed by all this shouting, not making definitions, but slow to move and hard to turn, North Carolina voted Whig with Henry Clay at more than one subsequent election.

The ancient jealousy which had prevailed before the Revolution between the western and the eastern halves of the state, was by no means dead. Even as late as the Civil War—some say even later than that—it remained a bar to mutual understanding. Just at this point there was so much lack of solidarity that government was difficult.

I have heard it asked why my state should be divided into so many counties, a round hundred of them; and I have heard it answered that this was a favorite strategy of the West in the long struggle for advantage. A petition would be brought alleging the greater convenience of some new center of local government. A village might aspire to become the county seat of something, and whatever party might be in power could thereby dispense just so much more local patronage. Then, if a "favorite son" of the East could be complimented in the naming of the new county, it was practicable to pile up the Assembly's vote for it. A simple expedient, only one of the political works and wiles long understood, and the result is easy to read.

There came a time at last when the constitutional convention so long overdue, so long held back by conservatism, could be summoned to consider the accumulated grievances of one section against the other, of class against class. This body came together in 1835, and while it did not wipe out, by any means, all the divisional jealousy existing for so many years of habitual dissension, it did accomplish a good deal that was needed.

While history outside the state and within it had been running thus, there had broken in upon our especial town and county a discovery of gold. This brought a small wave of prosperity locally, though it did not much affect the state at large. The finding of gold, even in the moderate quantities actually present in Rowan, was a chance that galvanized the community. It relaxed the restraint which the panic had put on all buying and selling and started things revolving again.

"GOLD IS CHANCY STUFF"

A little gold poured in to prime the financial flow would restore credit just so far. For forty years and more it had been known that there was gold here and there in the Piedmont, mostly in grains speckled through veins of quartz. Sometimes gold ore was in streaks of this sort, sometimes in pockets, sometimes in sands washed down by a freshet. A few years before this time, several large nuggets of almost pure gold had been picked up almost on the southern boundary of the state. The first of these was shown to a watchmaker in a near-by town, who could tell nothing about the "fancy rock," as it was called. Because it was so heavy, the finders used it to keep open their front door. A passing stranger saw it and bid for it the munificent sum of three dollars, and they let him take it away. This particular nugget was said to be as large as a "tailor's goose" (a good-sized flatiron), irregular in shape and of course very heavy. Several more nuggets not quite so large were found after that, enough to set the whole country around to digging and scrabbling.

In Rowan County a series of veins of quartz were traced out, and of these the richest and most continuous were twelve miles south of Salisbury at a place soon named Gold Hill. There was never any large area of gold field. Ledges were narrow; veins from their first discovery were seen to be intermittent. Gold is chancy stuff, a fact known just as well of the great California bonanzas.

Such was the change, such the gleam of prosperity which awakened the old town out of its lethargy. By 1844, the population of Salisbury had nearly doubled. Gold Hill had become a thriving village of never less than eighteen hundred people, including those who prospected, those who worked down in the mine, and those who profited by selling supplies to both.

The Gold Hill veins which cropped out at the surface had to be followed far into the depths of the ground, for they descended at a steep angle; and perpendicular shafts had to be driven down to cross the gold-bearing strata at a long slant. Before 1844, a good many shafts had been sunk. In going deeper to reach the ore, there came a depth where the cost of tunneling and timbering overtook the profits and made further digging no longer pay.

Between 1840 and the Civil War, wages were paid to a good many miners, who spent their money in the County. Besides this, farmers had the habit of adding to their incomes by placer mining, cradling the sands along creek beds when farm work might be slack. Also it paid them to rewash the tailings of Gold Hill Mine for a percentage of the gain, and anyone could do this in any spare time. Salisbury, because of the gold-mining, was in 1844 not only more populous but growing more expansive socially. By 1856, two million dollars of Rowan County gold had gone to the mint, and for the year 1857 the sum of $136,000 is recorded.

In the year 1844 the talk of new railroads and of surveying them had superseded all the old planning towards deepening and straightening rivers to make arteries of commerce, which had once sounded plausible. In Raleigh, the great celebration of the completion of the Raleigh and Gaston Railroad had taken place in 1840, and a few more miles had been added since then. Men were discussing railroad extension, perhaps as we today discuss air-mail lines to cross the ocean. But as yet no improvement in transportation had reached as far inland as Salisbury.

The bands of wagoners whose regular coming and going had been a boasted advantage of Salisbury were busier than ever, although their time was growing short. Their trade would die if a railroad was built, and the daily stage, which made two full days of the trip to Raleigh, would fall into the discard.

Meanwhile the town was gay again; the sporting men had fast horses and raced them; the ladies of Salisbury walked the streets in voluminous hooped dresses and wore on their heads those "Leghorn flat" hats which cost ten or twelve dollars each, untrimmed, at Richmond or Charleston.

By this time the Democratic *Western Carolinian* had given place to a Whig newspaper, the *Carolina Watchman*.

Even in this small community, there existed several well defined ideas of the way to live, the art of getting the best out of life. For example, the English fashion, which was like the Virginia ideal—easy, assured, self-sufficient, traditional—was inherited by some who thought this the only sensible way—a way very definite for all its apparent freedom. In such style lived the few pre-Revolutionary families who felt themselves to be leaders in politics and in social life as well. They loved good living and manly sport. They sent their sons to the University, whether the boys did anything there or not. They were proud, high-spirited, and punctilious in manners.

Another group came into town at a somewhat later date. They had a mixture of German heredity, some deriving from the Mocksville neighborhood, where a group of German settlers had been educated people. These had the German home-loving and thrifty ways, joined with the desire for more social prestige. The Beards, a purely German family, lived in Salisbury from the beginning and intermarried with the first set, for Lewis Beard, son of John Lewis, first comer, married the daughter of John Dunn, who inherited his property; and their daughter Christina married Charles Fisher, the elder, who was brought up in the country but moved to Salisbury to become a leading citizen, editor, lawyer, and representative in Congress. His son, Charles Fisher, was educated first at Yale and then at the new University of Virginia. He married a Caldwell, whose mother was a Henderson.

The third group, and the most numerous, had come into town from the various Scotch-Irish neighborhoods. Usually holding to Presbyterian tradition, they maintained a far more puritanic view of life than the other groups. Their ideal was austere, concerned with plain living and moral strictness. They were liable to be narrow, insisting on *thou shalt* and *thou shalt not*, and laying burdens too heavy to be laid, from the outside, on careless human nature. But these knew what they wanted and were astute in getting it. Their political power was great, and from them must have been derived the old saying, "When North Carolina votes strong, she votes agin' something."

The Scotch-Irish esteemed classical education and sent their sons sometimes to the University but more often to Davidson College, after the Presbyterians started it a score of miles to the southwest. They also maintained the schools in town, better schools than were commonly found in the North Carolina of that period. They had a male academy which was said to have inherited the charter of old "Liberty Hall," given before the University of North Carolina was founded. There was also a school for "little girls and young ladies," with some boarding pupils, housed in a dignified Georgian mansion standing alone in the center of a whole square of the town, shaded by spreading elms which had been planted in rows. Both these buildings are still standing.

I have seen the "Rolls of Honor" printed in the town paper, with names of children whom I knew as very old folk. It was said they received careful teaching there.

In 1839-1840 the first attempt was made to set up a free public school system in North Carolina. At least one-third of the adult whites were totally illiterate, and it was high time to remedy this. As a public policy the measure failed in Rowan because of a medley of causes. One of these was the indifference to any formal education at all, on the part of the German half of the County, but it would be of interest, even now, to know how many of the Scotch-Irish voted for the school bill. The Germans were skillful at handicraft, but they saw no need for schools. At Salem, only fifty miles away, the German-speaking Moravians set them an example of an industrial community with German folkways, and with education into the bargain. Besides the Moravians' primary school and academy for boys, the earliest school for girls in the state was in Salem. But from Rowan very few girls of German parentage ever attended this.

Beneath and around these distinguishable groups were the greater part of the people, who must work with their hands, without slaves to help them, and who attempted nothing beyond the day's work. By the slow development of better individuals here and there, some rose from these ranks, saw opportunity, founded independence. The texture of our society was called democratic, but, by this time, with its whole warp and woof were woven the custom and the tenet of definitely favored slave labor. Any newspaper printed in the South of this time will give you the methods of handling slaves, of buying and selling them, of advertising for and overtaking the frequent runaways; and, just as everywhere else in the South, this business was carried on in Salisbury. Trips were made to Charleston to purchase Negroes directly from slave ships. The descendants of some of these, as late as my own knowledge, remained recognizable among colored people who had lived more generations in America. Slavery as an institution was a thing unquestioned, although the numbers of black folk were not so great as they were on the broad eastern plantations.

Details regarding one's own father and mother are personally interesting. About one's grandparents it is pleasant to speculate. It is a happy chance if anything is known of those who lived neighbors to one's people, or if details about the friends they respected and liked can be rescued from oblivion. Here and there will be a little story or a trait of character. There is no accounting for what is caught in the memory. A child, listening to home comment, recalls it later, but does not give it the proper emphasis, perhaps remembering a passing remark as a sober judgment.

That great pit of silence which will soon engulf us all, contains most of the persons who made up the activity of Salisbury about 1840. Of the people who were walking its streets in 1844, when my parents came there to live, very few are today more than names on a list. Beside scanty records that exist, I will carefully lay my memory to recall here and there a personality. Somebody's eyes have to see what is to be seen. Until I can get myself born, and can have proper eyesight of my own, I must trust to a less definite vision by means of my parents' eyes. If some stickler for the true truth and nothing fanciful shall choke my trickle of narrative with some stony fact, I shall say, That's a pity, for my version of the story sounds so convincing I do hate to give it up! I declare on my own behalf that this is a sincere attempt to remember aright and to prove the memory as best I may—but do not expect of me any sworn statement, any assertion of perfect accuracy!

Let us begin again, then, almost a hundred years ago, with Frohock's millpond. I have told you about that. In those good old times malaria was as common in Salisbury as teething, while typhoid fever was a yearly visitation of Providence without known cause or remedy. In other disorders, unsanitary habits and poor drainage took toll. The cumbersome dress of the women, the habits of incessant tippling even among the best men, the quantities of pork consumed in an almost subtropical climate half the year, and the strange dislike (left over from the day of forest pasturage and mysterious milk sickness) of the free use of milk—all these things combined to make the town of Salisbury unhealthy. It was a pleasant town, but the death rate was high for old and young.

My father was a young physician, just graduated from

the University of Pennsylvania Medical School and ready to hang out his shingle and go to work. He selected Salisbury for his practice for two good reasons. First, he thought it the most hopefully developing town along the Piedmont; and, second, he understood that another physician was greatly needed there.

Just at this time, one old doctor, related to half the County, a man who until now had been able to discourage and disparage any younger man who tried to settle under his shadow, had been obliged by growing infirmity to give up all his country practice.

It does seem a bold thing and a risky, as we see it, for a young fellow to begin the practice of medicine first-off, immediately upon graduating from medical college; but in those days, no long interne-apprenticeship was thought of or expected.

III

A YOUNG DOCTOR FROM EASTERN CAROLINA

MY FATHER was born of the people, close to the real foundation of society where Adam delved and Eve span. There could be, then, no question over his lack of crest and pedigree or other rag of family prestige, and no expectation that he would be what is called an aristocrat. He did not need anything of the sort to witness to his quality. He just was himself. He was North Carolina born, in that part of the northeastern corner of the state which borders on Virginia and shares with it a portion of the Great Dismal Swamp.

Although, as often happens, he never lived continuously at home after he once left it for college, yet to the end of his days he loved to maintain that he ever remained at heart and by sentiment an eastern man; that he loved best the monotonous level landscapes and low-lying country of his boyhood; that in his dreams he always saw again its far-extended fields, with the nearest furrow aiming straight, like the flight of an arrow, toward some tall pine, or moss-bedraped cypress in the woods of the horizon line. He would affirm that, to his mind, the overgrown, swampy approach to some slow river, where the current was turned backwards twice each day by the tide, was better by far than all the steep banks and hasty water of our turbid streams. Sand, he would insist, is better for all uses than red clay except only when you want to make bricks. All his life he kept up this whimsical pretense. It could not have been long before he actually became so deeply rooted and fibered in Rowan County, and so absorbed by what he found to do there, that he loved it as home. But out of pure affection for the place he had chosen he required himself to speak of it with a mock depreciation. It was one of his odd ways.

Father was an only son, whose parents, as I have indicated, did not belong to an "old southern family" but to the lower middle class. The simpler folk of the southern states had in that time and place but two alternatives. They must thrive and attain the owner class, or they must sink to the status of the poor whites. Thus was eastern society divided, and this was the great reason why the Quakers could not bring themselves to remain there, subject to such limitation.

Of my father's mother I have no picture, real or imaginary. She was born in the south of England, in Dorset or Devonshire; and quite young she came over with two elder brothers. She married Grandfather Summerell soon after. Nobody has ever hinted in my hearing that she ever told anything of her old English home, or said just where it was or what might have been her family or breeding. When she came, she was able to read and write, and from her girlhood she had been taught housewifely accomplishments. Her two older brothers drifted out of sight, although she added the name of one of them to my father's given names. My grandfather, when he married her, had recently come to North Carolina from just over the Virginia line, out of a general region where there still live excellent people bearing his somewhat unusual surname. Neither of the young folk was of age when they were married.

It was always my grandfather's fancy to say of his own people, "I'm the best man I know of my stock, and as for the rest, let 'em rest!" Then he would add, as if by afterthought, "Except my mother, who taught me what is right." Of this mother we knew nothing except her name, which was Ruth, and the fact that she died when her son was seventeen, and that immediately after her burial he ran away from home by her injunction. Like almost any poor farmer lad of his day and place, he could read but little and write not at all, but his wife, being better schooled, at once began to teach her young husband. He was eager to learn, and afterwards he found someone to help him to use the arithmetic which came so readily to his mind. By equipping himself with this elementary knowledge, he was ready to become the overseer of a plantation, for his organizing ability was of the best.

All through the agricultural records in the South dating before the Civil War, recurs again and again the insistent demand for competent overseers; for any such men as were able to carry on a large farm, qualified to manage Negroes, and capable of rendering clear and honest accounts to an employer. A man of such qualifications was sure of employment, sure of being given inducements to better his condition. My grandfather had a natural genius for tilling the land; he loved to keep his dusky field hands sleek and hearty and in good humor with him and with each other; for all that, however, he knew how to keep them hard at work. He was kind but strict. His efficiency became known, and in the end he was made a sort of general farm manager for a wealthy man who owned a number of plantations.

At such employment money could be saved, and the opportunities for selecting and buying good land are easy to estimate. Grandfather John and Grandmother Mary systematically saved every dollar they could spare, so that in the end they could leave off the overseer job and set up for themselves on a plantation of their own. The new home was across the Roanoke River, some miles southeast of Weldon, and a move was made so far into what they considered up-country because the wife insisted upon this. She rightly attributed the loss of several young children of their early marriage years to living in the unhealthy swampy country farther east.

My grandfather was remarkable for his successful adjustment to his niche in life. He does not seem to have yearned for things impossible, but to have rather concerned himself with immediate conditions and needs. He seems to have been very active and to have enjoyed it. His methods were thorough, thrifty, and systematic, making a pleasant home out of the plainest of farmhouses by its cleanliness, order and perfect repair. His portrait shows a long oval face, keen, with penetrating hazel eyes and large well-shaped nose. Below the detached, appraising look of the eyes, a smiling mouth seems made for the savoring of the tasty things of life. He looks well satisfied, calm, and very astute—all characteristics of his nature. He was a tall man, always keeping that spare, supple build so common in Americans of his generation. Somebody has told me that my grandmother grew very stout in her later life. She was primarily a housewife, and a skillful weaver. She had a plantation to feed and clothe. Solomon's virtuous woman had to toil no more steadily or more efficiently than she found needful.

These two agreed that their only son must have as good a chance in life as anybody's boy. They would send him to a good school, and after that to the University; but while he was small, and because they saw every day how worthless the planter's young sons might become with too many Negroes to order about, they resolved that their John must be required to work, as well as to learn his book. So as soon as he was big enough, Father was required to "chop" cotton and to cultivate it, not too continuously, it is true, but obediently. Each night he found himself no exception to his mother's rule and requirement that everybody on the plantation from the Master to the small pickaninny should take the seed out of his portion of cotton before he lay down to sleep. Besides this it was his duty to reel off the endless lengths of spun yarn and make ready the warps. Only by the most regular, systematic work could the looms be kept running and the plantation clothed.

If at any time an old-field school was opened in the neighborhood, John and his sister must go. He turned out to be a bright scholar. If he ever played hookey it went badly with him, for his father was hard to deceive. On one occasion, a note from the teacher reporting an escapade of this sort was being taken home by his sister. John snatched it on the way and tore it across. Grandfather, riding that way, saw the scattered papers, and, picking them up, fitted them together. For the moment he said nothing, but the next day he rode by the schoolhouse, and calling his son out of school gave him a keen rating. Then he finished by punishing him soundly with his riding-whip. The boy did not rebel at the chastisement. I have heard my father say that this thrashing, and particularly what went before it, set him thinking as he had not done before and helped to make a man of him.

Besides the unanimity and good judgment of his parents regarding him, Father had no unusual advantages and almost no social contacts, for he was suspended, as it were, between two definite levels or classes in society. His parents did not allow him to play away from home with the neighbor boys, and they did not choose to have him follow after the sons of the richer planters as a tolerated inferior; so there were very few young companions in his life. He and his sister stayed at home in the plantation dwelling—a long, low, dormer-windowed house with huge holly trees in front. Their playmates, when they had them, were the Negro children. Grandfather was a fox-hunter, and gave his son a horse. When he thought the boy's seat in the saddle was secure enough, he would take John to the meets sometimes. There was one slave lad who belonged to my father after the usual custom, and with this "Dorsey" he sometimes slipped away to the cabins at night and heard versions of those pleasant fables the Negroes were in the habit of telling, all about Br'er Rabbit, and Br'er Fox and the Tar Baby. With Dorsey also he hunted and fished, but life was not idle for either of them.

There were no churches anywhere near. Formerly there had been many Quakers in that section, but of late they had been moving in numbers to Indiana, to escape the implications of slavery. My grandparents never went to church, and I do not know what church they preferred, except that they took no stock in the "hard-shell" Baptists of a crossroad six miles away. On Sundays and in rainy-day leisures, it was Grandfather's habit to read. He owned three volumes beside the almanac. Two of these made up a leather-bound Plutarch, purchased at somebody's vendue, and the third was a stout family Bible sold to him by a peddler. He used to plod slowly through these books and explain one by the other —confuting the Baptists out of the scriptures, interpreted in the light of Plutarch's *Lives*.

After the elementary terms of the old-field school, young John was sent to Halifax, North Carolina, to attend a classical academy. He would rise before daylight to ride over for a week or two at a time, taking with him a Negro companion to lead his horse back home. Grandfather did not intend to have a saddle-horse left at Halifax at his disposal to tempt him from his studies. On Friday afternoons the horse would be brought back for his return home. In cotton-picking time, in the fall of the year, it was Grandfather's custom to keep him at home and make him useful for a few days at a time, sending his son into the field to pick cotton and so establish the pace for the Negroes. Led by "Young Marse John" the pickers would go down the rows with flying fingers, but when the week's pick of each one was added together and weighed separately, not one ever equaled the young master's heap, for he could take out more cotton in a given time than any of them. "Old Marster," who felt a practical satisfaction in his son's nimble hands, would frown and grumble when Saturday came. He would pretend to be very angry because so little cotton was picked. He would talk of whipping "every man jack of them" for being so "shiftless and no 'count"; but Young Marster knew what was expected of him on this day also, and so he would beg them off. "They have done mighty well after all. Just look how many pounds on the scales." Such a Saturday usually ended by all the cotton-pickers filing along by the steps at the back porch of the "great house" to have each a dram poured for him out of Old Marster's jug, into the cocoanut dipper.

A boy so closely held to account, allowed so small an opportunity to escape, or to conceive himself a regular fellow, might be expected, when left alone in town, to seek out a little deliberate mischief, but it was not so. He had been so impressed by his common-sense parents with the design of making the best of his abilities, and his own nature was such, that he was decent, good-tempered, and studious. While he might look on at a horse race, for he always loved horses, while he might watch a cockfight for a time, he did not drink, did not play cards for money, and seldom made a bet. In my childhood I used to ask him endless questions, and he would answer me with perfect patience. Once he told me that the first thing he ever bought for himself with his own money was a pack of cards, and that previously he doubled that money at a cockfight, but he does not seem to have cared for what they called sport, or ever to have tumbled into the pitfalls of a small and naughty town. It really does sound goody-goody of him, knowing what such towns must have been like, but knowing him also, I conceive that it was an innate fastidiousness. It was not that he condemned others, but that he chose for himself. He was naturally the scrupulous gentleman. He loved good clothes and took care of them. His mother sent him to school neatly dressed, in such a quality of fine homespun as the political candidates liked to wear when they went campaigning. His homespun linen shirts, although coarse, were white as snow, but his boots afflicted his very soul. They were country-made, cowhide affairs.

At his boarding house there were no girls, until one day the landlady's niece came visiting, and to keep her company another Miss came in. The two made round eyes at John and set out to abash him. One whispered to the other, with intention that he should hear, "I don't know which is the thickest, that country boy's lips, or his shoe-soles." Of course this was hard to endure. Next day he had his measure taken by the best bootmaker in Halifax, for a pair of "fair topped boots," thin-soled and high in the instep, such as dandies wore who strapped beneath the foot their long, tight trousers. When the bill for the boots came in to his father, it was for no less than twelve dollars. That kindly man paid the account without demur, but notified his son that it would have to be "worked out" on the plantation that summer, and he saw to it that John paid in full for his fancy footgear.

Another story comes back out of that far-off boyhood. One morning in November, very early, before daylight, Father and his Negro Dorsey were jogging along the road to Halifax. It was a Wednesday morning, for there had been a delay in getting to school that week. On a lonesome bit of track, a narrow path along a swamp, they were riding, while overhead the starry autumn sky was as yet undimmed by dawn. Suddenly the whole arch of heaven was filled with falling fires, as if some enormous rocket had burst and scattered them abroad.

Black Dorsey plunged headlong off his mule, and kneeling on the ground tried to pray aloud between chattering teeth. "Young Marse John," as he narrated to me, was quite as terrified inside, but upheld the white man's dignity by sitting tight, although his horse was trembling and crouching, as frightened as the rider. A little later he said, "None of 'em didn't hit you, Dorsey, so get up and let's be on our way."

"Marse John," quavered Dorsey, "Is dem de sho'-nuff stars been a fallin' down? I heard say dey falls eve'y November."

"I've heard that, too," said John, trying to be nonchalant

about it, "but I never knew it was like this, nor so many."

Father described this experience and told of reading a newspaper account of it afterward. It was a mere chance that he saw the great meteor shower, but it set him studying of nature and causes and the world he lived in. He never wanted to be taken by the throat again by an insensate terror of the unknown.

Another event of my father's youth was the slave insurrection in southeastern Virginia, not many miles from his home. The leader and instigator was a freedman named Nat Turner, who set on the slaves. It was sudden and appalling, for a master seldom hated his slave, although many slaves hated the master who controlled their lives. A score or more whites were murdered in cold blood. The influence of this outbreak tightened up all legislation as to the legal status of free Negroes all over the South, and made the regulations for slaves far stricter. Grandfather, who had known Nat Turner and thought him a harmless fellow, considered the matter judicially. He said, "John, things are breaking wrong for slavery. Some day soon we won't have niggers any more. Somehow, the Yankees'll see to that. From now on, I'm done buying niggers. All my money goes in my old stocking-foot hereafter!" And to this declaration he held, raising great quantities of food, and not so much cotton, planting corn and fattening hogs upon it, and curing wonderful hams and bacon, which always brought far higher prices on the Norfolk market than any others. He specialized in seed oats, which he had a way of setting up in ricks, so that a wet June did not sprout the grain. Very warily, he would lend money to those of his neighbors whose methods of farming pleased him, and always he remitted a percentage of the interest agreed upon if payment was made in gold money. It seems that in his youth he once lost a security debt, and never again would he "go upon a man's note" either for friendship or interest.

In due time, John was sent to the University, not stingily, nor without adequate money allowance to enable him to hold his head up with other men's sons. Before he started to Chapel Hill, his sister had already spent one year in Salem Academy. True to intention, these children were having "as good a chance as anybody's."

During his first summer vacation, John's mother died very suddenly of an apoplectic stroke. By September he was again back in college, and present one morning at the compulsory prayers held in the little college chapel of that epoch. He spied a new bonnet in the faculty pew, with a pretty, unfamiliar face under it, and elbowed the boy sitting next to him.

"Jimmy, who's that girl in Old Mike's pew?"

"That's Old Mike's daughter. She's been up North a whole year, and just got back. She's a high-stepping brown beauty, isn't she?"

"What I know about her is that she's the girl I'm goin' to marry," answered John without hesitation.

It was not long before Miss Ellen Mitchell was being well chaffed on account of the conquest she had made, of "a gigantic but gallant sophomore," as one of her professor friends put it, and was herself a little thrilled by his quiet determined adoration. Miss Ellen was not only a very pretty girl, with all the love of admiration that pretty girls will have to the end of time, but she was a real individual and an interesting person in her own right.

IV

AND THE DOCTOR'S WIFE FROM CHAPEL HILL

CONVENTIONALITY has been demanded of women in each successive age of the world. Nowhere was it more definitely expected than in the South of the epoch where we now find ourselves. My mother's upbringing would be unusual for any time, but for her home and her day, it was unique. It is interesting to describe how she and her sisters had become the victims of advanced ideas, the subjects of experiment, and how their education had been conducted by their father.

Grandfather Mitchell's ideas were advanced regarding the educability of women, both as to what they should be taught and how much they ought to learn. Because his family ran mostly to girls, he had the subjects on whom to try out his pet theories ready to his hand. In many ways he was a remarkable man, but intrinsically no more remarkable than his wife, who shared with him his opinions on education and may have suggested them in the first place.

My grandfather's people had already lived for several generations past at Washington, Connecticut, and indeed, in 1937, the family still owns the old place and lives there in summer. A hundred years ago, they were intelligent, well-to-do dairy farmers. Today their dairy, greatly expanded in size and variety of products, is carried on under the Mitchell name in the city of Litchfield, Connecticut, a notable example of longevity in a business.

Grandfather's mother was Phoebe Eliot, in direct line of descent from the Apostle to the Indians. Jared Eliot, grandson to the Apostle, was her grandfather. She was as keenly intelligent and as hard to bridle into complacency as any of the strong-willed New England women of her day. She attended to it that her three sons were all sent to Yale College, where Elisha Mitchell, my grandfather, graduated in 1813. In the same class graduated also Denison Olmsted, who taught for a few years at the new University of North Carolina, and there were three southerners, Thomas Devereux, of Raleigh, North Carolina; George Badger, of New Berne, North Carolina, afterwards secretary of the Navy for the United States, and, better remembered, Augustus Baldwin Longstreet, of Georgia, the author of *Georgia Scenes*. It was not a large class. All the members knew each other. Grandfather was under the influence of Dr. Silliman, who initiated the study of science but was not allowed full professorship. On leaving Yale Grandfather became a teacher and one year was principal of a girls' school at New London, Connecticut. In 1816 he was called back to Yale as a tutor. Then his friend Olmsted and President Dwight, with Judge Gaston, of North Carolina, united to recommend him as professor of mathematics at the University of North Carolina. He seems in some interval to have remained long enough at Andover Theological Seminary to obtain license to preach as a Congregational minister. He went to North Carolina in January, 1818, to accept the appointment. The next summer he returned to New London to bring back his bride, Maria North. She too came of unusual people. Her father, Elisha North, was a physician and surgeon, a man far in advance of his time. Sir William Osler, in one of his printed monographs, refers to Dr. North's book on spotted fever as a very early example in America of keen diagnosis; and quite recently Dr. North's name was revived and celebrated as the first New England ophthalmologist.

When Elisha Mitchell taught school in New London, he had as one of his pupils his future wife. He was aware when he married her that she had a brain as well as a heart. Hers were not provincial people. In 1830-1831, her elder sister made the then seldom attempted tour of Europe, and her brothers were sea captains and New Orleans merchants. One of them married a French lady of an old "Faubourg St. Germain" family, and Maria's younger sister married a German, who was court bandmaster to old Kaiser Wilhelm. This aunt for whom my mother was named, faded out of her family's knowledge in a few years.

A little later, when my grandparents with their growing family were living in the Chapel Hill of that far time, they arranged to send my mother and her two sisters near her age to school along with the three Phillips children of corresponding years, two of whom were boys. All this little group were taught by the faculty professors. Before that, almost before they were free of the nursery, the three little sisters had been grounded in Latin, Greek, and French.

It was the time in the United States, but nowhere else in the world that I seem to know, when ideas had begun to stir regarding the higher education of women. Attempts at founding female seminaries had been made in various places —in New England, in Georgia, in New York State—and it was in 1830 that Mary Lyon began her campaign to endow Mount Holyoke. Much thought and discussion must have come before that.

My grandparents determined that their three girls should have instruction in any branch which would have been open to them if they had been boys; and in believing and maintaining this feminist heresy, they were ahead even of the forwardness of their times, and about seventy-five years in the future. Because Dr. Mitchell was more interested in science than in anything else, and because perhaps his daughters were too tempting subjects, too near him to escape his demands on them, he added to the classics and mathematics usually taught in the colleges of the day, subjects such as chemistry, physics, and botany, not a regular part of every curriculum and not, as an invariable rule, studied by the male students. With this life of really hard study, the Mitchell girls were given very little playtime. They were kept hard at their books. On that account they were not excused from the fine needlework in which their mother excelled, which was thought a *sine qua non* for every girl of any family.

Grandfather's eager mental curiosity ranged as far as the scholarship of the day would carry him, and suffered only from a lack of specialization. It was not yet the day for this, but his peculiar breadth of interest has been handed down and has reappeared in the third and fourth generations.

For his daughters' physical well-being he took the precaution to insist on their accompanying him on those interminable tramps he made daily, through woods and fields, for botanical and geological exploration. As regarded its natural constitution, the state was an uncharted country, and it was his mission to explore it. He would take along in his pocket some Greek or Latin author, some list of dates in history, and from this he would instruct the girls as they went on their way. On the return trip he would inspect and discuss the specimens they might have gathered, and make them learn all the names and data connected with these. Or again, he might turn human, and the girls and their stalwart father would go racing and tearing home, chasing each other over hill and dale, returning with ravenous appetites.

It does not appear what was his ultimate object in thus super-educating his daughters. In the society of the South in that epoch there surely was little enough room for bluestockings. No place existed where any part of such attainments would be considered useful or even tolerated, except in a teacher in an occasional academy for girls. By ability and stimulated effort, these daughters soon became learned women in their mentality. In their spirit they were at the same time carefree, jolly, healthy young creatures, brought up in the sex-conscious and animating atmosphere of a college town, and not without girlish anticipations and love interests. Their own object in life soon became to conceal as far as possible the fact that they knew more of the inside of books than did their young companions of the other sex. They dressed well, were laughter-loving, and, as they grew up, entertained their visitors with a pleasant frankness and clear-eyed comradeship unusual but very attractive to the swains of the college. Contrary to the die-away, romantic ideal for women, the sisters were not only healthy, but athletic. Thanks to the constant exercise Dr. Mitchell insisted upon, they were strong and active. An old story remains, how Aunt Mary, the eldest, wagered with half-a-dozen lads, that she could outjump all of them. Like a bird flying, she cleared a flour barrel set on end in the front yard, and by her agility won many pairs of gloves.

And so it developed that each one chose the good old way, the "long path" which girls have followed in all ages. Two of them walked directly into matrimony; the third was withheld only by a mischance. Grandfather could do nothing about it but fume and fret, and with pardonable disgust he declared, "I never in all this world took so much pains with my girls' education, simply for the sake of these young fellows they are marrying!"

Before he started to medical college at the University of Pennsylvania, Father had a complete understanding with Mother. Once I heard him tell a young friend how his own sweetheart's letters used to cost him twenty-five cents each, or fifty, if, as he preferred, she said a few words more, and how he rejoiced to get them. It was the understood convention that the man should pay the postage in a sentimental correspondence. In the year 1842, mail left Chapel Hill for the North only once a week.

Dr. Mitchell lived in a plain, two-story house with narrow eaves and a front portico or "stoop," which some of the oldest of us can well remember. It was one of the earliest built of the faculty homes of the University, and was shaded by locust trees instead of the oaks which grew on the campus. This house has been pulled down, and its place is now occupied by the students' dining hall.

In the old-fashioned parlour of the Mitchell home the young pair were married. Mother never would tell me anything about her wedding, save that Dr. James Phillips performed the ceremony. She was the first of the sisters to be married. To represent Grandmother's people, there came all the way from New London, Connecticut, her sister, Miss Eliza North. At some time during the previous year, Grandfather's mother had been to Chapel Hill on a visit. Ellen, my mother, was her favorite granddaughter, because she listened so well to the old stories the elderly love to keep telling. Mother told me that she listened to them carefully, because she knew how different her grandmother's life had been from what her own must be, and she added that the anecdotes did not interest Mary and Margaret, who had not spent a long year in New England as she had done in her seventeenth year. I wish she had set me an example and had written down all these family traditions, for Phoebe Eliot Mitchell's stories must have been worth hearing. Her memory went back to the Revolution. When she was a small girl, she is said once to have crept under a table with a low-hanging cloth, and listened there to British soldiers discussing their plans. But this is purely legendary. It is true that Dr. Mitchell's father actually enlisted in the American army a few months before Yorktown.

From what I once saw in an old horsehide trunk, I know what Mother's wedding dress was like. In color it was what we would now call a pale orchid. It was a stiff brocade, gathered so full to the tight-fitting whaleboned bodice that the skirt swelled and billowed in deep folds all around. The "second-day's dress" was a royal blue taffeta striped longitudinally in pale shaded brown, and having "real lace" undersleeves. Yards upon yards of silk went to the fashioning of such dresses. It was before the days of wedding silver and glass gifts and the wedding-present parade; but one of the seafaring uncles sent her a huge dinner set of canton blue, plates and platters for every conceivable use, and of this the greater part is still in existence, parceled out among the family.

Very soon after his son's wedding, Grandfather Summerell announced that he must marry again, if only because there was so much difficulty in trying to run a plantation without a mistress. Before he married, there were dispositions he wished to make. First of all, he would send to my father the Negro, Dorsey, who had been his servant and comrade ever since they were both children. Grandfather Mitchell owned a trusty family servant called "Uncle Summer," and as each successive little daughter was born, one of Summer's daughters, a little older, was assigned to her in the same way. So "Persia," Mother's maid, would join her mistress as soon as the young couple were established in their own home in Salisbury. After a short interval, my father's father set out to purchase a home for the bride and groom in Salisbury, and he gave it to his daughter-in-law, registering the deed in her sole name with no joint ownership with her husband, and announcing as his reason, "So that Ellen may keep her home and roof over her head, when John gets too accommodating and signs somebody's note, as security, and has to pay the whole of it."

This house, this home, was the same in which were born all my brothers and sisters and myself last of all. It was purchased from a Reverend Mr. Frontis, who built it. He was a French Huguenot pastor, who had charge of the Presbyterian congregation in Salisbury for some years before this, and was now about to leave town.

Mr. Frontis was noted for his odd use of the English language. Once he blessed a newly married couple after the ceremony, saying, "May the Lord peekle you both," confusing culinary matters in this way. This was also the Mr. Frontis who was so eaten up with pardonable curiosity as to the actual identity of Peter Ney, the schoolmaster, that Peter had carefully to avoid him, dodging his acquaintance for years. Indeed it has been said that Mr. Frontis was the reason Peter never taught school any nearer Salisbury.

Peter Ney was that Frenchman and schoolmaster about whom books have been written to prove that he was really Napoleon's Marshal Ney, escaped from a firing squad and come to America. But it would be hard to prove it at this stretch of time! . . .

When my father and mother finally settled, they first needed to make acquaintanceship with each other, for they were young people so very differently brought up as to be strangers to each other's way of living. My mother came from a home where, because her mother had been very delicate of late, a housekeeper had been employed to take all household responsibility from her. Hitherto Mother had spent her life in study, with a little sewing and drawing, and without much incursion into a kitchen. She had no knowledge of any household duty more exacting than making an occasional dessert or setting an especially inviting dinner table. Much company came and went in Professor Mitchell's simple and dignified home. It was conducted by southern methods, because such were the only patterns which could be ordered easily in our society. In Father's home, a more primitive way of living made more of a place for daily work, although the food was probably just as abundant and as well prepared.

And now, in moving to Salisbury, the young people were to live a little farther west, a little nearer the frontier, or rather, nearer the cruder, less established social community, where living as a whole was neither outwardly so polished nor inwardly so intellectual as Chapel Hill generally managed to be—a society where strictness was far stricter, where moral laxity was much more openly relaxed than it might be in the East. Luxuries proper and indulgences could not well have been more nonexistent in one place than the other.

Father and his bride began at once their married life in Salisbury and their relationship to the new community. Although they did not know it, they had chosen, once for all, the home and the life for the rest of their long lives.

My parents, to their elderly descendant, seem like strange ancestral babies. My father had just reached the ripe age of twenty-five, while Mother was six months past her twentieth or twenty-first birthday. They were married in the month of November and were driven in the family carriage from Mother's home in Chapel Hill to Hillsboro, there to take the stage for Salisbury. Durham, later to develop as a station upon a railroad not yet planned, was of course nonexistent. From Hillsboro, the young couple went on to Salisbury and there established themselves at the one passable hotel of the place until they could look about and find a suitable private dwelling.

V

A NEW HOME IN SALISBURY

THE HOUSE that Pastor Frontis built was long and low and very solid, being framed on beams and sleepers roughly adzed off square and thick and strong enough for a hay barn. Mother used to say, "I am sure the carpenter who built this house must have been a left-handed man who squinted, for there is not one level floor, and not one square corner in the whole of it." But while she was saying it, you felt that she doted upon the old house in spite of the fact, and enjoyed every constructional obliquity in it. Once a great bump appeared in our parlor floor, and the carpet had to be taken up and a carpenter brought to rip up the flooring. Beneath he found a cord of bricks, neatly piled as if brought for the building of a chimney and then covered over and forgotten. The floor beams had been laid above it, and it showed its presence only when the granite posts on which the sleepers rested had settled a little deeper into the clay.

The clay of our lot was very impenetrable and very bright red. The great southwest road to the Scotch-Irish settlements had once passed diagonally across it, and the first digging-over it was given had to be done with picks. The town was divided into four quarters by broad streets crossing at right angles at the courthouse square. This, the southwest square, had once been the common, the pasture free to everybody. Later, more town lots had been divided from it and sold, and the old road had been straightened and led along the street in front. At the corner, facing this street, stood our home place. Three quarters of a square was the large lot that went with it. There was an orchard, and a clover-lot separating the house enclosure from that of the next neighbor, for neighbors there were, when my parents bought the place, living both on Fulton and on Bank streets, the boundaries of our corner.

Our house was of that construction then called "a story and a jump," which means a story and a half in front, where the pitch went up much steeper, and had dormer windows to light the upper rooms. Behind, the roof ended in a long slope, low over the eaves of the back gallery. The ground plan was simple. Two large rooms, twenty-three or four feet deep and fifteen in width, were located on each side of an entry in front, these being the parlour and dining-sitting room. Each had a capacious fireplace. Behind the parlour was that smaller square bedroom used for guests, which filled the end of the back gallery and had a door opening on it. At the end of the back gallery opposite this, a door admitted to the two adjoining rooms of the ell, which extended southward, and these were used as my mother's bedroom and the nursery. This last, at the south end of the house, had an outside door both at the front and at the back, and indeed four of the five rooms of the house downstairs opened directly outdoors. Upstairs there were two more large bedrooms under the roof, reached by the entry stairway.

The first ell-room, used as Mother's bedroom, had been originally built for a "cocoonery," for Mr. Frontis' daughters raised silkworms. Even to my day remained the stump of one of the row of mulberry trees whose leaves gave them food. I once saw, taken out of the wall when this room was repaired, a great double-handful of empty cocoons, which must have been carried there by rats. This reminds us how, in the thirties, people in North and South Carolina experimented seriously in producing silk, as shown by advertisements in the newspapers of the time offering silkworm's eggs and mulberry stock for sale.

As the new home was situated somewhat at the end of the

closer-built part of Salisbury, it was a good long walk back to Main Street, where the stores were. The Presbyterian Church, built substantially of red brick, something on the outside pattern of the courthouse itself, could be passed on the way. Mother declared that, for all the ecclesiastical detail to be found in it, it might as well be a synagogue. Foursquare and plain it stood in its grassy yard, with grave cedar trees waving beside it. The columns were plain Doric, and for a belfry it had a cupola.

St. Luke's Episcopal Church, begun about the same time, was farther toward the old part of town. It was planned after the venerable pattern of some English parish church. It had a truncated square tower with pinnacles, and a raftered interior. Even when half finished it gave an impression of permanence with dignity and was like a stray bit of antiquity which had wandered into new-made surroundings. With all the passing of the years it has never gone out of fashion. My mother possessed no Catholic tradition whatever and had only a literary interest in the Prayerbook, but she admired this church building and said of it, "By grace ye are saved," although by that she meant only the outward appearance rather than any great gift of invisible inwardness as mentioned by St. Paul.

Just now, in these times, there were simple, roomy homes and space enough in which to set them. My parents, as any normal pair of young householders ought to do, took the deepest interest in the ordering and beautifying of their new nest. Over the Frontis house, with its surprised-looking pair of front dormers, there was sifted great beauty of lofty shadow. This was cast by its four enormous oaks, giants left standing from the ancient forest, trees which had never been lopped or mutilated. They stood in a group about the house they over-watched, the trunk of one of them coming very near the angle made by the joining of the ell to the main house. Always they rustled and creaked high above the shingles, making an undertone as the air moved them. In the autumn season they threw down volleys of acorns and windrows of brown leaves upon the broad roof spread below. In front of the house, somewhat out from the shadow of these great oaks, was the flower garden. To Mother and Father a delight of all delights was the planting of a garden. Mother's especial preference was for flowers, while Father's garden was all for food, for vegetables, for practical use. Mother set a formal box-border in double rows, leading from the house to the gate; she made a border of single blue hyacinths all around the whole front yard just inside the fence; she planted many ornamental shrubs, grouping English laurel and deodar cedar by the north end, for contrast of foliage; and she trained English ivy to climb the trunks of the oaks.

Father's vegetable garden was a comely sight, for even rows, perfect tillage, and neatness, and he produced vegetables and small fruits in abundance. He studied gardening in the best manuals obtainable, keeping his dozen books of horticulture on the most accessible shelf of that tall "press" where his medical books were ranged.

Behind the house was an unmowed enclosure, carpeted raggedly with that thick-growing grass which flourishes in the rich earth of house yards. At the side farthest from the house stood a long row of outbuildings. There was the storeroom where the feed bins and the cornsheller were kept, and over it there was a room for Dorsey. Near by stood a similar building which housed, downstairs, the kitchen, for kitchens in those days were commonly the width of the yard away from dining rooms. Over her kitchen lived Persia. It was a large old-fashioned kitchen, having a cooking fireplace furnished with crane and "spiders" in the good old style. A cookstove was not installed until one decade later at least. Besides these, there was a smokehouse, a chickenhouse, and the wash bench with its row of tubs, and a shed over all. Near this last stood the great outdoor wash pot with three legs set high on stones to allow room for a fire under it. Here clothes were scalded to whiten them, and here also soft soap was simmered slowly. The well was near at hand, just inside the yard gate, and was a huge one, like the dark shaft of a deep mine. Its windlass was a great beam. This concluded the row of backyard utilities, except for the woodpile, which was placed backward with wood corded solidly inside its high board fence in September and almost all burned in spring. Then there was the "ash hopper."

You left this yard by a gate which must invariably be shut, to go into Father's garden. Traversing that, you entered the barn lot, with the stable, and a clover lot beside that. It was a small farm, a working establishment, a home unit of industry organized to carry on all those processes which are now delegated to the baker, the grocer, and a dozen other trades.

On the front street at the middle of the orchard lot, stood the Doctor's office, which was the usual, detached, two-roomed cottage so often associated with plantation homes, except that in this case it was oddly varied by the fact that Mr. Frontis had bought four second-hand church windows sharply pointed. These he had used, not inappropriately, to light his pastor's study, but they made Father's office look like a tiny chapel.

In the years of the decade of the forties, it was true that a new prosperity had improved the old town, although throughout the decade of the thirties, people had been pessimistic about its future growth.

There is an editorial written by Charles Fisher, the elder, which declares a little wistfully of our pleasant part of North Carolina, "While our section of the country is declining, it is good to know that other states are prospering exceedingly." Because Calhoun had been brought up in the Piedmont and understood our needs, he had been the choice of our people. But now Rowan's revival of prosperity was independently on its way. Tyler's presidency, so well disliked by both parties, wore to its end, and in March, 1845, Polk came in with the distinct pledge of the annexation of Texas.

Polk was a Western North Carolina boy, born just over in Mecklenburg County, and his policies were thoroughly approved. What this could mean to us, what of favorable change would come with all the added territory of Texas, does not appear, although, as usual, our citizens rejoiced at the prospect. All along, the opinion had persisted, the conviction remained, that any misfortune or failure under the sun could be remedied by pulling up stakes and going West. It seemed impossible that all those wishing to go should move on and yet enough be left to work out the state's proper destiny.

Politics ran very high in Salisbury in 1844. I have heard that at first my father and mother were diametrically opposed, Father being a Democrat like his father, and Mother a Whig like her father, so that when one rejoiced the other sulked. The thing this shows is that Mother had a political opinion and talked about it, and it was different from her husband's.

The impression I get from the letters which remain, mostly letters between the pair when they were separated by Mother's going back home for a visit, is the certainty that these young folk were not bored for one moment with anything their joint life was bringing to them. Mother liked her neighbors, learned to cook, to cure meat and put up sauerkraut, and to make preserves. Anything that gave work for her skillful hands always entertained her, and to this point she did not too painfully miss the book-filled house at Chapel Hill. She was absorbed in the processes of homemaking.

Father could soon feel convinced that his profession would keep his family in comfort. At first he had some opposition from the tavern-keeping interests of the town, instigated by that influential old Doctor mentioned as having retired from practice. This was because Father had lately become an advocate of temperance. Such opposition Father countered by putting an advertisement in the paper, naming very moderate fees for the families of working people who had never before been able to have an educated physician, but had depended on grannies and witch-wives. He gathered a little cash by this and, what was more to the point, abundant experience.

My father's adoption of temperance as his rule in life took place in these earliest years. Coming as he did from a free and easy community, not deeply concerned about its sins, he easily became hail fellow with all the rollicking young bloods of Salisbury, and there were many such. Whiskey was their failing, as it was the failing of Salisbury and of the times in general. Father, being likable, shared in the usual entertainment provided for a congenial newcomer, and on several occasions went home the worse for it. He told me about this himself, how Mother said no word to him, but he found out that she often cried in secret over his growing dissipation. This at last aroused the chivalry which made a part of his devotion to his young wife. Unexpectedly to her, and entirely of his own free will, he came and begged her pardon and promised her, "Never, never again." So sensitive a lover as he kept his word then and thereafter. Mother knew her man, knew all his loyalty and his honor, but she felt that he needed some further allegiance to restrain him, more than his devotion to herself. She wished to commit him publicly.

When a man marries a woman more sober-mindedly brought up than he himself has been, she either converts him, or drives him into stronger negation of her opinions, while on her part she will either grow more forbearing as he draws her to himself or will stiffen her creed to resist him. Mother was the more thoughtful, but not necessarily the wiser of these two people, and she had been far more rigorously trained. It was by his stability of character that Father won the respect of his world, and if he could not maintain that, he was no better than the next man.

Since 1800, all over the Carolinas there had grown and spread a movement of revivalism in religion, and although at its first beginning strange extravagances were proved against it, these had dropped away long ago. The emphasis upon experience, begun from the first, had warmed up and intensified Presbyterian piety in a way that the liturgical churches did not emulate. Mother had been brought up a Congregationalist of the broader view, and when she and Father became serious and began to attend church together regularly, they sat under the Presbyterian sermons of Rev. Archibald Baker, who had succeeded Pastor Frontis. They finally decided to range their lives on the soberer, more inhibited side of the community's opinion, and after some hesitation they joined Mr. Baker's church together. They probably found it a loss in light-heartedness. It may have kept them out of a little pleasant sociability, but one has sometimes to come down on the one side of the fence or the other; and so, before habit had become rigid and decided the question for them, they chose their own alternative, and chose to live by it.

Perhaps it was not too simply Mother's influence. Perhaps Father, brought up where there were no churches, had felt the need of some religious anchorage. He had been a conscientious boy; his reactions had never been frivolous. He became as thorough in his religion as he was in other things, but his godliness was never according to any narrow formula. He cared nothing for ritual, and nothing for the determined aversion to ritual which was the pride of the Presbyterians. As his heart grew wiser, he loved his fellow men better. As he grew older, he learned to pray in secret over his patients, especially for those whose sicknesses were the result of personal wrong-doing. He rejoiced in the tender children who came under his hands, and every child in his

A NEW HOME IN SALISBURY

vicinity naturally gravitated to him. They climbed his powerful frame, rested in his strong arms, and trusted him. Along with a view of conduct which grew always more serious, never did he lose that broad jocularity, that sense of humor, that repartee, and what we call in North Carolina that "folksiness" of his youthful days when he did not think about his soul.

Mother slipped more naturally into the part of the community which was militantly religious, although I have heard her say that the rules of abstention were much more strict and more strictly defined in the West than they were in middle North Carolina, and very much more negative than her own family had taught her. She wondered why injunctions were so often, *Thou shalt not*, while positive loving-kindness was not stressed. People holding such strict opinions cared for no literature save religious books, and did not care for the march of human ideas. If they went to school, they weeded their minds of all imagination. In secular life they esteemed practical thrift in money matters. All these things were outside the habitual concern of both my parents.

How was it that the definite money objectives of his neighbors, as well as the easy unmorality of his youthful days had so little effect in modifying my father's character? I have thought about this a good deal, and with an idea of defining his faults, if I could find them. All I can perceive are a few eccentricities, a few humorous petulances, excusable preferences, distinctive sayings, tags of individuality. He was not ascetic. He loved good food, good clothes, and cheerfulness. He had a breadth of mind such as was once found in the fathers of our republic. He spoke plain Elizabethan English and was not mealy-mouthed. It must have been his one defect that his kindly toleration never extended to anything he considered unfair, unkind, or willfully untrue. He treated all such things with a scorn almost too rigid. He expected of every man the delicate sense of honor by which he guided his own life. But with other kinds of slips and failures he was sympathetic. Father judged no one so severely as he judged himself, and he was never afraid.

One of the image-breaking younger folk, one who happens to be a grandchild of his whom he could never have seen, read over the little packet of his letters with interest and, to my surprise, with reverence. She said at last, "Men like that do not live any more. I wish I had known him, Why, he's perfect! I mean it."

VI

A SMALL-TOWN NEIGHBORHOOD

The general environment has been laid out in the town where my father and mother lived all their days, and now the familiar streets they trod so often can be peopled with their intimate friends and their neighbors.

In the southwest quarter of Salisbury our house stood three squares west from Main Street, or two squares over from Innes, whichever leg of the tripod one followed, and on the corner of Fulton and Bank. Salisbury was put together by a definite pattern according to which the facing of the long lots which ran clear through their squares was always in the direction of the central square where the courthouse stood, like children in school fronting their teacher. This plan had its inconveniences. It made it possible that a householder looked out of his front window to perceive across the way his neighbor's pigpen in the back lot, while at the same time he was thrusting the pigpen belonging to his own domestic economy under the nose of the neighbor living just behind him. Of course the pig was the indispensable garbage can of the time, converting all the various vegetable leftovers into succulent pork and tasty sausage, costing little but a fattening ration of corn a while before butchering time; of course this necessary pig must be housed somewhere. According to the town pattern, the southwest side of Fulton would be called the "front street," while the opposite side, which for decades had no proper sidewalk, had tall fences to screen the back lots and was given up to a standing crop of dog fennel. Past our corner, Bank Street went on for a square, like a leafy lane, until the vista was closed by the big house where lived the Craiges.

Choosing to walk about the town for a time, and "dream true" as a little ghost not yet embodied might wish to do, I can imagine myself seeing the things my parents looked at in those days and meeting the people they knew in their early years together. Often they have told me of them in answer to my questionings, and so much of the familiar surroundings lasted through till I came to town.

Let us go out by our front gate which always shut of itself with an emphatic click, because it had upon it a dog-proof latch, devised by Father and forged by the local blacksmith. Going north along those picket fences invariably used, each lot having its especial pattern, the first neighbor-house would be that of the Bruners, square-built and very plain. By this time Mr. J. J. Bruner was editor and owner of the *Carolina Watchman*, a paper first set up to oppose the Democrats and uphold Whig principles in a town where for a long time the *Western Carolinian* had stood alone and stood for the other party. Mr. Bruner was an experienced printer, having been apprenticed very young under the care of Charles Fisher, the elder, who was his kinsman. Afterward he took employment with Philo White, a man from New York State, who edited and managed the *Carolinian* established by Mr. Fisher, and finally owned it. This man married a Brandon, and after his wife's untimely death went back North again. Mr. Bruner was one of those printers whose occupation was both education and culture to him, bringing out his natural ability, which was excellent. When my parents moved into the Frontis house, the Bruners were already settled. I have heard that from the first my mother found Mrs. Bruner a friend to be consulted about the many household matters and the ways of the town where she was ignorant. Mrs. Bruner was "Rowan County folks"; her mother was a Brandon, who had named her daughter "Clarissa,"

An essay could be written about the naming of girls in several epochs of our history, with speculation as to the primary cause of bestowal of many names once used, never given now. Our great-grandmothers craved romance, and their busy daily lives contained very little of it. They conned over the few novels that came their way and lived in the heroine's joys and sorrows. They dramatized these stories and cast their daughters in the parts; hence the scores of Amelias and Amandas, of Pamelas and Clarissas found in the generation after them.

Mr. Bruner had used his opportunity, but it was by his own effort that he became significant. In his youth he was a virile, combative man. "Fighting Joe" was the nickname bestowed upon him. Known to be the joyful fighter, he had a deceptive fashion of becoming ever quieter in demeanor and more soft-voiced the more nearly he approached the breaking point, before quick attack or open denunciation. Since his marriage he was a settled man, after a difficult youth. The house he lived in, standing so plain and homely, looked from the back into a delightful garden, where vistas of shady grape-arbors, bird boxes, and carefully tended flower beds could be seen. This was typical of the man. He never put much into the show window, but he knew more that was interesting about his town, more that was significant concerning Western North Carolina and its needs for development, more of the facts he daily observed, than any other one person. He was a great reader, and gifted, so it seems, with the true reporter's instinct, for by night or day, if anything out of ordinary occurred on our streets, Mr. Bruner would be first on the ground.

Next to the Bruner's came the Wilson's lot. Mrs. Wilson was one of three Slater sisters, perhaps the least conspicuous but none the less distinct in personality. Some years later she was left a widow and lived long years in the same little home with her sons, the quietest and most unassuming of women. Perhaps even then, for the reason that they take so long to grow, she had set out that double-flowering cherry tree which, in springs that I remember, filled one whole side of her yard with drifts of bloomy snow. Then it would suddenly shed its beauty to become, until next year, merely a huge cherry tree with green leaves, red-brown twigs, and not one single cherry.

Next door lived her sister, Mrs. John D. Brown, whose husband fitted somewhere into the pattern of Rowan County Browns. This lady strongly resembled Queen Victoria, save that she was better looking and indeed must have been very comely in her youthful day, when she did not wear snowy caps above her rosy face, nor have those neuralgic headaches which she expounded to her friends. These three homes made up the first block, all facing as our house faced, all looking at no particular other side of the way except the usual high board fence.

The next square had in the middle of it that colonial residence long used for a girls' school. Discontinued by this date, the place had been sold to the Overman brothers, newly moved to town to open a carriage-making business. On the far side of this square enclosure and next to Innes Street, the elder Overman had built a fine new home, and the young wife he took there was the third of the Slater sisters, and the prettiest one. Even by the standards of that day of early marriages, she had been a child wife. Her mother, after her widowhood, had married her overseer, and on this account all three Slater daughters made haste to marry so as to leave a home rendered distasteful to them.

Trees have always been friends to me, possessing individual characters. Out in front of the Overman house there grew one of my tree friends, the handsomest of those left from the forest which once invested the site of Salisbury. Around the base of its trunk the sidewalk had to be conducted in a semicircle to avoid its knotty roots, while acorns bespattered

A SMALL-TOWN NEIGHBORHOOD

the whole width of the roadway in front. Does it not tell something of a character which wishes a companion like that, rather than the lovely expanse of a straight and narrow sidewalk?

Innes, one of the two wider thoroughfares which cross at the center of Salisbury, passed between the Overman house and the Fisher home, so roomy and well shaded, which faced the same way on the corner opposite. Both the Charles Fishers, father and son, were as able and influential as any men our county bred. The father was continuously in public office, from the time he was elected sheriff, an office in which relations with constituents are very immediate, until he was sent to the legislature and then to Congress. Only once was he ever defeated for office. By his wife, Christina Beard, he had three children, two of whom were daughters. His son Charles was worthy of him. This was the year 1845 just passing, and both father and son were in politics and active, the son taking his turn at newspapering, assisted by another promising youth of Rowan County, named Burton Craige.

Farther down Fulton Street, but on the opposite side, there had just settled a second young doctor who would soon be forming a partnership with Father. His name was Marcellus Whitehead, and he and his young wife came from Virginia. They lived in a cottage which is still standing, a house with steep gables, very near the street, although not so near but that the huge magnolias that come between its windows and the world outside have had time to grow up tall and dark, to shade the house impenetrably. This was so when I was a child, and they kept the little dooryard perennially littered with their stiff, brown, castoff leaves.

After sauntering the distance of just these four squares from home, toward the north, open country was in sight again. Nothing to do but retrace one's steps.

At each crossing of the footway over the red clay of the street, unpaved and unimproved, were stepping-stones a foot high and set at intervals, so that foot passengers might trip or totter from one to the next and the wheels of vehicles might pass between. And we go back where we started.

The near neighbor and good friend whom Father esteemed as well as any friend he made, was Burton Craige. His people came early into Rowan, for his great-grandfather was a supporter of "Bonnie Prince Charlie" and escaped from Scotland, coming directly into our "neck of the woods"— and woods it must have been, for this was before there was any town or county, and before the settlers came from Pennsylvania. The Craige farm was on the familiar river road, and Burton's father married a first cousin. He must have been already Hon. Burton Craige when Father came to Salisbury. He had attended the Salisbury Male Academy under the Reverend Otis Freeman, had graduated at the University, where it is of record that his oration at graduation was on the unhackneyed subject of "The Proper Education for Women"; and had scarcely returned from college, at eighteen or nineteen, when he became editor of the *Western Carolinian*. He studied law, and soon after his twenty-first birthday was elected to the legislature. Later he was sent to Congress, and in between he was editor, lawyer, and leading citizen. Mr. Craige was a man impossible to ignore. His physique was more than commanding. He stood six feet-six or seven in his stockings. I can just remember him when I was a child—remember looking far upward into his fine face, lighted with clear dark-gray eyes, and crowned with white hair. I remember how I admired him, how in my child mind I thought he must be almost as handsome as God, and doubtless very like Him!

Mr. Craige was as eager a gardener as my father, and they kept going a neighborly rivalry in choice products. On a morning, as he passed our back gate on the way to his law office, he would deposit his largest potato, his earliest tomato, upon the thick gatepost there. The game was that Father should match it before noon, or surpass it if he could, and the two would foregather and discuss gardening across the fence. This gentle giant was beloved of all sorts of men, and even boys, a little more discountenanced than they are today, might take liberties. It could be told how a freckle-faced urchin would be edging warily up toward a wally-eyed, astute old billy-goat dodging about the street, not meaning to be captured. Mr. Craige coming out of his gate just then, the boy would yell at him frantically, as if he were one of "the gang," "Craige, head that goat, head him off" and they would have a successful round-up, all across the street. Mr. Craige had boys of his own.

My father belonged to the same political party as Mr. Craige, and their interests in that were similar. Mr. Craige, being actively in politics, would, as the custom was, be apt to partake too freely of that ever-flowing stream of North Carolina corn-liquor, considered so useful in emergency, so indispensable with a constituency; and he would come home like that. My father was himself full six feet tall, a man of powerful shoulders, but he told me how one night coming home very late, he encountered Mr. Craige in exhilaration, and just under the lamppost that stood on our corner. Mr. Craige was delighted to see him, hugged him up, beat a friendly tattoo upon his back, and told him in detail how much he loved him and why. Father said it was a startling experience. His friend was so tall, so powerful that he could not get free. Even my stalwart young father felt like a baby in his grip.

Like my father, Mr. Craige as he grew older became a temperance man, and on his death bed refused the stimulant recommended, saying, "I will die sober, even if I die a little sooner."

An unreconciled secessionist after the War was over, he knew no "duty of defeat," as Governor Vance phrased it. Mr. Craige had presented the secession ordinance for North

Carolina; he was elected a member of the Confederate Congress from our state; and after the surrender, like his forbears when they saw Prince Charlie's standard go to the ground, he held his allegiance to the "conquered banner," never asking to have his disability removed.

Our only banking institution was a private one, managed by a Mr. Davis, kinsman of that first North Carolina editor who lived in the town of New Berne. Our banker was a short-spoken, dignified man, typically and actually the oldest elder in the Presbyterian Church. Everybody referred to him as "Mr. *Bank* Davis." He was in Salisbury before my father, and the two were lifelong friends. His home was a square brick house just beyond Main Street, to the east, and it gave the name to our Bank Street, for part of this house had been built as a banking room, with counter and grating. Behind this and beneath was the strong room and bank vault, and in this office-cage Mr. Davis would sit during his leisurely hours of bank-keeping and find time then to do a great deal of knitting. When he had to put his half-finished sock away to wait on clients, he shut the work into the seat of his great chair which pulled out like a drawer. I have watched him do this when I was a little girl. During the Civil War, it is said that he turned out as many socks for the soldiers, knit with his own hands, as any woman of them all. He lies buried at the left of a line of four successive wives, and on his right sleeps the last wife, who lived to bury him. I remember his beautiful black-and-tan terrier, named Tyke. This dog accompanied every step his master made, except to church and to prayer meeting. Nothing could induce him to start church-ward. He knew when the time came, and not being a religious dog he never offered to start.

Another early intimate of my people was a Scotchman, Mr. William Murdoch. He was a master stone-mason, one who had been induced to come direct to North Carolina in order to help in the work on the Capitol building in Raleigh.

A SMALL-TOWN NEIGHBORHOOD 57

He was also one of the elders, and his home stood on the site of that "Cornwallis House" where Maxwell Chambers lived and where he was forced to entertain the English General that rainy February.

It was railroad building time. Roads were being pushed through everywhere in the middle years of the nineteenth century, and Mr. Murdoch's skill was called upon to construct the stonework for various bridges. It was said that no bridge-piers planned by him and built under his supervision were ever swept out in a freshet. He was the man who saw to the placing of the stone staircase in the Capitol at Raleigh, the one which architects come to look at, the one which is supported at the wall but has the outer edge free. After he became too old to take contracts, he became one of the most enthusiastic of the great gardeners of old Salisbury.

"Caldwell" has long been a name to conjure with; all over North Carolina. Joseph Caldwell, of New Jersey, was the first titular president of the University. Even before Joseph the first, there had been a Reverend David Caldwell who had a famous "log college" in Guilford County. In my time, Editor "Joe Caldwell" and his Charlotte *Observer* were what Western North Carolina almost to a man, both read and swore by. But our Judge Caldwell was another David, a member of the Iredell County family. In 1844, he was made judge of the Superior Court, and he married a niece of the first Archibald Henderson. His eldest daughter married young Charles Fisher and had a daughter Frances, afterwards well known under the pen name of "Christian Reid."

When my parents settled in the Frontis House, Judge Caldwell was living beyond us on Fulton Street. The Caldwell home was a square house set far back in an ample green yard and reached by a gravel walk bordered with box. Just as all the rest of the distinguished lawyers liked to do, Judge Caldwell handed down his learning by teaching students of law. He was an eccentric man, exacting and magisterial and a terror to the callow young fellow pleading his first case. Indeed, the Judge was apt to speak out his crochety mind to anybody. If ever he became angry or irritated, there would come out a spot upon his forehead between his eyes, a patch of flushed skin which grew more lurid as his anger grew. This oddity was spoken of as the "Caldwell Mark" and recurred again and again in his descendants. His granddaughter, Frances Fisher, had it, and I have seen it myself break forth suddenly upon the forehead of another granddaughter kept in at school for missing her spelling lesson!

In 1844 the second Archibald Henderson was still alive. Inheriting the Steele homestead through his wife, this man enjoyed a quiet life of study in his comfortable old house, which stood a little out of town near the familiar road to the river. He was never drawn into politics, and, oddly unlike his great Federalist forebears, he belonged to the Democratic party.

It was his sister Jane, who became by her second marriage Mrs. Nathaniel Boyden. She was the most delightful personality of all the young matrons of the town. My mother's sister Mary had lived under her roof a few years before, while she had been teaching in the Female Academy. There was a friendship already prepared with her for Mother when she came. The two women both loved good books, lovely gardens, and the odd individuality of the people around them. Such high spirits, such a keen merry wit, warmed by a sympathetic nature as Mrs. Boyden possessed have seldom been found. Sad it is that the ineffable quality of such a person becomes in a few years but a memory of a memory.

There was another Henderson, also a lawyer, not attaining the state-wide distinction of his brother. This was John L. Henderson, clerk of the Supreme Court, who died in Raleigh. This man's descendant, one Philo White Henderson, whose name attaches him firmly to old Salisbury, wrote the words to an old familiar tune, "Along the River of Time I Glide."

A SMALL-TOWN NEIGHBORHOOD

Among these people of excellent minds it is good to find even a little written down so that later someone can realize it. Life is always interesting even though so few records are produced. Hamilton Jones was another of the lawyers of ability. The founder of the *Carolina Watchman*, he edited the paper before Mr. Bruner took hold of it. He was a humorist of no mean order and used to write accounts of the amusing incidents he met in his law practice and publish them. In his old files, or rather referred to them when quoted elsewhere, is a story called "Cousin Sally Dillard," a sketch worthy of Judge Longstreet. It was so good that it was claimed and counterclaimed, but we know it was "one of Ham Jones's stories." I have seen another of his stories reprinted lately, showing the humorous sufferings of a man who went to Charleston to transact business and got tangled in social life which he did not understand.

"Cousin Sally Dillard" sounds as if it must have happened, for in the story appears a well known farmer down the river, a Captain Rice, whom Father knew quite well. Besides, there are the river, much corn liquor, Rowan County mud, and a picture, which must be true, of crude country manners in that time.

This does not give all the neighborhood. Besides these, my parents knew everyone in town, and must have lingered over their small traits and the peculiarities which made them interesting. My parents were not narrowly concerned with the few people of their own ilk, but had a democratic appreciation of real character. They enjoyed reality, whether it was pruned and polished, or whether it grew a little lopsided through environment. These are enough to show the kind of people they had come to live among, people whom no one now remembers, any more than are remembered those whom I knew best.

VII

DOCTORS AND PATIENTS IN THE FORTIES

My father, like his father, fitted snugly into the life to which he was destined. He was not one convinced that perfection had been attained in the social organization or the knowledge of his time; neither did he tear his hair over things he could not help set right. So long as he could serve those who had need of him, he let the world wag, while he enjoyed daily the practice of medicine. He was not a man afraid to speak his mind in condemnation of what he knew to be wrong, and yet he was tolerant and kindly toward ignorance and human frailty. He loved to discuss cases with his partner, Dr. Whitehead, an astute observer; and he took the greatest interest in consolidating the organization in North Carolina of a Medical Society. With all his might he opposed and derided the flood of patent medicine advertisement which then overflowed the North and the South alike. Most of all, he cared for his individual patients. He considered their problems and made friends of those who consulted him.

He and Dr. Whitehead shared between them the responsibility of the sick of the town and surrounding country. From the beginning of their association, each chose the work he preferred and the cases most likely to interest him. Dr. Whitehead was by skill and preference a surgeon, and was accustomed to declare that he liked to *see* what he was doing! He was a tall man, slender-fingered, cool, and competent; while Father, who was massive and jovial, understood better the characters of men. Early he began his prolonged experience in the care of young mothers and their babies—no simple task when germs were as yet unrecognized and when little children, in spite of all that was then understood, died like flies in the heat and damp of every sultry June. In this he found a cause worthy of the thought he gave to it. The normal routine of fevers and fractures, malaria and mumps, the two doctors shared as seemed best. If other practitioners strayed into town, as now and then one did, the two, like kind, tolerant big dogs, inspected the newcomer and perhaps passed him. There was more than two physicians were able to do, but scarcely enough work to keep a third man busy. This was decades before specialists were known.

The general practitioner who used to go about doing good in a horse-drawn buggy, is now as obsolete as the dodo bird, done away with by modernity even as the peddler and the circuit rider. Sometimes I think a service was rendered by the human understanding of such a doctor, a service sadly missed since his disappearance. In those old times his work was the one resource in sickness; his laborious days were occupied to the full, his nights seldom left undisturbed. Only because he found it impossible to detach his heart from his work and see it impersonally, did my father find his life too hard for him. He was so made that when his treatment was not effective he could not help worrying, not for his own sake but for the patient he wished to cure. When some father of the family or some mother of small children died in spite of him, it grieved him to his very soul.

Some humorist once named the general practitioner of the last century, the "wheel rotifer of infusions," alluding to the ever-turning wheels of the doctor's buggy as he made his rounds and to the drugs which it was then the custom for him to dispense in person. My father's beginnings went even further back in time and in manners, his early practice being even more remote, in a society more primitive. When he began, the Doctor's horse invariably wore a pair of heavy saddle-bags across; and the legginged and mud-spattered rider would be hailed from lonely farms, called in as he rode on horseback over tracks impossible for wheels. His devoted patrons would boast of him that "he kept three horses rode down the whole time, he was such a good doctor."

I have heard my father tell of chances he was forced to take; of fatal bleedings impossible to arrest, in a country dependent upon edge tools and far from resources; of the rough and unmitigated surgery sometimes unavoidable; of sufferings which make our queasy sensibilities wince. One day he was stopped in passing, called to a man whose leg, just below the knee, had been crushed by a falling tree. The place was fourteen miles from Salisbury, and Father had left his amputating knives at home. This was before chloroform had been heard of. He found in the farm kitchen a keen old butcher knife of good steel, and at the outdoor grindstone he thinned the blade to a razor edge. Then with a meat saw and with this knife he made the amputation, giving the patient, to ease his pain, all the morphine he dared administer. While it was grim and bloody surgery, the man's life was thereby saved to his family. Said Father, "I did a good job, and the limb healed with a convenient stump, so that when he strapped on his peg leg, he could go about his business, except that he could not get 'round on plowed land." This is by no means the only story that sticks in my memory as Father told it.

The kindly Germans of Rowan County seem to have had an especial interest for my father, because he had known none like them in his own birthplace. These people were still speaking a dialect made of German forms mixed with a little English. They were indeed speaking much the same jargon when I remember hearing them with my own ears, although in the interval between 1844 and 1880 their speech must have been somewhat anglicised. In cultural level these sons of peasants were much inferior to the ingenious and pious Moravians of the Wachovia settlements, and certainly they were less capable than the few families like the Beards, the Fishers, and the Clements who came to Rowan at the same time. But all these resembled each other in practical industry and thrift. If our Germans were illiterate, so were half the population of that time. The fact that food and simpler necessities were so easy to get, while refinements of any sort were hard to come by, made improvement in standards of living, over and above rough plenty, nonexistent in most places. In domestic arts these people degenerated after the time of the first settlers' skilled handicraft. In religion they still adhered firmly to the Lutheran faith, with a few who were German Calvinists. Always hard workers, they cared much for the trim appearance of their farm buildings, a mind their Scotch-Irish neighbors did not share; and every one of them was sure to have money laid away. They were primitive and very superstitious, believing in the magical and uncanny, in spells and witchcrafts. This is true of their kinsmen wherever they live close together in any part of the United States now, even after so many generations. Emphatically it was true of Rowan County Germans when Father came to Salisbury. In Rowan, such ideas have long passed away, since the race has gone into the melting-pot.

After the new doctor hung out his shingle, it was not long before he was called in to "conjure" a German patient. Here is the story.

Even in the 1840's, modern ideas were spreading, and the son of an old German widow, far down in the south of the County, becoming thoroughly alarmed about his mother's strange malady, instead of trusting to the old witch-women came to town to call in the new "drug-doctor." When Father reached her isolated farm, he found a woman introverted by her lonely life, indulging in as pretty an orgy of hysteria as any neurotic ward could show today. Her sons, tearful and solicitous, looked at her in despair. Sending them from the room, she told the doctor plainly that she well knew he could do nothing for her. She was convinced that one "Jim

Seyfert" had laid a spell upon her, and that was the trouble. Then lowering her voice, she told with bated breath how this man would walk by the house, shaking his head and stabbing with his forefinger against her; also how he had openly threatened her with magic spells, and how he had often laid crossed sticks in her path to the milking shed.

Being young and humorsome, Father made a wise face of it and listened attentively, with apparent respect, to the whole story. He told her sons that he could do nothing whatever for their mother, at least not just then. She could be cured only by means of a live frog, and this was February, no month for frogs. When they had captured one they might call him again.

It might have been April or May, when the round-faced young German reported at last that they had caught their frog. When the doctor rode out next day, he found a lively fellow making futile leaps against the side of the deep milk crock where it was confined. Father then sat down to have his "pow-wow" with the old mother. He told her that he would kill this frog and by its means would put a spell on Jim Seyfert, whose legs would be affected exactly as the frog's were when they were severed from its body; that this should continue until Jim Seyfert reversed the spell he had sent upon herself. And so, muttering a little medical dog-Latin, Father threw the frog legs after skinning them, into a basin of water which he had beforehand carefully salted in the kitchen. The sick woman looked on eagerly from her bed. When the twitchings and jerkings of the leg muscles began to slow down, she declared she felt much better already, and soon afterwards she rose and walked into the kitchen supported by her two devoted sons.

"But Doctor," she said at last, "I got me a good mind not to pay you nothin' because you never showed me the sight of that hellion, Jim Seyfert, a doin' of his *verruckter* tricks!"

Another of Father's medical stories had to do with a man

named "Cashdollar" out at the Gold Hill Mine. He was a mine boss, and was struck on the head by a flake of stone which fell a great distance down the shaft. He was of course taken up unconscious, and unconscious he lay, while a man could traverse twelve rough miles and summon a doctor to him. When at last Father examined the wound, he saw the substance of the brain exposed by the hole in the skull. He knew there was but a slim chance for the fellow to pull through, but he did his best.

"First," he recounted, "I picked out all the chips of stone and bone, then I made a silver plate by hammering out a silver half-dollar very thin. With this I covered the opening in his head, bringing up the scalp finally so as to hold all together. Then I left him, as I supposed, inevitably to die of the injury. For two weeks he lay comatose. Then they told me he came suddenly to himself and took up the string of curses he had been shouting out, down in the mine when he was struck, and continued from where he left off. He recovered finally and lived six years, to be stabbed in a drunken brawl. Some folks take a lot of killing!"

Then there is a story of the man whose ear the mule bit off, but this can only be referred to.

My father in observing conditions became thoroughly convinced of one fact. He could see that wrong diet was affecting both young and old to their injury. Whenever he could, he preached certain truths about simple digestible foods, even though, in a population such as ours, people's dietary preferences were the articles of their belief hardest to alter. Fruit was plentiful, and he used to recommend the use of it ripe and uncooked. Milk was plentiful, too, but was regarded with strange suspicion. He tried to assure people how necessary it was for both the young and the very old. He came to recognize also the strange individuality of body chemistry by which one man's meat is another man's poison, and by careful experimentation with the food easily attainable he is said to have preserved the life of many a baby that would have died without his care in the heat of early summer. It was by his precept and providing that a great variety of vegetables and comparatively little meat was the rule on our family table.

Soon there were children to be cherished in his own home. The eldest was a girl, the second a boy, and this little fellow died very suddenly when he was three years old, of something they could not then remedy, membranous croup. Of this little first-born son, named after my father, there remained no picture and no memorial save one. On the floor of our old back gallery used to be visible the outlines of a baby's foot and hand, around which grooves had been carefully cut with a pocketknife. "It's all I have left of little John," Mother said. "He stepped into a little spilled water and then stumbled, leaving a wet foot-print and hand-print so perfect and so characteristic that I sat down that very moment on the floor and cut out the shape so they could be traced."

Mother sought some means of easing the pain of her loss and found it in mental work. She must long have been missing the stimulus of her scholarly upbringing, for Grandfather had kept his girls busy, teaching them that their minds, as minds, were as good as a man's. As far as success in study was concerned, he proved his point, but at first Mother had been glad enough to be free of this constant mental effort. It made her seem too old and be esteemed too different; and it isolated her in her gay normal girlhood. Now she needed some of it back again; she wanted intellectual effort to help her forget the heartache; so she turned to the nearest thing. She began in earnest to study Father's medical books. Of course a mere book knowledge was not of supreme worth. In a year or two she mastered with Father's help all she could learn in this way. She insisted upon his subscribing to all the best medical journals, both English and American, and upon his buying the newest medical books as they appeared. She it was who read these exhaustively and who made notes of everything new. Father was a very busy man, often too tired out to feel able to read at night, often so exhausted that he fell asleep in his buggy, or even on horseback, losing consciousness for an instant, then jerking back into awareness. So constantly on the go, a man could not dig and delve in study, after a day of such exhaustion, but Mother enjoyed doing his studying for him. She read aloud to him what was novel and important; she came to know his problems almost as he did himself.

While in all this she must have been, like him, deep in the intimate knowledge of the secrets of the community, never was there the least allusion, never the trembling of an eyelid, or the set of the lips to show what she knew. Her way was never to let friends know that she studied anything. She "sometimes read to the Doctor in the evenings," she confessed.

It was due also to her encouragement and close economy that Father was able to turn his practice over to another physician for an entire winter while he went to New York to study the new medical discoveries, especially the use of anesthetics.

During this sojourn, he was invited to spend the Christmas holidays visiting Mother's relatives in Connecticut, and he loved to tell of his experience of a New England winter in all its snowy beauty; of the alertness and witty vigor of one of his wife's grandmothers at eighty, of the serene comeliness of the other, not quite so aged. Old Dr. North, in New London, too deaf to converse, was still very friendly to his young southern colleague. He made him free to read any or all of his seven barrels of "thoughts," that stood in his office. Whenever Dr. North had a thought he considered worthy of careful expression, he wrote it out on a slip of paper, corrected it, and placed it in a wallet he always carried. The wallet being filled was emptied into a barrel. By this time there were seven barrels of these, one would think worth exploring, if indeed they had not been carelessly burnt after the old doctor died.

That winter Father also went to hear Jenny Lind, whose concert tours in America were managed by Barnum. She sang in New York before huge audiences. Father liked to recall the power of her soft notes, which were not damped down or lost, but kept their sweet distinct tone.

When after this winter of study Father returned, he was ready to refute all the local wiseacres who insisted that any relief from pain by means of anesthesia was "against the Bible" because not mentioned there. They believed that no woman should be spared the pangs of birth-pain because of the ancient curse of Eve. But, after all, people were not so bigoted or so piously determined that their relatives should suffer all the pain possible, if there was relief at hand. In the end they all asked for it.

In order to permit of Father's leave of absence, Dr. Whitehead had been overworked, and, being of a highly nervous temperament, he stimulated his faltering energies in the regular fashion of the time and place. I have not heard what really passed, but I feel sure he became offended because of something Father found occasion to censure. Certain it is that the close friends suddenly broke their partnership and at the same time their friendship. The two would be continually on the road, but they would pass without a greeting or a glance. When one glimpsed the familiar buggy of the other round the turn of the road, he would begin to lay on with the whip, which was necessary, because the horses had never quarreled at all. They looked forward to their old custom of equine fellowship, and the long rubbing of social noses, while the two doctors talked over cases. These friendly animals shamed their owners and showed the way to reconciliation and a new understanding, which took place after a while. The renewed friendship lasted all the joint lives of their masters, but the formal partnership lapsed. This made little real difference save that the accounts were separately kept. Father's favorite work continued to be the care of mothers and infants. Dr. Whitehead still practiced his skillful surgery, and still they arranged their practice to suit their predilections, and talked over together all their difficult problems.

Father used to have his habitual bedside jokes. He required, so he said, that whenever a new baby-patient appeared, it should immediately have a regular name given it, to call it by. When families disputed, as families always will, as to which grandfather, etc., Father's reaction was invariable: "And so you haven't named this child yet?" he would say. "I see I shall have to name it myself," and if it was a boy, he consistently referred to the little wretch as "Abinadab" but if it was a girl, she would be "Minadab."

"Doctor, don't you *dare* to call my lovely baby by that awful name!" the young mother would cry, and Father would say, "Very well, madam, very well. Give the poor infant a better one and I will try always to remember it."

VIII

ABOUT RAILROADS AND TAXES

It was the very first summer that Father and Mother spent in Salisbury, the summer before they moved into the Frontis House. They lived for a time in a rented home which stood somewhere opposite the postoffice of 1936. That year, there occurred a prolonged and disastrous drouth.

Anyone interested in ancient histories of long-past weather might cull from old journals and letters notices of its foregone vagaries. There were in our section, the "good crops of 1780," the "cold year of 1816," the "cold Saturday and Sunday" of some time in the twenties, "the big snow of 1857," but just now there was the "drouth of 1845."

In this weather dispensation, the crops of the entire western half of North Carolina were nonexistent. The yield did not amount to even scanty fruition—there was no yield—and the price of corn went higher and higher, until shelled corn brought the preposterous figure of a dollar and a half a bushel, instead of the usual forty to sixty cents. The trees of the forest, those whose roots did not tap the deeper watersprings, withered and died for lack of moisture. The poor half-starved cattle tottered around dusty pasture land in search of a little grass or ranged the woods to eat leaves. Very many beasts died of starvation. All this dismal scarcity came in a year when the crops of the eastern part of the state were never finer; so plentiful were they that they were scarcely worth the gathering, while in that same year the fisheries had been so abundantly productive that not half the fish taken were ever laid in salt. Fat roe-herring had been used by farmers to fertilize the hills of corn, after the old Indian fashion, and so helped to produce a part of this superfluous abundance.

All these conditions, so unbalanced, so difficult to meet in a measure of relief, pinched the pocket nerve sufficiently to set our whole people wondering. If only there had been a railroad running through the state from east to west, these inequalities could have been made nearer even by distribution. The penny wisdom, the lack of foresight, the actual imbecility of the way policies had been shaped while politicians wrangled and repeated the same old slogans, could be discerned by any "impartial" observer, but that nobody was really impartial was shown by the continuance, even after an object lesson like this, of the same old disputations. Political trends are very hard to alter and persist by inertia of tradition long after they have lost every shred of the reason for existing which they must once have had. A change is hard to influence, even in the face of such an emergency as this long and terrible drouth.

Outside events must be mentioned which give a wider background than can be seen in the limits of our corner. When the state of Texas was annexed and opened to settlement, the wagons of the movers rolled all the faster. Soon there were not going to be people enough left in North Carolina to enjoy the advantage if the railroads were all built at once. The treaty with Great Britain in 1846 adding the far Northwest to our continental area had been concluded, and two years later the United States rounded out the Southwest into the Pacific. The Mexican War had intervened, but not many of our townsmen had gone into the American Army. It would have been natural for soldiers from the southern states to enlist because of climate and because southerners were so eager for the extension of slavery to the great empire that is Texas. President Polk had fulfilled his election promise of annexation of Texas and made his name a rallying cry in North Carolina. By this the Whigs were disorganized and the Democrats reassured.

In the year 1846, Grandfather Mitchell, at the request of the North Carolina Assembly, made survey of a tentative route from Raleigh to Salisbury the course of which indicated very nearly the exact line later followed by the North Carolina Railroad. This road was intended to be a state-built highway, a graded turnpike with a rounded contour, and a road from Fayetteville was planned at the same time to join it in Salisbury. Then the connection might be carried farther west. It sounds strange to say so, but as yet there was no proper wagon road to Fayetteville, the head of navigation nearest us. After forty miles or so east, the track dissolved into a skein of alternate paths over the wire grass and shifting sands of Moore and adjacent counties, winding across the open "piney woods," where every man chose his own turnout. The deep sand and the hard pull of it against wheels bespoke a plank road. It was a general opinion that no railroad which went through such poor country could ever pay for itself. But something had to be done. North Carolina had definitely come to the end of its tether. There was no way of getting from one part of the state to another, no rivers suitable for commerce, no tolerable roads, only one line of railroad which stopped at Raleigh, and no more. Transportation was continually being better organized everywhere else in the United States, but here everything was lacking which had not been in use when the eighteenth century closed.

It was during these middle years that the movement West began to include rich people, who took large bodies of slaves to new and fertile lands in Alabama, in Mississippi, and, farther still, to the virgin prairie lands of Texas. There the raising of cotton began on a larger scale. The fine homes, the broad-winged plantation houses which had been built before this time in the eastern part of the state, date their first decline from the forties quite as much as from the ruin of the

Civil War. When their builders went West, the old homes were apt to change hands for the worse and be allowed to run down. Our state, never so proud of family, or so used to luxurious living as her next-door neighbors, lost far more of her most distinguished citizens than she could afford. Grandfather Summerell's old patron was one of such rich planters, who about this time emigrated to Mississippi, taking his entire household and his full hundred of field hands, and forsaking his level acres, where the drainage ditches promptly filled with mud and rank growth until they became worse than the wilderness from which they had at first been reclaimed.

To go back a little to the beginning of this chapter, it was in the autumn of the drouth, that wagons loaded with grain came through all the way from Weldon to Salisbury, sent by Grandfather Summerell and others, a venture which brought a good profit. Grandfather had made huge crops of corn and oats, and he was always a man who, when it began to rain porridge, set out his bowl. He accompanied one of these wagon trains to Salisbury, and at that time he had traded in person for the Frontis house, which he presented to my mother.

Two years later it might be perceived that the portion of the nation called Rowan County had forgotten the drouth and had taken heart for a new day. The old town of Salisbury had given her blessing to those who needs must leave for Texas, but there are always many who prefer to stay in the well-known home scenes where they were born.

In an isolated country, isolation breeds provincialism. The western half of North Carolina was very provincial, and although half the Southwest had by this time been seeded with our stock, no new blood had meanwhile come in to us.

The so-long-acclaimed economy in tax assessments which was the whole text and teaching of the political leaders, might have been an excellent thing if it had not ceased to be a method and become an object, a fetish. When Assembly after Assembly met, organized, took its pay, and spent its whole session voting to do nothing at all except return home in complacent satisfaction over its extreme good management, the entire subject was getting ludicrous. Long before this, there had been a sample of just such legislative economy, which led to the loss of that art treasure, the Canova statue of Washington, which was destroyed by fire in 1831. This happened because the legislature thought the state could not afford to place the heavy marble upon a movable platform, so that if need arose it could be rolled out of a building well known to be inflammable. It was destroyed in the burning of the first Capitol, only a few years after it was placed there, and a few pitiful fragments of calcined marble are all that remain to testify that it ever existed. This is but a parable of the cheerful absurdity of the country legislator confronted by something not in his party platform.

My mother saw this statue when she was a little girl and described it for me before I had ever seen an engraving of it. But the disaster of its loss had been a fact of history for a good many years when Miss Dorothea Dix came to stay for a time in Raleigh and recorded that the lamps beside the beautiful new Capitol were not kept lighted because of the persistent practise of the greatly admired virtue found in strict Democratic economy.

Miss Dorothea Dix was a lady from New England, who was traveling all over the civilized world, advocating the cause of humanity for the insane. These unfortunates had hitherto, all over the world, been confined in prisons or thrust into cages, often maltreated, and oftentimes endangering the sane. Miss Dix had now come to visit North Carolina out of pure zeal for her cause. She proceeded as she was accustomed to do. She gathered the facts for herself, wrote them into a memorial, and this she referred to the representatives of the people assembled to make their laws. She urged that North Carolina should reform her own deplorable conditions, which were as backward as any.

Just now, the governor was a Whig, a wise man from Alamance, a western county. In November, 1848, he addressed an Assembly which, by this time, had become predominantly Democratic, and so opposed to him. It was shortly before his retirement from office, and he felt impelled to tell them plainly the dismal story of their failures with transportation problems. He described how the Raleigh and Gaston, and the Wilmington and Weldon railroads both were at this time fallen into disrepair, and were financially well toward a bankrupt condition. He described their equipment as out of date and neglected. The "strap-irons" which in those early times were screwed down upon wooden stringer-rails to make a surface upon which the car wheels ran, often became loosened, and the ends of these metals, called "snake heads," would detach themselves as the train ran over them. They would curl up under the wheels and penetrate the flimsy wooden coaches, stopping the train and endangering the lives of passengers. I have heard it told how some friend of my parents narrowly missed being impaled, when one of these ripped through his coat, pinned him to the ceiling, and only by good luck passed up inside his clothing, escaping the body of the man.

With only two unconnected lines of railroad built piecemeal, even so late as 1848 we might be said to have no proper transportation system whatever; and, according to the parsimonious policy of those who voted the taxes, no greater expense could even be proposed without the strongest opposition. How often the best contrived policies of one era degenerate into the intrenched error of another!

Now if the assembled statesmen had not the imagination to see, or the influence with the voters to justify the spending of money for a railroad which could really haul a freight car or transport a passenger to some destination, how, by any stretch of vision, could these same men realize an altruistic cause such as Miss Dix's proposed asylum for the insane? The first was a purely economic question to be reasoned out in dollars; the second, by all the standards of those times, was a visionary absurdity. Governor Graham, however, made his second recommendation to the Assembly, after discussing the urgent necessity for more railroad mileage, and this was a recommendation inspired by Miss Dorothea Dix. She had woven her ascertained facts about the care for the insane in the state into a memorial to be presented to the Assembly. The Governor had read it and was fulfilling his duty in endorsing it, having no idea that any reform would ensue, but wishing to clear his own record. He reflected that as he was a Whig and the majority of the members of the legislature were Democrats, he was not expected to conciliate but could "hew to the line, and let the chips fall where they may."

This old story, as illogical as invention could construct, describes the adoption of both the reforms, the economic and the benevolent. Miss Dix was boarding at the old brick hotel in Raleigh, the very same building that stands at the head of Fayetteville Street to the left, as one walks out of the south door of the Capitol, the hotel where most of the representatives of the epoch stopped during the session of the Assembly. Here she became acquainted with Mrs. James C. Dobbin, of Fayetteville, the wife of one of the legislators; and in the long leisures of that legislative winter, the two ladies became good friends. Mrs. Dobbin fell ill, and Miss Dix immediately visited her and soon became her nurse. They talked at length of the cause which Miss Dix represented, a cause which had brought her, at her own expense, to North Carolina and was keeping her here with small expectation of success. A few weeks later Mrs. Dobbin died, with Miss Dix at her bedside.

In the weeks of Mrs. Dobbin's illness, the representatives of both political parties had finally assured Miss Dix that it was useless to talk further of establishing an asylum for the insane in the state, and at last she began to think she would have to give up her cause and endure a failure.

From the deathbed of his beloved wife came James C. Dobbin. He returned to the Assembly, disconsolate, manifestly struggling with his sorrow, dressed in the deepest mourning. Immediately he began an impassioned campaign for an asylum for the insane in North Carolina. It was, he declared, his idolized wife's last request as she lay dying. She had been convinced by her devoted friend, Miss Dix, and by her insight his had grown clear. He must fulfill his promise to the dead, and to the living. A genuine orator, his grief and his passion mounted until everyone capable of human sympathy was overcome. It is told how at one time he had the whole Assembly dissolved in tears. This was the turning point, the beginning of a broader vision, and a more liberal spirit.

After Dobbin's speech, Miss Dix was called to appear and be presented to the Assembly. She came in on the arm of Governor Swain, then president of the University. She brought with her a strange compulsion. The bill she advocated was passed by a vote of 101 to 10, and every man looked at his fellow in wonder how it had been brought about.

If the economy of this reform had before this never been discussed, now that it was adopted it could be shown that the expense of caring for the insane would be lifted from the counties, and this saving, added together, would go far toward maintaining the new institution. Now they could see it all as plain as print. Now they could go home and say to their constituents, "Justice to all, special privilege to none."

You will say quite truly that there is nothing about railroads in this story; yet somehow the adoption of one liberal measure meant the breaking of the ice, the riving of the stone. The hard shell of the political deadlock was gone, and people felt a glow of freedom, a rivalry in progress.

The Assembly now turned its attention to railroad bills, of which there were many waiting. The city of Richmond, among the rest, was seeking railroad connections to feed its trade, and, with the necessary capital already subscribed, it came asking a charter to extend a railroad straight across the western half of North Carolina from the Virginia to the South Carolina line, from Danville to Cheraw. This line was not to cost the state of North Carolina one penny, and the Virginians thought they had an argument which would be a clincher and would ensure them all they wished.

Very much to the contrary, their proposition aroused our fathers to bitter resistance, for, as it seemed to many of them, nothing less was being asked of them than the selling of their birthright. The Virginia bill was killed, many alternatives were discussed, and all the bills were voted down one by one, until there were left only two. One of these advocated a state-aided railroad to be extended from Raleigh westward to Salisbury, and there to be divided into two branches, one going south and one west. After all the speeches, the vote, as canvassed, seemed to stand equal, 55 in favor, 55 against this plan for building up the West. No one had the least inkling which way the speaker of the Senate would vote. He was a silent, noncommittal man, and he had taken no one into his confidence. It all hung upon his decision. He broke the tie by voting "aye" for the North Carolina Railroad.

It has been said by those who were present that the applause fairly rocked the granite Capitol, and that it was echoed by the whole state when riders, who had volunteered to spread the good news both east and west, spurred into each successive town. The measure, insuring a continuous central connection along the length of the narrow state of North Carolina from the ocean to the foot of the mountains, had for the first time united our commonwealth in interest and might be expected to do so in sentiment, making of us one people.

The route which the new road was to follow was almost the very one which had been laid out by Joseph Caldwell, the first president of the University, when, long before the days of steam locomotives, he proposed a tram-road to be constructed as a central highway for hauling merchandise. This course was re-indicated in general by Elisha Mitchell, when just before this he surveyed for the turnpike which was advocated, as mentioned a little earlier.

More than anything else, this step forward arrested the drift to the West and Southwest which, year by year, was depleting our population. It gave the whole state new hope and aspiration, employment in the building and expectation of trade to follow the railroad connection between the East and the West, and into South Carolina and beyond. The branch over the Blue Ridge was longer in being surveyed, for it had to traverse so much difficult ground, but in the year 1856 the first train ran clear through the state from Goldsboro to Charlotte.

Why was the lane so long in turning? Largely the difficulty must have come from an inexorable geographical position—the shape of the land, the course of the rivers, the sand-bar barriers of the coast with a lack of good harbors. Slavery had nothing to do with the lack of initiative, for slavery was universal in the South at the time. The roughness of pioneer living and the crudity of pioneer conceptions of comfort had passed away. Political stubbornness in a people is not necessarily an evil. North Carolina has never taken kindly to dictation, but has been unforeseen and unpredictable in her politics. There is a natural conservatism in our people, a certain shy sentimentality, a reluctance to desert the wisdom of the fathers, a preference for our own obstinate opinion, and a restive refusal to consider what other people choose to say of us, unsolicited. All these things may have entered into these events.

Father told me, when I was a child, how the County folk watched the railroad grow past us from the river, southward, as the work went on, day by day and week by week; how the Negroes who worked at the grading and filling sang newly rhymed railroad chants, and answered one another to the strokes of pick and shovel; how farmers selected their soberest, staidest mules for the perilous task of plowing in those fields nearest the track, and how these ancients, one and all, lifted heel on that day when the iron horse actually snorted into view, and ran away with plow-chains jingling, followed by the panic-stricken Negro plow hands.

For a long time after, wagoners kept on traveling. Their trade was doomed but not at once superseded. The movers, such a disturbing and sorry sight for more than twenty years, dwindled in numbers, as fewer and fewer families now took the road to the Southwest. If some young men did go, they went singly and by rail.

In the year 1857, "Porte Crayon," a newspaper man and an artist, was sent to Salisbury by *Harper's Magazine*. His article, one of a series called "North Carolina Illustrated," may be found under its date. He drew pictures of Gold Hill and its miners, and described a picnic and daylight dance he attended out by the river, where they had fitted up a brand-new station warehouse for a dance hall, to which the whole festive company traveled by the new railroad. He put up at the "Rowan House," then the best hotel. He gives a cheerful picture of Salisbury, not yet come to its best, but a pleasant, wholesome place in which to live. The standard of living was far more comfortable by this time. The town had even begun to reform itself. Public opinion began to consider that the swilling of unlimited quantities of whiskey was something less than respectable, and not a mere weakness to be condoned. Everywhere houses were better furnished. Judging by the shapes of the beautiful old mahogany pieces which, in our town, were never replaced at all by knobby walnut in the eighties, nor later by execrable "golden oak," we may see that most of the furniture must have been brought in after the railroad was running, after 1850. The huge sideboards, the long old sofas with rolled ends could not have been so easily handled in wagons over the roads of the time.

In Salisbury, the neatness of our homes, outdoors and inside, had always had a German quality. We did not endure dilapidated fences or sagging gates. Outhouses were whitewashed, gardens kept neat. Any down-at-heel appearance was far more common in more aristocratic sections, in those places where the best people lived in the country and the small town was only a convenience for trade. In Salisbury lived the usual professional men and merchants, but with them there were no homes of the wealthy, nor were these in the country. We were undeniably middle class. We had refinements, but no pretension. We were not wealthy planters. But in this decade the more prominent citizens had their portraits painted. The portrait of my father, which I possess, was done in 1853, and it is one of a good many I used to be familiar with in old Salisbury; and people bought silver, and sent to Richmond and Norfolk for carpets for the best room, and set marble clocks on their mantels.

All over the land a second "era of good feeling" had come to pass, with all the grisly old skeletons shut up in the closet, and everyone in honor bound to look the other way from all old bones of contention. Railroads were the introduction to, the instrument of, all this comfort and prosperity. North Carolina people could now be going places with the rest. Few wished any more to forsake finally the homely scenes, for the restless elements were drained away, but many were glad of a chance to visit the northern cities, and see the world.

Our people had become more happily stationary than most American populations ever are. Whole streets of homes in old

Salisbury remained for lifetimes in the hands of their first purchasers; farms were handed down from father to son. There are families living in Rowan today who were living just there long ago when my father and mother were young householders newly come to town.

IX

HER OWN BRIGHT SPIRIT

SPELLING OUT the reasons for other people's thinking—that is what most biography is about and what all fiction tries to do.

My mother had very little chance to leave her native state during her married life, and seldom went even as far from Salisbury as Chapel Hill. Summer jaunts were, by the fifties, very much the regular thing among the best people of South Carolina and Virginia, but in North Carolina traveling for pleasure did not come so early into fashion, certainly was not usual in the West.

Mother used to say, although the phrase was not original with herself, that North Carolina was "the valley of humiliation between two mountains of self-esteem." Our people of the West were what must be called provincial, sometimes with a tone of contempt, and although wealth and fashion existed in some places in the state, in Rowan we were homespun enough, and generally quite unable to afford a season at the White Sulphur, or at Saratoga Springs.

Inevitably, my father and mother took on the ideas of their time and place. They were comfortably off, but by no means rich. They, along with those with whom they associated, believed in the southern side of all current political questions. They believed, as I have been told, but with a few reservations, for they did not consent to the doctrine of nullification, nor did they indulge in tirades against abolition propaganda as conducted in the North. Reviewing passions long spent, we can see how our social organization, like any other carefully maintained scheme of living, must have had its good points as well as some bad ones, and we can see how those who lived in and by it were constrained to assent to all that it brought, by old custom, by habit, and by the influence of environment. Inside our own minds, I suppose, we knew our intentions and knew them to be good, though often misconstrued.

All over the United States, good prospects for the future were believed in, and no retardation of development was feared. With the locality, the rosy pictures of progress might vary, but everybody, everywhere, was certain that things must keep on growing better in the best world that had ever existed.

My mother had an uncle by marriage, living in Cheraw, South Carolina, a man from Connecticut, one who had lived so long in the South that like a religious proselyte he had come to profess in exaggerated form all the ideas which passed current there. He would call the Abolitionists evil names and declaim about them until Mother would have to laugh heartily at his tirades. Then the two grandmothers and the aunts in New England, a little afraid to tackle Grandfather Mitchell but willing to stand up for their opinions, would cover both sides of large letter-sheets with denunciations, and blame their southern descendants for being southern. This sort of thing, too, would have to be laughed off. Mother failed to see, as did many another in her time, what of inevitable severance was at work in these long-enduring oppositions, in the diverging social and political thinking of the two sections.

In such an atmosphere, in times restricted by it, Mother craved to know how and why the world outside had come to think so differently from our own little world. She believed that climates and natural conditions were the greatest influence in forming men's opinions, stamping them to an especial pattern. She could see this plainer than most, because she could see it in her own people. She would ridicule her New England kinsfolk for their tender concern for the Negroes they understood so badly, declaring these a thousand times better off now than when they were savages in Africa. She declared that these had never been deprived of anything they were capable of using, but she had at the same time an uneasy feeling that what was so good for the Negroes was somehow depriving the white people who owned them, or who worked in competition with them, of some essential of self-development. There was something disturbing at work in her mind. She would say, "The Negroes are getting plenty of the very best schooling, for are we not, all of us, taking turns in teaching them?" And indeed in our section this went far towards being the truth. She herself was a kindly mistress, as shown by the way her own servants behaved after freedom came to them.

Restless my mother was, with active mind and ever-skillful hands. The sense of restraint and inefficacy, the desire to use some of her abundant vitality beyond the bounds of her environment, made her thoughts widely wandering. She bought, about this time, a great many new books, especially books of travel. She conned them well. Just then the world was interested in exploration, and because for her the "only courser was a book," she doted on narratives of adventure in far places and descriptions of what existed there. On one crowded shelf, I remember the *Abbé Huc* on China and Tartary, travels in Siberia, in Africa, in modern Egypt, and in the Holy Land, as well as many volumes on better-known Europe. She could afford the new to keep company with the old leather-bound classics in Greek and Latin, and the English poets which she brought from her girlhood home. Then, too, she would beset our congressmen, Burton Craige and John W. Ellis, to procure the geological reports of the United

States, all about the newly explored western wonderlands, about the chasms and the geysers and boiling springs, now frequented as the Grand Canyon and Yellowstone Park.

Mother never let her Greek grow rusty. During the whole of that year she once spent in New London at her grandfather's, she studied the Greek dramatists under the tutoring of one of her father's old college friends who was teaching at Yale. I have seen the letter to Dr. Mitchell in which he wrote to the effect that Miss Ellen was quite as good in Greek translation as himself, that he felt it to be "something of a farce, my undertaking to instruct her."

In the old days "before the War," in many well selected private libraries were preserved the record of their owners' mental excursions, for there were no other sources to obtain books in the South. Next to the Greek and the Latin would be ranged Shakespeare, thoroughly studied, quoted with discernment. The long row of Scott's novels would come next, for this was the best beloved story-teller. Mark Twain expresses it as his opinion that it was Scott who unfortunately formed southern society according to a feudal ideal, and greatly to its detriment. This may be true in a measure. My mother's library included old copies of Dickens' and Thackeray's novels bought successively, as reprinted in the United States. It was not destitute of New England authors, Hawthorne, Emerson, and the genial "Autocrat," whose books were read almost to tatters. But Mother really enjoyed the unquestioning English reliance on the foundation of Church and State more than she sympathized in the freedom of Unitarian speculation. Provided she felt sincerity, she was inclusive in her likings. In poetry, Tennyson was the one poet then called modern who most delighted southern taste, but I never saw a line of Browning until I was a good-sized girl, and only then did I encounter a complete Tennyson, with all his later work. Charles Lamb was Mother's choice among all essayists. While she admired Thackeray greatly, she found Trollope better suited to her lighter mood than Dickens; but most of all she doted upon Jane Austen. These will specify her mental quality, fastidious and discerning. The immortal Jane had not at that time gathered to herself that widespread adoration which has since then grown so great.

Biographies and histories were, in proportion, by no means so plentiful as they are today. I remember the familiar ranges of the backs of Bancroft, of Irving's *Life of Washington*, of Macaulay, and of Prescott's "Conquests." Then a few French memoirs, a tiny leather-covered "Mme de Sévigné," and a *Télémaque*, in French. Besides significant books, Mother subscribed to *Harper's Magazine* and *Godey's Lady's Book*, and handed them all around the neighborhood. Now and then someone presented her with one of those gilded annual anthologies then fashionable, such as the *Poets of America*.

Too much mental activity in a woman is still considered a nuisance. In those old days, learning might be perhaps pardoned in a man but was a monstrous excrescence upon a womanly personality. Accordingly, neither then nor later did Mother talk much of her mental excursions. The charts of them as stratified in the various bookcases and old-fashioned "presses" around the house, I have indicated. She never arranged a formal library, set out in an especial room, although there were enough books to fill one. "I just have my few books to read and to lend to my friends; I have no library," she would say.

Mother's taste in style was for a simpler, more colloquial English. Her own talk was always vital and unforgetable. I say this because I have encountered so many sayings of hers unforgotten, in the hearts of her friends, since I grew up to be told. While she was disconcertingly different in more than a few matters from the ideal of her day as regarded women, she ignored the fact and thought of herself as being but little unusual. She always spoke disapprovingly of the "strong-minded" sisterhood!

To show how normal she was, one need only mention the children, the little family which had filled up rather slowly as the years went by. A second baby boy had died in infancy, and only lately had she succeeded in bringing through his "second summer" a little son whose two sisters were good-sized girls when he was born. Around the unconscious heads of her children her hopes and fancies circled, just as they do with any mother. Once I glanced into a locked diary to which she had confided her analysis of each child's character as it was revealed day by day. The list did not descend to myself, and I perceived after a page or two that it was not meant for me, and closed it, but, devoted mother that she was, she also could estimate each one's character keenly, and write it down. I used to know well I was not up to her standard, and she herself must have been forced to listen to a perpetual inner dialogue between the reasons which her mind saw plain as print, and the excuses her heart advocated. Besides her inner life, she was a person who wanted to do visible things. Who says it is the passive nature which is deepest?

Now in the midst of a slow maturity she came to know her power. Because it had always been a trait of her family to develop late, she had changed entirely from that normal, girlish, systematically trained, but somehow rather emotionally superficial young matron, who had come ten or twelve years before to Salisbury. Her mind had then been filled with book ideas from the outside; now and in the future it partook more of vital wisdom. Her self-imposed study of medicine had developed her. She was aware of the growing importance of science. Although not very much of current thought seeped in to confirm her in this, she was not afraid of new ideas when she encountered them.

One thing was especially able to fill her family with admiration, and that was Mother's extraordinary dexterity in all her varied handicrafts. She could carry on almost any of the fine needlework then considered so refined and so useful, with the least possible apparent effort. She had an unusual capability and habit of sewing a white seam rapidly, by the sense of touch alone, not glancing at one stitch out of twenty. She would sit with her book in front of her, paying all attention to that, but setting her stitches with uncanny regularity. So rapid was her sewing that when sewing machines began to be common, as they did after the War, she continued to sew up her seams by hand and fell her edges perfectly and nonchalantly as she sat with her Greek Testament or her new novel spread before her on the table; indeed, many an evening through has she read aloud to me without a break, and without even a hesitation in her hemming or overhanding.

In one of those fortunate years, Mother took lessons in painting from some itinerant portrait-painter, and learned to copy neatly. She produced a few carefully detailed pictures from originals in "Dodwell's Greece," a giant folio of colored lithographs of Greek ruins. One of these efforts, representing a fine perspective of columns of a ruined temple, stood one day upon the hall table, newly framed to hang on the parlour wall. Captain Rice, the identical farmer who "gin a treat" in that immortal story of "Cousin Sally Dillard," came in to see the Doctor. As he stood waiting, he gazed pensively at the picture. What he said was, "Now I reckon that mought be a plan of the new courthouse, ain't it?" After that the picture was spoken of in the family as the "plan of the new courthouse," for the courthouse built in that decade had columns, massive ones, across the front. It is now the old courthouse, standing nearer the center of Salisbury than the new, and used desultorily for a library, a community house, and a depository of records.

In this building, in the beginning, Sunday schools used

to be held for the purpose of teaching poor people to read. There were no public schools as yet, and in these makeshift classes it was Mother's habit to teach faithfully, not that she thought herself accomplishing much good, for she knew how ineffectual and condescending the whole attitude of it must be; but because she wished to show her desire for something better, and her concern for the underprivileged. I have heard her quote the words of a white girl she once took into her service for a nursery helper. This child, of a poor family and degraded, asked her, "Miss Ellen, what kind of a man is you got? Why, the Doctor, now, he don't cuss none, an' he don't drink none, he don't fight none—Why, he don't do nothin'!" Intrinsically, "Jincey" was a "right sharp gal," and Mother said of her, "Why do we sit here and allow people around us to form such ideals of living as this, and let them alone in their ignorance, while all the time they are just as *white* as we are, and probably as good, save for opportunity!" She knew families whose ancestry was as good as any, who had been marooned in pioneering times in lonely neighborhoods or on poor land. She wished earnestly that these might be taught in practical fashion so that they could come out of Egypt. Her concern was for the poorer whites of our state, growing ever poorer in their poverty, and more numerous. With such folk she had a way, never condescending, level, tolerant, talking with them of the basic interests which concern all men and women. The plain people cried out to her sense of justice, the "forgotten men and women" of whom Walter Page was to remind his state fifty years later.

Mrs. Spencer, over in Chapel Hill, Mother's girlhood friend, was also eager for education, but took a more aristocratic view of the subject. She believed that the University could make its lift felt from the top, like an educational force-pump, and she disdained such primary schools as would be needed to reach the common folk. She could not endure the uncultivated. She declared, for instance, that she could not admire Andrew Jackson because he was such a rough diamond; and as to that famous North Carolina editor, W. W. Holden, who came of the humblest extraction but was a man of extraordinary mind, she had not the slightest patience with him then or later. It is true that only after the War did he come into obloquy because of treachery to former friends, those men of the state who alone would be able to steer through a difficult situation of that era. My mother maintained that he would have trusted the best of these if he had not been so set back and snubbed in his youth for being the self-made man that he was, with the hatchet marks of his making all upon him. Who is able to read the page of the future, or declare that the past might have been shaped to something better!

She took the view that the neglect of common schools for common people, so general at this time, had something political mixed into it, that it was the disingenuous policy of those who deliberately neglected this training of that white man's intelligence which they lauded and flattered so regularly. She declared she wanted common schools to come first, and ahead of University expansion, a heresy indeed!

I well know there must have been some connection between the ideas Mother professed in these years, and those of a pioneer in popular education, of the years from 1840 to 1850 and onward. He was a personal friend of hers, often staying in Salisbury, where his kinsfolk were friends of our family. It is evident she knew him well. In his youth he published two novels, and of these he gave copies to her. I have seen them, bearing friendly inscription. The lines of thought these two people followed, the confidence they both felt in the dignity of the plain citizen, the idea of his needs, were the same in them both. It was in Salisbury that was held the first educational rally for the beginning of a public school system.

Before the War intervened to wreck his work and to destroy both endowment and revenue, there came to be a hundred and fifty thousand children enrolled in the public schools of North Carolina, under Dr. Calvin Wiley's leadership; and, for those times, his system was a good one. Especially was his manner of intensively training select young women for teaching in country schools, in sufficient number to set the machinery going as soon as possible, a practical scheme. Our habit is to compare this early beginning with those schools systems which come later in development; but in this day of small things in many states of the Union, the comparison would have been found in favor of North Carolina at this time. Our public school system was initiated in 1839-1840, and by 1860 was well on the way.

In his later life I knew Dr. Wiley. The work he had tried to do for his state had all been lost in the grievous wastefulness of war. Late in his life he was ordained a Presbyterian minister, and for his last years was employed by the American Bible Society. He was a gentle-spoken old man, whose face was a maze of intricate wrinkles and whose eyes were kind and weary.

Mother's urge for education used constantly to give her the desire to instruct this one and that. Her own children were, as children usually are, her most resistant pupils. Much of the thorough instruction she gave them could not well be avoided, and she did instill into them some interest in the things of the mind. As she was always trying to make her ideas count, she took it upon herself now and then to help young preachers prepare. I have heard her say that she found their minds too stiffly set, and got little response from them. But children, especially small boys, were always happy in my mother's company. She talked to them of their own concerns, with interest, as equal with equal. Older young folk were made uneasy by her. Her keen direct look daunted them.

As for the servants, they were frankly afraid of the keen incidence of her glance.

"Don't do it right, Miss Ellen gwine ter look right straight th'o you, ontell her eyes come out yo' back." That is what they said.

Father used to laugh at her by way of reproof of her unrestful eagerness, and would say roguishly, "My wife's a striver and a driver, but as for me, I'm a la-a-zy man!" meaning that he took things as a little more matter of course than she could.

A part of her revolt was shown by her reaction against conventional phraseology. She liked to say things oddly and teasingly. An old friend told me this story: how a very rigid religionist was inveighing in Mother's presence against dancing, as a wicked exercise. Mother declared, "I believe we do not give our young folk enough innocent fun. We should allow them to dance a great deal, and we should go ourselves and see them do it."

Said the objector, "That is a dreadful speech from a woman like you, a Christian woman!"

"But they danced in the Bible, and it was not wrong as we read it," said Mother. "Don't you remember how David danced? and he danced 'before the Lord' and he 'was girded with a linen ephod'? In other words, he danced violently, and in church, or what corresponded to it, and half undressed besides, and it was not counted against him as a sin!"

"If you let them know it is just *your way*, you can say anything short of calling people liars," was her saying, which must have covered the silence that fell after this sally.

A tearful speech reconciling an unnecessary death she called "Praising the Lord for your own stupidity." To one of her children, sulking, she cried, "There you sit, as glum and obstinate as a bull of Bashan," which sounded like the peak of frowardness. Her version of a sermon on a queer text from a minor prophet (preachers used such texts far more in those days), was; "The preacher gave us a good sermon from the holy text, 'Oh Ephraim, your cake's all dough'!" Mother's speeches were at times almost impish.

But she read and pondered long in her leisure moments. Being of a planned industry that brought to every task its time, she salvaged many an hour for long thoughts. The vexatious problems of the country she loved, the things she could not help—she lost them all in the timelessness of great literary perfection. Great thoughts from many minds grew familiar and slipped into her speech, as Biblical phrases were used unwittingly by pious women of old time.

It is hard to conceive how bitterly she must have chafed under the limitations of her life, so pleasant as it was in most of its conditions. She had only narrow opportunities for doing the work she was capable of accomplishing. As the decade wore away, she perceived the dim twilight graying many a fair prospect. Most of her friends, both men and women, knew very little of her mind. She did not choose to show them her thought. Character for her was the one touchstone, and she liked all good people. She kept her house well, she ordered her family with diligence, loved them, tried to give them good counsel if they came to ask it, and laughed heartily with them by way of sympathy. But her well furnished brain she used as an intangible retreat from all the things she would wish otherwise, not so much a home of dreams, as a school of pure thought, where she lived in retreat with her own bright spirit, alone.

X

CHANGING WEATHER

THE YEAR 1857 began apparently quite as normally as any of those serial years of progress and prosperity added to the calendar about them, save and except that it brought with it a real snowstorm, such as our mild climate seldom sees, making New Year's Day notable.

The Christmas season of 1856 was spent by Mother and her little folk at Dr. Mitchell's home in Chapel Hill, where her sister Mary's presence with her family made a family gathering. Father, who stayed behind to look after his practise, before January first, snatched time enough to ride on the railroad as far as Hillsboro, and thence drive over to Chapel Hill. He would see his wife's people, and be ready to accompany his own family back home.

The railroad had been kept a good distance from the University village because the sober authorities of the day could not consent to have it pass nearer, to spoil the collegiate calm, or to furnish the students too easy opportunity to go excursioning and neglect their books. Chapel Hill was twelve miles to the side of the main road. I think it was a Friday that Father arrived, and on the Sunday night it began to snow. Monday and Tuesday, two days and nights, the flakes flew, and every flake added to the mass. It was a snowstorm unprecedented, with a keen wind which kept piling the drifts; and when at last the snow ceased falling, the freezing cold came creeping down.

By the next Tuesday, New Year's Day, Father felt compelled to return to his patients, leaving his family to come later, as they were able. So, borrowing one of the big bay mules belonging to the University, which were always kept in Grandfather's stable, and taking black Uncle Summer to accompany him on the other mule, he set out bravely for Hillsboro.

As you leave Chapel Hill, going west, a long sloping road slips down away from town, formerly steeper than it now is. Encumbered by the heavy rider, the mule waded unwillingly to the crest of the hill and sidled gingerly downward. Very soon, it stepped off the road into a drift which reached its shoulder, for the snow was so deep that there was not a fence post visible to show the road. It was in the deep side ditch, therefore, that the mule wallowed about, my father having managed to leap clear of it. Finally it regained footing at the place where it fell in. A highly disgusted animal, stubborn after its kind, the mule persisted in turning homeward. It had filled both ears with snow, a thing no decent mule should be asked to endure, and when Father remounted and spurred his beast onward, he was whirled with determination back in the direction of Grandfather's stable. The mule won the debate. Next day when Father tried again, he managed the journey but was so chilled and fatigued by it that he was taken sick when he reached Salisbury. Mother was notified, gathered her children, and posted after him. This illness laid him low for months. It was a rheumatic fever, which left him with joints of the feet and ankles so tender that he never again could walk any great distance. This hindrance never passed away for the remainder of his long life. After this sickness, Father's youth, his genial early maturity, was definitely over and done. It was this disability which prevented him, a few years later, from serving in the Confederate Army and left him at home among the few thousands in the whole state who were of military age and were never enrolled on either side.

CHANGING WEATHER

That June, when Commencement was over, according to his regular custom Dr. Mitchell mounted his horse to ride out into the less frequented parts of North Carolina, to penetrate the Blue Ridge, and to enjoy himself thoroughly in scientific ranging through his beloved wildernesses. As he journeyed westward, he stopped the night with his daughter in Salisbury. He was undertaking the journey this year, so he told her, to correct a mistake. Between himself and Senator Thomas Clingman had arisen a controversy regarding comparative altitudes of the various peaks of the Black Mountain Range in Western North Carolina. This great mountain range makes a huge clot, two score miles long, with a number of separate peaks rising from it, not very different in height. To one of these, called the "Black Dome," the Senator had transferred the slightly greater altitude of what was subsequently called Mitchell's High Peak, which came next to it in order, a summit which Dr. Mitchell had surveyed when he surveyed all the sixteen peaks of the Black in former summers, and had singled out as being the loftiest of them all. This mistake could be corrected easily, being now well verified. He wished to do so in time to keep it from being recorded wrongly in the government map now being engraved in Washington.

Dr. Mitchell was a man very vigorous for his sixty-five years, and an untiring walker. He was really sentimental in his delight in the pristine unhackneyed beauty of the mountain solitudes. In repeated summer excursions among them, he had come to respect and understand the mountaineers, those solitude-loving, self-reliant people who had come somewhat to resemble the Highlanders of Scotland. He had been a welcome guest at their cabin firesides and had enjoyed their folk wit and quaint phraseology. His journeys across the ridges were so strenuous that he took only mountaineer guides who were used to the steep wilds, when he did not go alone.

Accordingly, he met such a companion in Asheville, ascended the eastern slope of the Black, recalculated his altitudes, and spent the night in a cave or under a deep shelving rock a few feet below the peak afterwards named for him, on its northwestern slope. Next day he sent back his guide and plunged down the western declivity of the range to the home of "Big Tom Wilson," afterward the most celebrated of the guides and hunters of all that region. Staying the night at this man's cabin, he awaited his son, Charles Mitchell, who was to join him next day. When the young man did not appear as expected, Dr. Mitchell started on alone, and a little late in the day, to tramp back across the range. About the middle of the afternoon, a bewildering fog settled thick among the rocks and trees, veiling all distance, so that his best practice was to follow downwards some mountain stream and thus extricate himself by nightfall.

Following this plan, he seems to have gone down a ravine, a short way past the ridge, along which a nameless little river plunged and foamed. Then he came suddenly to a place where it had leaped for many ages, sheer down a cliff, and had worn for itself a deep pothole or basin in the solid rock at the bottom. On the brink of the waterfall, he must have slipped on the wet stones, and fallen headlong into that deep and silent pool. He must have been stunned by the fall and drowned immediately in the icy mountain water. But no one will ever know. His watch stopped at half-past three.

When that same day, a little late, his son arrived to find him gone already, he did not follow on foot, but on horseback rode the long way around and back to meet his father in Asheville. When Dr. Mitchell did not appear next day, nor the day after, and when none of his regular guides had word of him, the general alarm was given, and the whole country turned out for the search, beating up the bristling thickets, following many dim trails through the high balsam woods bedded with moss.

It was days later when Big Tom Wilson pointed out some marks on a mossy root which he said might have been made by the hobnails of Dr. Mitchell's shoes. He was jeered at by his comrades, who by this time were getting weary of the search.

"We've been a-follerin' bar-trails now for a week," they said, "an' there's bar-trails a plenty 'twixt here an' Toe River."

"Yes, there's bar-trails," Big Tom Wilson replied, "but when did ever any one of you see a bar with his claws on his heels?" By this hunter's superior observation, the new trail was followed and on the eleventh day after he must have fallen, Dr. Mitchell's body was discovered, perfectly preserved in the cold water and fortunately unmolested by wild beasts.

All this makes up a tragic story, and those who venerated the teacher or who loved the husband and father shared the suspense, the sorrow, and the loss. But at this remove of time, it may be seen how merciful was the call, how fortunate for him. He was taken out of life in the twinkling of an eye, while the shattering forces which were even then gathering to disrupt the world he loved were still inoperative, when trouble for his chosen institution was still unthought of.

In one of his letters to my grandmother, written during the explorations of a former summer, Dr. Mitchell described a deep, lonely, forest dell he had visited, a place seldom trodden by a human foot. He pictured the peace of it, the dumb resignation of creeping beneath some friendly rock, there to die solitary, as the ageing animals do when their time overtakes them. "To breathe out mortal breath in such a place, alone, would not be a hard way to die." So he had written, and so now he had his wish.

The year 1857, just passing, was the year of the Dred Scott decision, in which the Missouri Compromise was declared unconstitutional. In Congress, for the second time, a bitter war of words was being fought over it, with both sides in the controversy more determined and more abusive than ever. There was nothing as yet of visible disunion, nothing of actual destruction, although in South Carolina, the most sensitive of the southern states, mounting sentiment for secession was growing, and the measure was being openly advocated. Persistent prophecy, then and now, is the way to assure a thing's happening. And this is the background of our chapter, this national struggle swelling on the horizon like a storm cloud with grumbling thunder, looming always higher and darkening the future.

A young man born in Rowan County, Hedrick by name, was a member of the faculty at the University, a professor of chemistry. He had first graduated there, later studied at Harvard, and was recalled to his Alma Mater, where he had been teaching for several years. In a private conversation, he chanced to state that he disliked the institution of slavery to which he was born, that he had come to oppose its extension, that if he was convinced that a vote for Frémont, who was running for president with a free-soil plank in his platform, would avail anything at all, he would be ready to vote for him. He spoke rather casually and wistfully to one he counted his friend. The person who heard repeated the remark, making it sound harsh and bitter, rather than confused and regretful. Professor Hedrick was confronted by a report of his words.

In that year, so inflamed was sectional opinion, that uttering such a remark was about as prudent as casting a lighted match into a keg of powder. Hedrick did not deny saying the substance of what was reported. Unfortunately, he was unwise enough to write out, and to have published in the newspapers, a reply, and a statement of his exact words and sentiments—a manly and candid enough article as it reads today—but by it surmise was crystallized into certainty. In this he wrote of seeing, in his youthful life near the River at Hedrick's Ferry, a thousand slaves in a single year, taken across in their chains, being ferried over on their way south to the fields of Louisiana and Mississippi, where they were wanted for hard labor. Most of them were young men, sifted out from their kinsfolk, to become part of great plantation gangs organized for sugar production. This sight, so he stated, and this knowledge, had been ever since at work upon his mind.

The hot and hasty sons of the planter-aristocracy bitterly resented this criticism of the life they called the best, and even the implication of his adverse opinion. His students became a mob and rioted against him in his classroom, and outside also, until he lost all semblance of authority over them. The trustees accepted his resignation when he proffered it, and with him there also resigned M. Henri Herisse, a young Frenchman who returned immediately to France, where afterwards he became a historian of note.

Even after this rebuff, Benjamin Hedrick did not seem to realize what a pogrom had been raised against him, or what kind of genie had been let out of the bottle! It may be laid down as an axiom that any political system or religious creed which requires that a palisade be built to protect it from encountering adverse opinion, is, by that very fact, to be considered a dangerous explosive. The maintaining of a tightened and riveted consent is something that has never long succeeded in keeping away change, but at this particular time any tiniest exception taken to our southern views was considered an attack on the foundation of society and not to be permitted. Hedrick should have known all this perfectly well. Self-preservation should have warned him not to go to the State Educational Convention held in Salisbury in October by Mr. Wiley. The young men of our town heard of his presence. They hanged him in effigy in front of his lodging. This insult proved decisive enough to send him finally out of the state before a worse thing should happen. He took the train for the North the next morning.

It was this event which made all that was being discussed as possible, into a probability, something expected by all, and, by some, seriously desired, indicating that all the yarn was spun, all the fate prepared. These things rush down a steep place irresistibly.

It was in 1852 that Mrs. Harriet Beecher Stowe published *Uncle Tom's Cabin*. This was a prohibited book at the South. That Mother owned a copy, I am witness. The volume must have been sent to her by some of her northern relatives, who were vigorously aligned upon the opposite side and who did not fail to write and tell her how diabolical were all the works and ways at the South. Once when a small girl, I saw my mother take a parcel out of a trunk in the attic and, removing the wrappings, produce a book. She took it downstairs, and as she sat by the fire read it and burned each leaf as she finished it. Deeply impressed, as a child would be, I asked about this. She replied, "It's a book not true, written by a woman who should have known better, and great trouble came of it."

A second book, published in 1857, was even more indignantly relegated to the index of forbidden writings. Oddly enough, this other was one of the few literary products of Rowan County. In the years of its censure, anyone might have run the risk of being tarred and feathered who even remembered its existence. It was entitled *The Impending Crisis* and was written by a country boy born over Mocksville way, in what was then Rowan, but now is Davie County. The author was of German-American parentage, his full name being Hinton Rowan Helper, his parents spelling it "Helfer." His book in its day was a firebrand, nay, a stick of dynamite. Its main thesis was the argument that slavery was irretrievably degrading and perhaps destroying the poorer

CHANGING WEATHER

white people of the south, mentally, morally, and especially economically. It took away, so he said, their right to work, by making out of manual labor, slavery business, and by bringing down the man who owned no Negroes to the level of the slave. The book was written with intense animus, not only against slavery but also against the Negro race. This man hated a Negro. As a boy he must have been humiliated in some way by some Negro. His father is said to have owned slaves, and it is impossible to imagine what could rankle in his son's mind so bitterly. Even along with its spirit of animosity, the book was stuffed with irrefutable facts, and contained a measure of truth told in such a way that no southern man could bear to read it. Cool appraisal, which can only come much later, asserts that Helper arranged his statements and statistics and suppressed many aspects. But what man proving a point by figures gathered from historical data has ever done otherwise? The southern press went wild. A man who undertook to distribute the book in North Carolina was promptly put in jail. Nothing was too evil to tell against this country boy and his book. He did not deceive himself. He well knew he could never come home, no, not for an hour!

W. W. Holden, who was well known as the editor of the *Standard* in Raleigh, himself led the attack on Helper and excelled his own record for vituperation. His editorials on the subject fairly sizzle with anger and condemnation. Slavery as a topic was about this time pretty well loaded everywhere. John Sherman, gone home to Ohio to "mend his fences," lost the election merely because he recommended Helper's book to somebody; but by 1860, that squeamishness was past, and antislavery crusaders were using it as a campaign document. And so, in 1850 when Hinton Helper gave up his job in Michael Brown's store and went to California to dig gold, no one would have picked him out as the man to light so great a fire. Kinsfolk of these Helpers are remembered by friends of mine as good quiet country folk, and Hinton was considered, when he started West, a fine hardworking fellow with a bright future, but one to whom no exciting adventures were ever attributed.

Long afterwards, when I asked her, Mother grudgingly replied that a good part of the book was undeniably true. It was plain that somewhere she must have read it, but in the later fifties I verily believe the possession of a copy would have sent even a respected mother-of-a-family permanently out of community standing, if not actually to prison. As I have said, both my parents adhered to the southern side of the cause. Besides giving to it everything they owned in money, they argued for it, loved it. It was their own.

Grandfather Summerell, who had always done his own thinking, seeing his ancient predictions regarding Negroes coming literally true, began to call in the money owing to him. If it was paid him in gold, he would remit a good percentage. Always he had been in the habit of allowing some discount for this. Always he had been known to love gold money for its indestructible value. He kept his own counsel and was cool and wary. When the time came, he invested sufficiently in Confederate bonds to avoid all suspicion. Then with his own hands he managed to secrete seventy-five thousand dollars in gold coin, and this he did very soon after South Carolina had fired on Fort Sumter. There was no one to call him disloyal, for no one knew. Father and Mother held nothing back. In our garret, on top of the great horsehair trunk where Mother found Mrs. Stowe's book, sat Grandfather Mitchell's hat, which was found floating on the pool where he was drowned. Inside it was a mass of parchment paper, and once I looked at this. It was a bundle of Confederate bonds. Somebody collected these in after years, and Mother sold her bundle for about three dollars, I think she said.

CHANGING WEATHER

In 1859 came the John Brown Raid. The decade was closing in lurid light.

My mother, in her after life, disliked talking of these rushing years, and would not describe her own reactions save to reaffirm her loyalty to the main body of southern doctrines. Ruefully she laughed at the determined vigor with which her New England grandmother first tried to reason with and convert her and, failing, just as vigorously repudiated her. She said that if anyone ever wished to know how wartime really *felt*, there was a perfect description, written by her own dear friend, Cornelia Spencer, in a little book too much neglected then, and now forgotten, called the *Last Ninety Days of the War*.

Of all the early confidence and swagger she said never a word. Of the eager marching away, not a word. Of the end, never one word. What she did tell referred to the tasks she and her neighbors accomplished in keeping the home fires alight. She had relatives fighting on both sides, as well as many friends. In the old Mitchell Burying Ground in Connecticut, a long row of flags are set on Memorial days. Father would inevitably have enlisted if it had not been for his lameness. On that account he had to be the one doctor left behind to care for the sick at home.

All the leading young men of Salisbury enlisted early. Among the very first enrolled was the younger Charles Fisher, then president of the North Carolina Railroad. Immediately he was given a colonel's commission, and he furnished out of his own pocket the accoutrements of his men. The young men, John Steele Henderson, and his brother Leonard, the tall Craige boys, Burton's sons, young Dr. Caldwell (the son of our neighbor, the Judge), the young pastor of the Salisbury Presbyterian Church, Rev. Jethro Rumple, all these went, and company after company of Rowan boys beside. The oldest son of the Overmans was in the Junior Reserves and went later. On the first list were Beards and Brandons and all the way down the alphabet. Entirely of one mind were now the Scotch-Irish and German families, and both sent their best. The beginning of the war was unanimous. It was stirring and hysterical with glee and glory anticipated, just as it has been over and over again, but as we hope some day it will cease to be, ever and ever again.

Charles Mitchell, my mother's only brother, a young physician, enlisted very early, and in the first year he died of fever, without seeing a battle.

XI

"TIME OF THE WAR"

AT THIS POINT in the narrative begins that struggle which all the oldsters agree to call "The War." Wars have been fought since this one, and its turmoil would have been utterly silenced in the reverberation of the last one, war so stupendous that our paltry strife is scarcely to be mentioned in the same sentence; but still we old folk speak meditatively of "The War." This it was which shattered for our fathers their scheme of things entire, that changed the whole course of their children's lives, and has never ceased, even at this late day, to be called by all southerners, "The War," without an adjective. By and by students of history will wonder how we were so childish as to think it so overweeningly important.

We, in Salisbury, felt greatly distinguished above the state outside; our town was the home of the first war governor of North Carolina, John W. Ellis. From a young man he had astonished the easygoing town by his ambition and industry. Always diligent in business, in law, and in politics, he had now come to stand as a leader in a great crisis and was looked up to as a sagacious counselor. He moved very slowly. He knew that our people were proverbially deliberate in making up a united mind, and that in their usual hesitating fashion they had not yet determined to take up arms.

Ellis was a follower of Calhoun, a Democrat. He had been elected by many Whig votes as well. It is uncertain who traded, if anyone, who welshed, or to whom the final plunge into secession was due. My father always thought Ellis to be cautious in this, but I have been told that he is now proved to have been deeply committed to it from the very first. What of it? After the state had made up its collective mind, he could never have held it back. Late in joining the Union, North Carolina was sentimentally loath to leave it. Ellis knew his people would refuse to be stampeded, and he made delay until his Fabian tactics came to a sudden dramatic end.

Lincoln's call for troops tipped the balance for him, just as it did for Zebulon B. Vance, who succeeded him as governor, and for the whole state standing behind them, and opened the way to secession in one short moment. Some states were like Kentucky, rent in twain; some like South Carolina had long wished to go against Federal dominion. North Carolina was like neither. Belief in States' Rights, and the indomitable self-determination in which experience had trained her people, would not brook dictation from outside. But they could not visualize themselves fighting Virginia, or South Carolina, and this issue showed the only alternative.

Every town which has persisted long enough to have a history, develops specific character as well. The town of Salisbury was stubborn with a Scotch-Irish determination, and added to this they possessed the German phlegm. Never overenthusiastic, ever mindful of old days and ways, the citizens wished to live up to their idea of the older heroes. They felt confident where, if these should be alive, they would be ranged. Our fathers followed Governor Ellis into the valley of decision. The time had come and they must take up arms along with the rest of the state, not so eagerly as some, but conclusively enough.

Welcoming the inevitable, our town organized its citizens to meet the crisis affecting everyone. Just as it always happens, it was the young men who answered the call with most alacrity, considering war to be a sort of glorified picnic. As soon as anyone was designated to write down their names they enlisted. Having thus chosen their part, the enlistment was like that of one of the County boys from Old Thyatira Church, "For the War, and for forty years if necessary." This united sentiment was an experience truly glorious at first, for this was the first year when all the boys went marching away, with drums tapping, with shouting and rejoicing, because the thing they had been anticipating as an adventure was now a reality. After the first contingent had gone, life seemed duller, and there remained very much that was not especially exciting to be done by those who remained at home.

Our leading citizen, Colonel Charles Fisher, who had enrolled and outfitted his regiment largely at his own expense, was killed at Manassas, leaving behind him a family of orphan children. By the end of the second year, such losses were becoming all too common, and many a family in turn received its sad news.

My father's business was cut out for him. It was his part to watch over the health of the community as best he could and be of service besides to such families as were carrying on without their husbands or their stalwart sons to work for them. This sort of unofficial office continually brought up new problems. Never before had he been so learned in the troubles of other people, and often, by knowing true conditions, he could become a clearing house for the providing of assistance, for the bartering of this one's resources for the goods of another who could not obtain their value save by such exchange. My mother had always enjoyed doing something new. She and her nearest neighbors, especially Mrs. Craige and Mrs. Bruner, immediately began the business of stretching ends to cover family needs, so that they could spare more to give to the "Cause." Of course and at first it was like a game. That was the time when flags were embroidered, and presented with speeches; the blank days came later. In the second winter the needs of daily living began to pinch a bit. It was now time to ransack the attic and bring to light sundry pieces of old-fashioned machinery stored there years ago, to bring down and learn the use of them. Those days were far nearer in time to the old textile process, and some few women still lived who remembered how the routine went. Mrs. Bruner had been brought up in Rowan, and in her youth had been taught how to spin and weave. She could now instruct her neighbors. Mother obtained a pair of cards somewhere, and soon learned to keep them constantly at work. Once she showed me how she used to card cotton rolls, which were piled up by great basketsful for the spinning, for under Mrs. Bruner's instruction she had soon learned to spin.

A short while before the war, a yarn mill had been operated in Salisbury, and stocks of cotton yarn had been accumulated, which furnished material for the first bout of that diligent knitting always revived with each successive wartime. After this stock had been all used up, there was no alternative but to spin more on a hand-driven wheel, for stockings the soldiers must have. And indeed the knitting of stockings by hand had never been so completely laid aside as had the weaving industries.

At Mrs. Burton Craige's a loom was set up, and among them the neighbors kept it running. An old Negro woman was discovered who had not forgotten how weaving should be done. Upon this loom was produced cloth with warp of natural cotton and with filling of walnut or butternut-dyed wool, woven with a twill into a tough jeans of a dirty mixed brown color. Such cloth was of course quite hideous, but oh, how durable! and it sufficed for the outer clothing of the older children and the servants. This being a forced industry in emergency, there was no time to experiment with the old-fashioned dye pots and mordants.

It was not very long before all sorts of minor supplies and necessities began to wear out and give out, with no possibility of replacement. Such smaller deficiencies can become very vexatious and be felt keenly. For instance, buttons were quite unobtainable. Persimmon seeds, drilled with a red-hot darning needle make pretty little brown buttons for smaller children's clothing, and a few buttons of largest size could be whittled out of dogwood rounds by the fire of winter evenings; but who was to make the new darning needles, or the knives, or the new steel knitting needles so absolutely indispensable, or the combs, or dress hooks, or any of the myriad small wares hitherto imported from those who manufactured them? As to such articles as dishes, or glasses, or spectacles, there were never going to be any more of any such things until the War was over. If some child or servant dropped a plate or dish, it was a catastrophe which the whole Confederacy was unable to repair.

Then the Confederate hospitals had to be supplied with bandages and lint, and for this all possible stores of old material and finer cotton and linen rags—anything fine or soft —must be used. Bandages were rolled of the better fabric, and each fragment of old worn linen must be picked out into its threads for lint. Blankets for the soldiers were contrived by raveling carpets and washing the woolen thread, to be rewoven. Silk dresses were taken apart and re-sewed into gores for war balloons. Garment after garment, treasure by treasure, everything was put to some use, either at home or in service of the army.

My mother's great blue canton dinner set, sent her from China by her favorite *North* uncle, the shipmaster, was kept carefully packed away, and never used save on state occasions. She had common dishes for everyday, and in my time the set was almost intact, save that there were no soup plates at all of the pattern. Mother explained to me that these had been the only possible utensils in her possession in which she could bake a pie, during the early part of the War when pies were still a possibility. In this homely use the china plates had been cracked and broken one by one.

Some coarse pottery must have been made here and there to use locally. It soon became next to impossible to ship anything weighty upon railroads whose carrying capacity must be fully utilized for transporting supplies for the armies in the field and which were already overloaded.

All through and beyond this feverish indoor business must go regularly forward the all-important agriculture, the planting and harvesting of food crops to supply the troops, while by skillful gardening, the women and children could be largely nourished on garden products not readily transportable. In the war years it was first discovered how good a food for man as well as for beast is the cowpea, and how useful to balance the too great proportion of carbohydrate contained in our white southern corn-meal. The standard sweetening in wartime was the sorghum easily made from Georgia cane, and this was used to flavor and make endurable the "coffee" and "tea" concocted out of all sorts of queer substitutes, such as diced and parched raw sweet potato for the first, or dried raspberry leaves for the second. Everybody went to work to demonstrate how much food a small plot of ground intensively cultivated could be brought to yield; and among the rest, my parents, who had long been enthusiastic gardeners, were not behindhand.

In the last year of the War another care was added to the responsibility of those left behind in Salisbury. Refugees began to drift in, old folk, women and children whose homes had been destroyed or who were too uncomfortably near the routes of armies. Some came accompanied by their faithful Negroes, driving wagons laden high with household goods, and others came nearly destitute; but whoever they were and whatever they brought, places must be provided for their shelter, and food must be given them when they were unable to buy it. A development of community order and helpfulness arose to the new occasion. People were not slow in coming to their aid, and in the latter months of the last year a score or more of such families came in as refugees.

In addition to the continual activities of the women, and

to the doctor's work of alleviating sickness, work and aid must be ministered to those whose men were away at the War. Though the main concern was with the great object of trying to win the War, these people must be given work to do, and so new objects and industries were devised. Nothing that could be dried and so made longer available was wasted. Queer substitutes for candles were concocted out of resin and beeswax. But enough of this.

Being far inland, being situated on a main railroad and in the midst of a productive farming country, depots of supplies were gathered together in Salisbury. Provisions of corn and bacon were warehoused, to be drawn upon for the troops in the field. There were storerooms of blankets, and a great number of bales of cotton accumulated to be shipped by some blockade runner like the "A. D. Vance," whose cargo would pay for the manufactured articles the South had never made and just now had not time to attempt. Besides all this, there was an arsenal of small arms which were beginning to be skillfully made.

About midway of the struggle, it was announced from Richmond that the Confederate government had bought the old yarn mill previously mentioned and that it would be used for a military prison to receive some of the prisoners now overcrowding all possible barracks in Richmond.

Prisoners are a pitiful by-product of all wars, and an issue with which no military organization likes to be annoyed. Prisoners are taken to cripple the enemy; they may be exchanged with the enemy for those men held by them in the same durance; but by the action of the paroling system they cannot take up arms again when restored to their government, and more men make more mouths to feed when already there are too many. If soldier-prisoners are in enemy prisons, guards are needed to hold them in check, and more resistance is to be quelled there than if they were being opposed in open field. Prisoners of war are never anticipated, never prepared for beforehand, and are liable to be treated as negligently as possible. Between the Federal authorities and the Confederacy there was a good deal of jockeying and fencing as to whether exchange negotiations were not in themselves a recognition as of a lawful government, rather than the byproduct of rebellious conspiracy. Then, on the southern side, it was in the same way questioned whether prisoners could be exchanged with a power which did not recognize States' Rights or the choice of secession, and which called the South a rebellious province. Meanwhile prisoners became very numerous, could not be properly guarded in Richmond, and frequently were making escapes.

Salisbury did not want the prison, did not want northern prisoners in her borders, did not want the odious task of guarding them. Warm protests were made against the plan, but the objections were overridden. The factory was a substantial building of brick, out on the southeast edge of town. Men began to be sent there. Some of those taken on the battlefields of Virginia came first, sullen, dirty fellows whom their own mothers could not have recognized in their squalor. Just at first the building was large enough to house their number. No one was detailed to guard them, and the townsfolk had to volunteer for this disagreeable duty. Later, more and more prisoners were pushed in by droves and hundreds. All sorts and conditions of men, herded together, high, low, good, bad, all equally miserable. The place was too small for them, both outdoors and in, the wicked ones abused the more decent ones; the thieves stole from the weak. It was true that prisoner officers must be better kept and watched because they were worth so much more in making exchanges. After a time a detail from some brigade was spared for the purpose of guarding them.

It was a horrible, disorderly den, crowded to the limit with men half-clothed, cold, dispirited, often sick, fed on food they were unaccustomed to eat, the more unpalatable because they had no cooking vessels fit to prepare it. Even this doubtful supply of food was growing always scantier. Every prisoner was filled with bitter hatred, scornfully recognized and repressed by their jailors. A military prison at its best would not be a place of any ease; at its worst, set in a community unwilling to tolerate it, in a country already drained of its resources and strained past endurance, indignant and hostile, it became a pit of misery unspeakable. Do not forget it was no more so than were sundry northern prisons of the same sort! The only possible excuse for such a place lies in the *tu quoque*, if indeed some additional excuse for the destitution of Salisbury Prison is not to be found in the grave scarcity of all subsistence, which was now invading the homes of the South in far greater measure than the North ever experienced.

Some good women of the town (I know the names of some), did at first out of their dearth send food to the sick prisoners. Some ministers of the Gospel did visit them, but the relief was so small, the power to help so slight that at last the town attempted to forget altogether this presence on its borders—attempted, but never could quite succeed in doing so.

Why these prisoners did not break out of confinement, burn the town, and take to the woods, is hard to imagine. The danger of such a thing was ever a fear. That they did not do so must have been the result of their utter weakness and depression and of the lack of unity among them. Sometimes they rioted, and the town would know about it by the staccato of shooting in that quarter. Always they kept dying by scores, of starvation, of disease, of homesickness, until nobody could endure to contemplate the horror of it. They had always to remember, some of those townspeople, that they had sons, brothers, friends, enduring the like despair in a prison somewhere north of the boundary.

Prisoners did sometimes escape by twos and threes. They committed depredations. Alarms were constant and were raised by evil men in town, who committed crimes and shifted the blame to escaping prisoners, so that by this means there would be no investigation.

But at long last, the War was drawing dramatically to its close. Sherman came up from the south to North Carolina in the spring of 1865. General Stoneman, one of Sherman's lieutenant generals, marched north from Georgia, through South Carolina, and had orders to turn west, and destroy the Confederate stores piled in Salisbury.

Sometime in the late autumn of 1864, my mother planted a long row of grapevine cuttings all along the back fence. She made Dorsey dig a deep trench and bed it well with compost, and then she brought out the cuttings she had rooted, and laid them ready. "Wait a moment, Dorsey," she cautioned. "I must get something more." And going back into the house she came out with an apronful of decrepit old shoes which had been worn until even the Confederacy was sure they were of no further use. Did her apron sag rather heavily? If so, Dorsey did not notice it. His "Old Miss" had ways past finding out! In a row all along the trench she set the old shoes, went and brought a second apronful and filled out the number, saying finally, "Plant the vines now, Dorsey; they say old leather is the very best thing to make grapevines grow, and so I saved these old shoes to put under them." Actually she went in the house and left Dorsey to finish filling up the trench alone.

The silver spoons marked with our family initials, which I possess today, lay inside those old boots and shoes until she dug them up, a year later, and restored their contents to the sideboard. Dorsey's eyes would have bulged out of his face if he had seen what he was planting.

That same week that Mother planted the grapevines, Father, on his regular visit to the County poorhouse, gave old Mrs. Kress a stocking foot into which something heavy had been sewed, and directed her to attach it firmly to the waistband of her full dress-skirt, inside.

"This will not put you into any danger," he told her, "for they will never look for the Doctor's gold watch on you."

"I know it, Doctor," she answered, "But I'll be tickled to death when I see them thieves riding by, to think how I'm fooling them," snickered old Mrs. Kress over her toothless gums. And so the family, having protected its few treasures, sat back to await the final catastrophe. Such secreting of valuables was entirely necessary, for the conquering army was becoming always more obstreperous and unrestrained, looting, and destroying what they could not carry away, acting like irresponsible, wicked boys. Sometimes, however, even looting took a humorous turn.

Mother's friend, Mrs. Vogler, unexpectedly found herself provided with a shining pair of gold-rimmed spectacles which exactly fitted the needs of her vision, when anything of the sort was unheard of in those destitute times. "My niece who lives in the country near Greensboro brought them to me," she told Mother. "And when I asked her where on earth she could have got such things, she said, 'Stole 'em, Aunt, stole 'em from a thief'!" And Mrs. Vogler went on to narrate how the niece was at home when a troop of Yankee officers had stopped and ordered breakfast at her house. While the men were eating, she heard them laughing and peered in, to see them passing these spectacles from hand to hand. The joke was that one of the group had snatched the spectacles in question from before the eyes of an old lady in South Carolina, as she stood ruefully watching the Yankee ranks march past. Just at the moment when they all burst out laughing at this pleasantry, one of their horses broke away from the branch where it was tied, and the whole group went out to see to their mounts. On their return the glasses were not in sight, and they went away, each accusing the other of having pocketed them. But they fitted Mrs. Vogler's eyes to a T!

When General Stoneman was drawing near, Father sent away a young horse he had raised, as the very first thing certain to be commandeered. Over the hills to the west of town, there was a wood beyond Macay's, once Frohock's millpond; and, beyond that, a deep, rocky dingle or ravine. The Craige's old family manservant went over to feed and water a dozen or so of horses picketed there among the boulders. No mules were taken there, because a mule will always bray and betray his whereabouts, while horses are companionable and do not nicker if they can see each other. One of my kinswomen tells me that their folks saved their mules in the same fashion, but that they tied their mouths almost shut for two days, with hemp ropes. A mule must open its mouth to bray.

The little group of horses described were never discovered by Stoneman's "Raiders" but were brought safely back to town, by night, after he was well on his way. The General stayed in Salisbury for three days, being ill in his tent the most of the time. Nevertheless he managed to give personal protection to all who asked it of him, saying he was not there to make war on noncombatants.

Poor Dorsey, who had received a donation from some young soldier who had lately been at our house, of a few Confederate rags, was peremptorily stopped on the street in front of our house by half a dozen Yankee troopers, who felt so hilarious that they rode round him, and at pistol's point forced him to take off his remnants of uniform. Mother heard the fracas, and walked calmly out to see what was happening. The terrified Negro fled in his scanty under-rags and fell at her feet for protection.

"What do you young men think you are doing?" she asked indignantly. "These clothes are all the poor Negro can get to keep him covered, and he is not responsible for the fact that they are gray!" One of the soldiers leaned down and picked the garments up from the dust, with his thumb and finger, and threw them over in Dorsey's general direction. They then rode away somewhat sheepishly. And it was then that Mother herself walked to Headquarters, and asked that a guard be assigned to her.

That same afternoon, a man darted into the back gate and across the back porch, a man not in uniform, but wearing a blue army cap. He came in and walked directly to the sideboard, and, jerking open the drawers, fumbled after possible silver, while Mother stood and glared at him. All he could find were two thin silver tablespoons which had been kept out because there were absolutely no other spoons of metal to take their place.

"Where's your silver?" the man asked. "Where thieves will never find it!" answered Mother. Then, "Did you ask my guard whether you could come in here?" "Guard!" said the man, striding to the front window. Sure enough, there was a blue uniform, his gun at rest, looking over the front gate into the street. The camp-follower jumped back, seized one of the spoons as he passed the sideboard, and slipping it into his pocket was gone.

That night and the next, fires went up. Cotton and supplies were burned, while country folk were allowed to take away what they could "carry in their hands" of food. Some of the townsfolk, who were "disloyal" enough to accept from the officers quartered upon them a goodly present supply for their own use, and something over, had their covetousness, excusable as it was, remembered against them for years. Last of all, the small arms were loaded into wagons and taken away, when the main body of the raiders left.

When Sherman had been reported as nearing North Carolina, most of the prisoners were transferred northward, except the deserters, who were moved south. Everyone was glad to see them go, and no one was sorry when the Yankees made a bonfire of the evil-smelling empty, dolorous prison, the scene of so much unalleviated suffering and so many deaths.

That chapter could only be appropriately closed in a purification by fire.

One of the greatest deficiencies in the Confederacy had been in the matter of drugs. My father had hoarded his supply for the town and county and made it last as well as he could. He happened to have some ounces of that unclarified, black, gummy substance which is opium in its first condition as dried poppy juice. One of the army doctors came along and demanded to look over the store of medicines in Father's little office on the street, and he commandeered the lump of opium, entire.

"I have many people to serve," remonstrated Father with dignity, "and it will be a long time before I can obtain any more, while you have all the Federal stores of drugs at your call." The army doctor looked at the gummy mass before him, thought a moment, and, dividing it with his pocket-knife, handed back the *smaller* portion. Father took it with a smile and a shrug and was thankful.

Salisbury was not unduly incensed against General Stoneman. He obeyed his orders and destroyed the stores, but also he gave guards to all who asked for them. He restrained looting, and little unnecessary havoc was made in the dwellings of the town. Although he was a sick man while he stayed in Salisbury, he found means to prevent such burning and destruction as took place so wantonly in Columbia, South Carolina, and with impunity in many other less important places.

One thing of destruction, however, was done in such a way as sadly to hamper me in preparing these pages; for when it is desirable to verify reminiscence by referring to local record, there is none to be found. Soldiers occupied the printing office of the *Carolina Watchman*, and printed and issued proclamations thence, while Stoneman was in town. Some of these men remained in charge after the main body of Stoneman's Raiders was gone. Finally, on leaving the place, they made a scornful gesture of hatred. First they burned all the files. At present very few issues exist for the years of the War. Next they threw out, and mixed all together in an inextricable heap of confusion in the middle of the floor, all the fonts of type. Lastly they wrecked the presses. Such is war, such the way of the victor.

By the time that Jefferson Davis passed through Salisbury on his way south, everyone knew the game was lost. The final surrender had taken place near what is now Durham. Very soon the men from Appomattox would begin to come home again.

XII

AFTER THE SURRENDER

"The War" now being over, as regarded the actual fighting, there remained only the accepting of the results, the most difficult of submissions, for these as well as for the whole South. All had followed the same opinion, backed it by the same arguments, partaken of the same disasters, and now were called upon to drink the same bitter potion of defeat. This they must do, and must besides accept the ideals of the victors, at least definitely enough to be controlled by them. All wars end in some such fashion, not only in material loss for the conquered, but in the forcible changing of customs.

General Stoneman left behind him a guard sufficient to enforce discipline in the town, so that swaggering troopers in trim blue uniforms could be seen any day, spurring along the street in a cloud of dust, mounted on such spirited horses as could never have been furnished them by any army quartermaster. These soldiers were much in evidence, taking pains to indicate that the townsfolk were entirely at their mercy and disposal. The citizens had no remedy save to avoid them, and if that was not possible to look the other way as they cantered by. The sowing of hatred on both sides, during the years of the War was yielding a harvest which would need long to gather. Even at home, between our own people, aching resentments were born, evil suspicions rife. If anyone was believed to have accepted presents from the northern soldiers quartered in his home, if empty larders appeared to be too suddenly filled or too abundantly supplied, whispers went round, and such a householder would be regarded with mistrust. Such a rumor, such a hearsay, would ruin a reputation with the whole town, and in this fashion there were reputations which were badly damaged. If some young girl, bored by the sober wartime, even once looked after a handsome young officer, without a scornful grimace, she would be accused of flirting with the enemy, an offense unforgivable. Even the simplest complaisance toward them from the women of our homes was utterly frowned upon, and this drove some things under cover which might have been innocent enough. Although conquered, the town was by no means subdued. Rumors such as these passed from mouth to mouth, with a sneer, and in some cases such censure has persisted far down into the days of my personal memory.

When Lincoln was assassinated everyone paused, gasping, wondering, and lived through a week rigid with anxiety; but after tension has lasted for years and has been the experience of an entire population, emotion of any kind is soon exhausted, and fear brings no panic. This also passed into numbness before it was contradicted by the course of events.

In the minds of everybody the thought stood foremost that they must pretend not to care too deeply, that they must carry things off as gaily as possible before their military rulers, and appear to forget, assuming a cheerfulness hardly plausible. The Negroes, being now freedmen, were no longer to be relied upon, and their former masters were obliged to do their own home drudgery and to plant their own crops if crops were to be planted. In many instances, devoted old servants refused to listen to the fairy tales the younger ones told them and remained in their homes for a little wages; but the younger ones had the phrase, "Forty acres and a mule," to be bestowed on each one by the United States government, so firmly wedged in their minds that they would not work a stroke. Awaiting this donation, they drifted aimlessly with free foot, trying to find out where it was to be collected, and in order to live meanwhile they stole all they could lay their hands upon. A sorry change this was, coming after the wonderful record for faithfulness the Negroes had established during the actual warfare. Perhaps they, too, had been tense; perhaps relaxation had made them also indifferent to the future. Their former masters had neither money nor credit; deprived of Negro labor, they could not raise the food to feed themselves, much less their ex-slaves. That first year it was hard to induce Negroes to do any regular work, even with the advantage of the exhaustion of the world's stock of cotton, which made it bring such fabulous prices then and for some years after the surrender.

Our Dorsey had more intelligence and industry than most of his race. He was an excellent carpenter. Before the War, when building was going on, Father used to hire him out at day wages, while a less skilled man worked on the home lot. During these periods, Father encouraged him to work for his own profit, outside his regular hours of labor, and to save every penny to buy his freedom. This cash he had carefully hidden away, and now that he had been set free without price, he had a sum of money which made him the richest member of our household. Very soon, in decent respectful fashion, he bade goodbye to his master and his old home, and moved to Arkansas, where he invested his money in a good farm. Father never saw him again, but years afterwards, two of his sons, fine, upstanding, brown young men, came back to Salisbury on a visit, and walked up to the porch to make themselves known to us.

Persia, Mother's maid, was of a different stripe. At first she begged to stay. Then she found a new lover, left her husband, who was Dr. Whitehead's driver, grew impertinent and careless, and finally flung off between daylight and dark one night, a temperamental flighty woman. More than once she came back, for in her own way she adored Mother.

I remember her. One night, by the fire, someone knocked at the door which went out of the sitting room to the back

AFTER THE SURRENDER

gallery. There stood a tall, handsome black woman, who cried, "Miss Ellen, Miss Ellen!" and threw her arms round my mother and began to weep aloud. Mother drew her in and told her to sit down with her by the fire. They talked until late, and Mother made her a pallet to spend the night. That was Persia.

The first summer was a strange, unreal one. Soldiers came drifting through by twos and threes, and somehow, in spite of dire poverty, life inched along in melancholy defiance of privation. Welcomes were given these men, sorrows were ignored, unaccustomed work done with bravado. In the time of waiting, many things were talked over of the past, and the future was anticipated, none too comfortably. Our South Carolina cousins came back from Lee's Army and stayed awhile in Salisbury. It was hot weather, and Mother made for them inviting beds in the little bedroom behind Father's office, thinking this would be a treat to men so long in the field. Next morning the boys were discovered sleeping out under the open sky, on the ground in the orchard behind the office. They could not endure the softness of a bed after so many months in camp without tents or proper bedding.

Salisbury gave many parties for the returned soldiers. "Cold-water Walk-arounds" they called them, and "Starvation Sociables." There was frolicking and flirting, and almost hysterical mirth. One of the cousins was mightily taken with my eldest sister who had grown up to young ladyhood in the War years. A year later they were married and went to South Carolina to live. Young people who were mutually attracted got married at once. There seemed no use waiting for better prospects.

The narrow urgencies of home took every moment of my mother's time, and besides, her boys were growing up, must be educated and prepared for college. She could easily do this for them. But she was an exacting teacher, and she aroused friction, for after a certain age no boy will do his best in study with only his mother to instruct him. Davidson College, that Presbyterian institution accessibly near, was the place for which my brothers were destined. The University of North Carolina had fallen on evil days since the surrender; by 1870 it was closed, as everyone feared closed finally.

Life in a narrow groove, life as lived in my home town, was slowly becoming organized toward getting a bare livelihood, although the irritation of constant clashings with a government which not only disapproved but actually hated those whom it must rule, went interminably on, and took all that was endurable out of life. In after times, nobody who experienced it liked to describe the reconstruction revenge taken upon the entire South. The experience would be described by allusions, by single instances, by shrugs and shudderings. We are made so that we cannot actually recall, although we may remember, the fact of severe physical pain; but chagrin, disappointment, insult, defeat, and that hatred which emphasizes them all, can be recalled very much as we felt it at first, when we think back to the cause and the effect. The memory is almost as insupportable as the reality. For this reason we have, inside our souls, crypts, morgues, inclosing dead sorrows which we keep shut, and which we pass as the townsfolk of Salisbury used to pass the Yankee officers swaggering on our streets, with averted glance. But the worst of everything was the sick boredom, the curtailing of ambition, the uncertainty of the future.

When the young men came home they found little to do. They sat around and witnessed the fantastic tricks of the Freedmen's Bureau, and saw how the gaping Negroes were by it indoctrinated in hatred to their former masters. Carpetbaggers swarmed in and purloined from the government that favored them. Our men recognized that sinister combinations were forming, which would sometime have to be defeated, but against which they had not forged the proper weapons. They needed employment, but were hampered by all sorts of political disabilities and limitations unremoved, as well as by the sort of association in which they might have to work. They refused to be made mere laborers on the land, and nothing more. Somehow the time must be helped to pass, and they did what all Americans like to do. They organized a club, a society to include the like-minded. That was what they thought they were doing over in Tennessee, and in a few months the idea had spread like wildfire. To their new brotherhood they gave a Greek name reminiscent of the college so many of them had been forced to leave so young, and to this they added another, Gaelic, mystic, alliterative with the first. The circumstance of its actual existence they kept secret and unverifiable, because the Yankee government was unfavorable to secret societies for white men. Our young soldiers enjoyed the setting at naught of their odious interference. They met at night and wholly in disguise, choosing for their assembling deserted buildings. If any lonely old house was reputed to be haunted, so much the better for their purpose.

It is an interesting speculation to wonder how many of those horses which Grant permitted "Lee's Miserables" to retain and take home after Appomattox, may have been subsequently ridden in those queer ghostly cavalcades.

It was the winter of 1866. Everything was out of joint, and the Negroes, getting cold and hungry, were helping themselves to everything they could lay their hands on. It was then that the rumor first became current that ghosts seven feet tall had been glimpsed riding after midnight on dim white horses. The Negroes recalled that never, when they lived on the plantation with "Ole Marster" had they been terrified with such nightmares. They fared back to the old place, or what was left of it, and, being assured of protection, were set to plowing for next season's cotton crop.

What was true generally was true of Salisbury. Many a fine young man who escaped alive and returned after the surrender could find nothing whatever to do. By the second winter he would be heartily disgusted with sitting around and living off his women folk. He seized the idea of this secret organization, and hidden away somewhere he would be sure to have the paraphernalia of the North Carolina division of the Ku-Klux Klan. Mother told me of a young Rowan County farmer she knew about who once allowed himself to fall asleep in his sheet and mask. His wife found him next morning, and almost blurted out the truth to a neighbor. The same story may have happened more than once, in other places.

Down in South Carolina it was worse because conditions were more acute. My sister, recently married, lived near Cheraw, and wrote home of doings there. A carpetbagger was encouraging the Negroes to steal cotton, which they picked out on moonlight nights and sold to him below the market price. Cotton continued to bring a high price for some years after the War. This carpetbagger was duly called upon one night by the Ku-Klux. They came silently along the road, their horses' feet muffled, their steeple hats upon their heads, holding up the white draperies which added so much to the impressiveness of their height, the horses being disguised as well as the men. Before the culprit's door they formed in a half circle, and their leader called the man out to them. At first he showed a bravado, but when he saw a black pistol barrel steal out between the white folds muffling his accuser, it was time for him to shiver in his night clothes and become more docile. A paper was read to him, recounting his misdeeds, item by item. After each sentence came a solemn pause, when the whole assembled crew bowed gravely in unison as they stood in the moonlight. Finally he was sentenced to leave the country, being given three days to make his exit. This sentence was then affixed to his door, signed with three bloody K's. Immediately the phantom riders melted away, parting at the crossroad where my sister, her eye glued to the crack of the window-blind, saw them separate.

Next day, ashen with terror, the Negroes came to whisper about it, and the day after that, the carpetbagger's house stood vacant.

It was all too dangerously simple, this method of control; it was too easy by this means to resist what was so unwisely attempted by that revengeful reconstruction Congress at Washington. Ku-Klux became a concealed weapon ready to any hand. It was not long before it was made a means for executing personal hatreds as well as resisting wider injustices. Abused by private revenge, it could become a two-edged sword, so dangerous that the original organization, the men who had formed it, tried to disband the company they had called together. But after this was supposed to be done, it was still a long time before the sheets and ghostly trappings were discarded for good and all: meanwhile every outrage—and outrages were frequent in times so unsettled—was laid to the convenient and vague instrumentality called the Ku-Klux Klan.

In the year 1869, W. W. Holden, formerly a leading journalist, now reconstruction governor of North Carolina, a man who had gone over to the "Black Radicals," prompted by his advisers or commanded by them, judged it necessary to call in some military police to correct the disorders and offenses of the middle part of North Carolina. Nobody was intimidated, only made angry to the core, so that fuel was added to a fire already burning. The man he chose to command his "Army" was named Kirk, who was formerly a "Bushwhacker," one who in wartime had kept some of the mountain counties terrorized; for in the remoter sections of the West there had been more Union than Confederate sentiment. This man was empowered to recruit a regiment of mountain boys, daredevil fellows. Eventually they did march into central North Carolina, as will be told later.

Grandfather Summerell, after the surrender, found himself possessed of more cash money than any of his neighbors. He also found it impossible to do anything with it and still live at peace, in a society which had no money at all, just as he would find in the reverse condition if he had tried to hold up his head in a rich community on nothing. People managed to borrow of him, and were careless to pay him, for they could always say of him that he had acquired his wealth illegally, and they would generally be believed. Although the world was not in his confidence, perhaps the more on that account he fell under suspicion and his money became Dead Sea fruit to him. It also demoralized his family by his second marriage. One of his connections was once haled into court and indicted for a felony. The proud old man would not have him stay and face trial. "Jump your bond and run away, and take care to never show your face here again," he insisted. "I'll pay your bond! I'll have no thieves nor jailbirds in my family connection!" So Grandfather paid the boy's bail bond with some of his hoarded dollars. It was told besides how he was glad to come to the rescue of the man who gave him his first start in life. This was the aged planter, now living in Mississippi and left entirely destitute. In the old days, Grandfather had been his overseer in Eastern North Carolina; now he was able to send his old employer the wherewithal to make his last days comfortable.

The story of the wrecking and dragging down of the University, of the difficulty in initiating a fresh start afterwards, all this I have written into a book called *Old Days in Chapel Hill*, founded upon the journals of my mother's old friend, Mrs. Cornelia Spencer. And that is another story.

As to original Union men in Rowan, there were not many. The sweeping sentiment which arose very early in the War, drove them out, made them recant, or simply go under cover; but Judge Nathaniel Boyden, husband of my mother's valued friend, was always for the Union and no nonsense about it. That by no means prevented his only son from galloping off to war with all the rest. In reconstruction times, Judge Boyden was associate in the Supreme Court, of which the Chief Justice, Richmond Pearson, also came of an ancient Revolutionary family of Rowan County.

When Judge Boyden died, a conspiracy of silence, possibly entered into to spare the feelings of his wife and son, told nothing whatever about the real meaning of his life. The obituary notices gave only the date of his death, his office, and told of his phenomenal memory and his grasp of the law. In another column, a notice stated that his successor was appointed, "Before his flesh is cold"—a study in revenge, that!

When the economic life began to settle, after buying and selling were resumed and life went on in predictable order, my father arranged his fees to suit the times, and undertook his full portion of charity practice. For one-third of his work, he did not ask or expect to receive any money compensation whatever. All Negroes able to pay him were charged, for the same service, one-half as much as white people. To this ratio he held for the rest of his life.

Father was soberer, lamer, older, but still a fairly happy man. He had his beloved profession. His sick folk were always with him. Whether successful in collecting his fees or not, his success in the saving of life was known of him, and people were thankful. After a short time of adjustment, a bare living was not too difficult to manage. Father, then, was much the same, not much sadder, only kinder.

Mother, on the contrary, chose to deprecate her former self and to starve it out. Except that she could prepare her sons for college if they would allow her, the disjointed world she now inhabited did not seem to need her help in any way, save as it always needed those daily services that some woman must always supply. She had allowed herself to look forward; she had built up aspirations for her country and her children; and now they stood all on the threshold of a far more puzzling world than the one into which she had been born. She was a woman (nowadays we begin to know of many such), who needs both people to work for, and ideas to work with. She would have felt it shameful to complain. She cared for her family, she did her work well, but hers was a nature which needed a greater space in which to function.

One small circumstance is significant of her sense of limitation, and that was her loss of all interest in any sort of personal adornment. Formerly she had enjoyed suitable dress, but from the end of the War, she never at all varied the cut of her clothing or the fashion of her hair. It remained in the plainness of forced economy. She used no lace, she wore no ribbon. She took from her bandbox the same black bonnet of straw for nine consecutive summers, and in winter wore one just like it, made of black silk. If she owned a modest best black dress, it would be cut in exactly the Quaker pattern of her new black calico. She grew massive as she grew older, and she was a tall woman. Her plain clothing became her as I remember, but her children all disliked her studied disregard of fashion. I think we perceived in it something which had happened to her inner nature.

In a stern, inexpressive way, she became very religious. It was her Greek Testament, and not her Euripides, which always lay open upon her sewing table. To pray, to execrate—one who cares too greatly is obliged to do one or both on occasion, or lose sanity of outlook while watching the "contrariousness" of things. It is happy for a person to lose the self in faith and compassion, and make prayer the choice.

Physical suffering is not a thing to be denied, but a real ordeal. The mental revulsion of a deep-thinking nature, brooding over the mischances of poor fellow-humankind, is the worst pain of all.

The years just after the surrender saw our county, once as hopeful and as fruitful as any other place in the world, peeled and stripped, and all to build over again. The once tidy farms were a sorry sight. Roads were uncared for; bridges were down. The railroad, sadly out of repair, was being restored at a heavy cost, and a burden of taxes was being expended by political graft.

Gaps in the population seem to close readily. If men are not seen for a time, they are forgotten by all save their near kinsfolk. But this loss, this kind of disintegration weighs on maturer folk who survive and makes them see themselves as a separate and older race, far older than they wish to be considered. Life in Salisbury was depressing, until, in the course of events, another younger generation should be born and, growing up, bring in cheerfulness and hope for the future.

PART TWO

XIII

I COME TO LIVE IN SALISBURY

IT SOUNDS conceited to write of the date of one's birth as if that day was in anywise significant, but my first milestone happened to be set up at a crossroad of danger for my home town. I was born on that very day in the summer of 1870 when "Kirk's Army," having finished mustering in Morganton, was beginning its march down the mountain to deal with the Ku-Klux Klan. Kirk's Army had been summoned by the reconstruction governor, the renegade, W. W. Holden, and was composed of a body of Union guerrillas recently disbanded, recruited with rough mountain boys spoiling for a fracas. The military demonstration was supposed to be needed to quell disorders stirred up by the Ku-Klux, to which several recent murders had been charged—murders not at the time, then or since, proved against it. Indeed it was a turbulent time, and people on principle gave to a hated government all the vexation they dared, without actually incriminating themselves. Today, a person may justify this military expedition or may condemn it, according to the set of his opinions; but old Salisbury, situated directly in the line of march, was of one mind. Salisbury was enraged, and Kirk's Army fully reciprocated their indignation. I have heard it said that the soldiers had planned seriously to burn the town as they left it, and that they were diverted from their purpose only long enough so that they might take care of the stock of whiskey they found there. Enough was ready at hand to fuddle their purposes, and for the second time in its history Salisbury escaped this fate by the same ruse, the first time being during the Revolution, when the invaders were a large band of Tories, who are said to have fallen drunk along Main Street beside the barrels of liquor shrewdly rolled out in their path. And so, with Kirk's Army, there passed away the final mutterings of the devastating storm of actual warfare. Its effects remained and were to be reckoned with for many a day. A desolate time it was in which to begin life, and a poor prospect.

As always, when the Recording Angel draws a line and casts up the final score of an epoch, new days and changing times were already opening new accounts. In 1870, the older folk had come to the full realization that they would all be needed to help in the rebuilding of the commonwealth. The returned soldiers were still war-weary, and the children of the new day too young to look at their future not realized. It was going to be difficult to gather together what little impulse there might be for sane restoration. Upon the middle class of the South the Civil War had fallen most crushingly, and it was these who would have most of the rubbish to clear away. It was a time of dubiety and discouragement, and, as to prosperity, it was a pinching time.

That reconstruction baby that grew to be *Me*, was a healthy enough young scion, and at first too placid to be called a properly insistent, demanding infant. Treated from the beginning with a good deal of that sort of neglect which is wholesome because it does not deprive a child of vigor, although placing no premium on self-assertion, I am said to have taken my earliest life with great serenity and decorum. Some aunt once declared of me that I should die of old age before I was grown, and this was a good thing for everyone concerned, considering the gray times I was born in. Father was an elderly physician, Mother was no longer young; and I fear neither of my parents was too overjoyed at having me, a little afterthought, pitched into that home where for a dozen years they had been thinking of anything but babies.

I COME TO LIVE IN SALISBURY

My brothers and sisters were so much older that they must have seemed like uncles and aunts, while my parents were like grandparents in their quiet tolerance.

Outside the home in which I was growing into an individual, all the trappings of life wore more and more threadbare. There was every excuse for things remaining neglected and out-at-elbows. Although great plantations laid waste and dilapidated mansions did not belong to Rowan County, where society had been so much simpler, our County had gone to rack and ruin in its own kind and degree. Only the glorious sunshine of the Piedmont, pouring down on the rolling red hills and the ragged woods, was bright as ever. The one-horse farmers who had gone out so willingly to fight the rich man's battles, returned to find themselves less regarded than before. In Rowan County proper, Negroes had never been numerous compared to the eastern districts. In the town of Salisbury there remained leading citizens, the lawyers, ministers, doctors, and now and then a merchant who had somehow kept alive a feeble spark of his business.

The problem of each was the problem of all—how to get a living in difficult conditions. Some were beginning to wonder also how they were going to procure any opportunity at all for their growing children; and that education which they had not so much regarded for themselves now seemed the one advantage needful, and something impossible to attain. Some of these people had good background; all had a sort of desperate ambition.

The dreary comedy of the reconstruction government was working toward its end, so men hoped; but there seemed little possibility of hastening the final overthrow of this government by carpetbagger and scalawag rule. Our proud and dogged people could only wait impatiently, grimly enduring their poverty. They had the unbreakable pride of those who would keep control by the sheer determination to dominate. Many of them held family traditions of having weathered other troubled times in former stormy centuries, and they kept silent, resolving to be ready to attend to the instant need of things just as soon as the opportunity came which was surely coming.

I have described already the sort of mother I had, a mother I have never lived up to in all my long life. She was regarded as the town prodigy, without being disliked for it. From the first she had known how everyone expected, because of her learning, that she would be highly unsuccessful as a housekeeper and as mother of a family, and she took pains to disappoint them on her own behalf. She would shell peas for dinner, and give her son a lesson in exasperating exact translation of Horace from the Latin, while she rocked the cradle in which her little daughter lay. Best of anything she did, I like to remember her gift of pungent speech. She had her own proverbial philosophy and was entirely independent. She would say of the Quakerish clothing she liked to wear, "Nobody with any judgment will think less of me for dressing as I please, and as for those who have no sense, who cares what they say!" The beauty of it was that she really did not care, which is the first requisite in a dress reformer in any age of the world. Mother had a tall, uncorseted, figure which looked well set up in plainly cut, unfurbelowed clothing. Her eyes and brow indicated her mental vigor. She carried with her a kindly atmosphere with no sentimentality, a feeling like that of a calm, cool morning. She did not have to scold when she wished to reduce a child or a servant to order. She opened her eyes and looked intently, not with a bullying frown, but appraisingly, analytically.

Father was jollier and more impulsive. He joked and he petted; although he was first of all to be loved, he was to be respected also, for he, too, had a firm core to his character. By such parents I was not spoiled. I was brought up by the clock on the mantlepiece and never pampered. My brothers

I COME TO LIVE IN SALISBURY

and sisters might expect too much of me, but if they were too exacting Mother was there to check them.

As I grew out of babyhood, I seem not aware of my family except as background. Much clearer than any countenance, far more distinct than the interior of my home, comes the memory of a wonderland outdoors, shared with an enormous rag doll for companion. This dolly, "Sister Kate," was as large as a four-year-old could conveniently lug about. I used to pity her, they say, because she was "so hebby." Mother had made her well and shapely, She had a "store-bought" head, her neck was stiff, her trunk quite solid, but her knees bent equally well both ways, and careful propping was needed to set her upright. Mother had made for her clothes of well sewed muslin and calico exactly like those I wore, with real buttons and button-holes. These clothes could be removed and laundered, so that dragging along garden paths, and feeding copiously with bread and milk at suppertime did not render her permanently crocky.

With so many grown-ups around, I did not think of the house as mine. I claimed only the nursery, just off Father's and Mother's bedroom, and under their great bed in the daytime was rolled the trundle bed, where I slept at night with Sister Kate. Far above me I could hear Father snoring, now and then. This noise, he assured me, was made to drive away "Booghers." Tongue cannot express the sense of blissful security with which I heard him begin to breathe hard and regularly, and then to snore!

In the daytime, life always went better out of doors, and I never willingly played inside. On most of our milder winter days, I was bundled warmly and sent out. When it rained, I loved to sit at the very edge of the back-gallery floor and watch the little rills of water run down the channels of the hard-packed paths to form spreading shallows. I considered the leaping circlets made by raindrops crowding and drifting on these pools. I loved the good rain. I loved to sit with the soothing rush of it in my ears.

I cannot remember when I first began to notice the four huge oaks which swayed and creaked at a great height above our house roof. They were giant companions to me. When I lay out upon the grass, I could plainly see how the blue sky rested directly upon the tops of them. Their trunks were clothed with ivy as far as the main upper forks, and the vines came dangling and dribbling downward in long festoons and streamers. On the ground grew box-bush borders, set around flower beds. ("You mustn't pick Mother's flowers!") The hyacinths and violets grew temptingly low, and very close to my eyes. Among the pleasant garden things appeared also some which appeared to me deeply questionable, and mysterious: butterflies that came and disappeared utterly and strangely—and those flowers called snapdragons—I was afraid of them, because if I pinched one, it would gape so hungrily that I dropped it with a shudder!

The great vegetable garden behind the house belonged entirely to Uncle Harry, our colored man, who could be very cross. No flowers grew there. I remember it at first as always sunny, and filled with the drone of June bugs making a warm sound. I hunted June bugs there—green iridescent beetles which flew about and came tobogganing down the blades of the corn. When I caught one, I turned it upside down under a firm brown thumb and looped a sewing thread around its wavering, imploring, last leg. When so tied, my June bug could be launched into the air, to buzz helpless at the end of his tether. If he pulled away, if he left his shining green leg in the thread, I did not care. He began with so many; one leg the less could not matter.

If Uncle Harry was not in sight, I would select ears of corn just formed, which made delightful baby-dolls with long blonde hair. "Chillun', ruinin' my good roas'n years!" That was what Uncle Harry would say to me when he caught me.

I COME TO LIVE IN SALISBURY

In the undefined, misty country of childish awareness, things well known are glimpsed dreamlike at first, and afterwards congeal, and become real memory. Always I have had a companionable second self to discuss characteristics with me, and my family declared from the first that I was an odd little thing. It must have been when I was about five that one of my aunts, returning from her first trip to New York after the War, brought me the present of a new book for children. It was called *Alice in Wonderland,* and they told me about it when they put on my new pink calico frock—and my birthday hair-ribbon. This was in June, and after breakfast I took the new book out to the front porch to look at the pictures. Alice with her curls and apron I could not admire. Evidently she was not a desirable companion to make mudpies with—but the White Rabbit! Instantly I was absorbed. That June day and that book jogged my memory broad awake, and it has been continuous ever since. Life, too, still retains even now its wonderland quality because I keep looking at some familiar scene on a well known road, and I am certain somehow that something interesting, something unaccountable is just around the bend waiting to happen to me!

And so that morning, while I was looking at the delectable "Alice Book" on our front porch, I raised my eyes and gazed around. Our four towering oaks upsprung as always, mingling their shadows on the roof. From the second story of our house, the two dormer windows peered down at the box borders of the flower garden like a pair of astonished eyes. All was utterly familiar, but all was quite new and freshly perceived on that day.

"Jennie" came presently. She wore a white dress, and a deep white sunbonnet starched stiff as a board, and when I ran to meet her with, "Now we can play," I spoke eagerly, but Jennie met me with ceremony. She was a little older and far more worldly wise than I was; she said primly, "Mamma told me to give you a birthday kiss; she says this is your sixth birthday."

I pulled back, and the kiss landed on my freckled nose. "I wore my white dress," continued Jennie, "because I thought maybe you'd be having a party. Are you?"

"We're going to have apple-float and cake," I replied, "but Mother says we are not going to call it a party. Come on now, let's go down into the garden and play Indian."

Jennie was disconcerted. "I am just *not* going to let you paint my face all up with red rose leaves, and I *won't* do whoops on my mouth. I am company and I don't want to be any Indian!"

"All right, then, let's go in the garden and fly June bugs."

"I thought the next thing would be smelly old June bugs," sniffed Jennie. "I can feel 'em tickle in my hand this very minute!"

"I'll hold, and you can tie," I answered.

But Jennie's mind was firmly set on a party; so, the doll dishes being taken out, she began to enjoy herself, pressing food on imaginary guests and talking "lady talk." Then my naughty self thought of placing one of the tiny doll's cups upon the tip of my pink tongue and trying to talk with it there.

"You ought to act nice, even at a play party," exhorted Jennie. But all the cake being eaten, the two of us trailed down to the fence at the lower end of the long vegetable garden, where grew a row of neglected quince trees bristling with suckers. Each little girl chose the longest switch she could find, and then we measured them together.

"Your switch is the longest," said Jennie, "and I think you ought to give it to me because I am your company."

"I'm going to keep my longest one because it is mine, and because this is my birthday besides," I rejoined. Jennie was peeved, and made a vigorous swipe in my general direction, and her switch wrapped smartly around my chubby bare legs.

I COME TO LIVE IN SALISBURY

I returned the blow with emphasis, and instantly there was a whirl of screaming, snatching little girls. Aunt Mary, our cook, heard the fracas and did not even stop to slip on her shoes. She shuffled down the garden path in her bare, cushiony brown feet. She shook us children apart. Then, interposing her substantial bulk between the combatants, she dragged us both panting, back to the house.

"I'm gwine to tell yo' Ma how ugly you is!" she said shaking my arm as she held it. "Why cain't you play pretty wid yo' company?" and having shoved us up onto the back gallery she let us go and dived back into her kitchen.

"You never will play a single thing I want to play, and I'm goin' right straight home!" cried Jennie.

"I don't care if you do," I answered.

So Jennie lifted up her voice and told the world that she was "going home, and never coming back again in my whole life, you mean child!"

"Oh yes, you will! You'll be back again this afternoon," I answered pertly. Jennie began to cry or rather to wail, and Aunt Mary, whose sympathy was entirely on her side, came out to pacify her. I feared that, after all, she might be persuaded to stay; so deliberately I administered a good, twisty pinch in a tender place, but on the side away from Aunt Mary's observation. Jennie went home screaming loudly with outrage, and I went into the house and reported blandly to Mother that Jennie was tired of playing and had gone home. "I think she's coming back this afternoon," I added. Mother smiled and said, "Well, if you are tired of each other already, the sensible thing is to part." I opened my mouth to tell frankly the story of the switches, but closed it on reminding myself that Aunt Mary would tell all she knew and interpret it as she chose.

Was it because of the story which I left untold which was but a half truth, or was it because Mother believed me and smiled so unsuspectingly, that the place where my graceless conscience should have been and was not, began to burn me? True it is that I can always remember the look of her at just that moment. The clear picture of my mother, smooth-haired, quiet, and serene, exists for me beginning with that eventful day.

Then Father came home to dinner. I felt sure he was the most important person in the whole world. He had a buggy and kept two horses. He would hold me up to pat the soft nose of the gentler of these. The feeling of live velvet, shrinking and twitching under my hand will always come back to me, and the way "Old Wat" would snort and sneeze if a finger was laid on the border of his soft brown nostril.

After dinner Father smoked his long-stemmed pipe, and I came to him, as he sat on the back gallery. I told him about the birthday, about Jennie, and about her going home. Then he questioned me further till he had the story of the switches, and even of the pinch. He was very grave, and shook his head. He said he was sorry that I had been so naughty, and commanded me sternly to go over and beg Jennie's pardon, so that she would forgive me and come back some day soon.

"I would make you go right now," he continued, "but just look, what a heavy cloud is coming over. It is going to rain hard in a few minutes." Sure enough, a great June thunderhead had swollen up above the quince bushes at the bottom of the garden. Thunder was grumbling, deep-toned and continuous. What Father called "the Corn Wagon" had begun to roll. Immediately there began a long afternoon of copious rain, and after that, a sunset of clear shining. Early bedtime, and the birthday was ended. Life had become self-conscious.

XIV

I FIND THINGS INTERESTING

AFTER A KITTEN once gets its eyes open, there's little it does not sniff, or attempt to make game with. From this time forward, impressions came to me in such full tide that it is hard to lay them in order. While I had been growing out of babyhood, family changes had taken place. My eldest sister had gone with her husband to live in far-away Texas. My brothers were struggling for an education in needy southern colleges, teaching alternate years to raise the money; and my second sister had survived a long illness to drift into chronic invalidism. I felt a strange horror of her sickness. In playing in the garden among the rows of corn, I had encountered something repulsive. Instead of being the usual tapering, plumed thing, an ear of corn had burst, and in the gash could be seen purple, swollen masses. Mother told me, when I asked, that it was a "sickness of the corn," and with this livid fungus in mind I imagined something akin to it as the cause of my sister's sickness, and so dreamed ugly dreams of it and never lingered near her bed.

My interests began to change. The friendly outdoors no longer satisfied me entirely. I craved playmates to my mind, while because of my sister's illness children could not be asked in. I had to invent a playmate, and it was a little Indian boy. Most imaginative children have such invisible companions, and mine was named "Little Acorn" and liked to play at all my games, while I chattered away for both. Afterwards I have concluded that I never could affirm that I saw him, although I believed that I could hear him speak. At times I believed in him implicitly, while at others I knew well enough that he was but a projection of my more unruly self. When I wished to speak plainly to grown folk, it had used to be, "Sister Kate says." Now more revolutionary sentiments were prefaced, "Little Acorn knows."

When I was obliged to stay in the house, pictures made the deepest impress upon my mind. The illustrated Shakespeare that excited me toward I knew not what, the pictures of weird goblins in my fairy book, a dilapidated Macaulay's "Lays," with classic figures in line-drawing, all these I would pore upon, striving to interpret them to my eager mind.

The most disconcerting of all my silent observings was "Billy McGinnis," who lived shut up in Father's office where the walls were all cupboards and where you could see him grinning derisively behind the glass. This was but the head of him, for all the rest of his bones were laid neatly in a box in the cupboard below. Of him also I dreamed, and of what dreadful thing he must have done to become such a horror.

Mother was terrified with all this uprush of imagination, and troubled to find me turning into such a very queer little girl indeed; but burdened as she was with the care of her sick daughter, she could not herself do much to help matters. It was characteristic of my parents that I did not discover why Father suddenly began to take me with him on his shorter drives out of Salisbury. I would feel overjoyed and elected, when he would say meditatively, "I wish I knew of a really good little girl! If I could find one I would take her out into the country with me this morning." Hopping on one foot, I would cry, "I'm good, and you could take me!" Coming back from some apparently abstract thought, Father would say, after a long inspection, "Well if that's so, I *will* take you. I reckon you better ask your Mamma for your hat and jacket." Released thus from the deadening hush of sickness in the house, I took refuge for many long

I FIND THINGS INTERESTING

mornings in the companionship of my dear father. Often on weekdays, and invariably on Sunday afternoons, I went with him as he drove out into the country.

Most children then were confined to home boundaries, and as they were in my day (but are no longer), could form little idea of what lay beyond their daily range. Now I had opportunity given me to know the town as it really existed and formed a continuous whole with the surrounding country. I came to know the direction of the well traveled roads that radiated like spokes of a wheel, from the Sherrill's Ford Road that went west, and passed Frohock's old millpond, to the Trading Ford which crossed the River on the northeast. All during the autumn of 1875, and through most of 1876, I went with Father every pleasant day, sitting alert and upright on the buggy seat beside his kindly bulk, having a box for a footstool on which to prop my chubby feet. The habit then formed, persisted for years afterwards and became one of the blessings of my childhood.

The Salisbury of those years showed a far smaller town, whether you approached from Dunn's Mountain, or came down a slippery hill long since graded to a gentle slope which is the extension of Main Street southward. No snaggled row of provincial skyscrapers was visible. Rank above rank of clustering trees met the eye, for old Salisbury has always cherished its trees. White houses peeped archly down through their second-story windows, and here and there a steeple pointed skyward, or there was a tuft of deeper green.

It was my father's custom to give as much of his Sunday as possible to those who were unable to pay him, the old "chronics" who did not need frequent visits but were accustomed to expect the Doctor on any pleasant Sunday afternoon. The drives were always leisurely. This so that "Old Frank" or "Old Wat" might take Sunday relaxation also, and travel without urging. The country was lovely, although it was sad—lovely in spite of its neglected fields.

The soil was exhausted and washing into gullies, or growing up in valueless timber, but somehow the country was wild and sweet. To a child, woods suggest romance. There were cedar thickets, red clay banks crowned with blue-green scrub pines, persimmon trees with their grotesquely angular growth, while in autumn the great golden hickories filled my heart with joy.

The two of us would swerve aside from the uneven ditch which in those days was called a road, would cross some small stream trickling across our track, and turn in between weatherbeaten gate posts whose gate was long fallen away. Always it would be a poor home to which we came on one of these Sunday afternoons.

Father might say, "Sit right here in the buggy. I will try not to keep you waiting too long." I would understand that there was something painful which he did not wish me to see. Father, his medicine chest in one hand, and a basket in the other, would stride up the ragged path. Returning, the basket would be empty, his face grave. But more often, he led me in with him, and the "Doctor's Baby" would be made very welcome. Invariably, something would be found as a treat for me. It might be nothing more than a handful of "scalybarks," a few wild plums, or lovely little red June apples. Once it was three tiny pullet's eggs.

All my life I have remembered with a tug of pity the utter bareness of some interiors. I have perceived the indescribable foetor of hopeless poverty. Some poor homes, by reason of incapacity or the weakness of extreme age, degenerated into rural slums. Usually, however, they preserved a self-respect that made them keep the place scoured clean to the bare bone.

I have never forgotten in all my long life the story told by these cabin homes of surrender to hopelessness, the tedium of life, and lack of comfort. Such things make the heart ache. Last of all we would go home by way of the poorhouse. It was built of logs, whitewashed, and its bare yard systematically swept clean of every sprig of a green thing growing; but the row of cabins stood in a sunny enclosure. People could be certain of a rude plenty of food and could have companionship of their own sort, with little work exacted. But my father's hard-bitten poor patients preferred to cling to their sad homes under rotting shingles, hoped to die there, and did die, perhaps alone, rather than take advantage of their right and place provided.

Do not ask me to tell explicitly the here and now regarding these impressions of childhood. I must sum them up as best I may, giving the general view. The exact time is never certain unless there can be found some definite recorded event to pin it to. This is the way we must assemble most of the panoramic recollections of long periods of our lives, whether we will acknowledge it or not. I can close my eyes today, and see the fields of my childhood still enclosed with rail fences, into the corners of which no plow could go; and the banks beside the road with their sassafras bushes, thickety masses of blackberry canes and rag-weed. Every fence post would be wreathed with poison ivy. This last is a deep green vine, and all its stems are furred with hairs as stinging as those of a noxious caterpillar. Sometimes when I would get out to gather flowers or berries beside the road, Father, waiting in the buggy, would call out cautions to me regarding a careless touch with its poisonous, three-cleft foliage.

The red clay of each cut bank or fill, was not the thinner, orange-tinted soil to the eastward, but a darker richer ground with the stain of iron rust, deepening to reddish chocolate color. With such finely powdered clay, the rain would have its will, once the binding of forest roots had been broken. Little trickles of water soon excavated channels, and these grew deeper with every summer rain, until there were great gullies which could not easily be filled. In long neglected fields, these ditches became a study in waterways, and at the same time a lamentable kind of devastation which Father used to discuss with me. He said things had grown worse more rapidly while the men were away at the War, and when many fields lay uncultivated which formerly had been well plowed; but the washing of the land, he thought, had been shamefully neglected from the first. Then he would moralize a bit, comparing the progressive deepening of some great gully to the growth of a bad habit.

Somewhat later in my childhood, I visited one time near the very worst of these old fields that I can remember, where denudation had gone so deep that a man on horseback might have been lost to view riding along the bottom of some of the washes. Following the lay of the land, such seasonal waterways joined and parted and formed a network, isolating the few islands left undissolved because of rocky structure or interlacing of tree roots. On one of these islands my playmate and I had our castle. We climbed up cunningly by small footholds and swinging roots. Once arrived, we were in an impregnable fortress—"The Yankees could not get us there!"

County roads were like the weather, a dispensation of Providence. Soil like ours could never be made into a roadbed stable for all weathers. The autumn was the only time when our roads were really good, for then the wheel tracks shone like polished mahogany, and a trot was better than a walk. The badness of the going in all other times was a fact enforced like Squeers' method of teaching spelling, by sad experience, by lurchings of springs and wrenchings of harness. All these adventures of the old dirt road have gone with the making of the cement highways. I could tell you where there existed notable great mudholes like open sores, never entirely dry save in time of drouth, and then scarred and knobbed by crossing wheel ruts. In wettest seasons, people in wagons might even have to remove a panel or two of rail fence and take to the woods and fields to pass at all. The popular method of mending roads then practiced was to cut down many pine branches and immerse them in the morass. The larger ends, the size of a walking stick, would bend upwards under the passing wheel and beat a tattoo upon the spokes like a boy drawing a stick along a picket fence. In my childhood, even inside the corporate limits of Salisbury, I remember redoubtable mudholes which I could diagram today, mudholes which no loaded wagon dare attempt.

It was in these times of serene joggings about the country, with the best companion I have ever known, that I learned the way things looked in each successive season, so that I can never forget them. Father answered my questions—and always I have asked very many—as equal to equal. We would indulge in sage speculation as to whys and wherefores. He never laughed at my ideas, and we were quite serious together. Then he was possessed of such entertaining accomplishments! He could make the most delightful flutes that spoke on one repeated note like the clear voice of spring. These could be made only in March when the sap was newly come up and bark could be made to slip easily, and I would ride home tootling blissfully. He could tell me the wonderful Tar Baby story long before Joel Chandler Harris wrote it down to charm everybody. He could sing Negro songs. He knew that one about "Patteroller ketch you," and another I have never heard elsewhere the words to which were,

> "Snake 'e bake a hoe-cake
> An' sot de Frawg ter min' it,
> Frawg got ter noddin' an'
> De Lizzud come an' stole it!
> Ah, bring me back ma hoe-cake
> Ya long tail Nanny!"

There remains from these childish adventures a composite of many afternoons of pure felicity, pictures of wood roads, of quiet pools where the road accompanied a "branch" for a little way, and of openings which showed ancient house plots, with the inevitable dooryard cedars, where the heavy "grass of graves" and of old home places grew rank. The figures in these pictures were sometimes benignly polite old Negroes, but more often were white people of country neighborhoods —bent old women in calico, queer unwholesome aged men.

At last it would be time to turn homeward, for the evening sky was turning clear lemon-yellow with fiery wisps. In the autumn the evenings would be growing crisp. When home was reached, there would be Mother, sitting reading aloud to my sister as she lay on her couch, while the fire snapped and glowed. After all these dolorous abodes, how glad I could feel, knowing that this was my home, and that it held Mother and all the picture books. Our plain sitting room would be to me like Heaven!

These good times came to a sudden conclusion, for my poor sister had been growing gradually weaker and paler for more than two years. Late in the summer when I was seven years old she became worse. Nothing was said to me of what the family must have known was coming, but I remember the tenseness over all. One night I awoke in my low bed and was startled to find myself quite alone in the room. Rushing through a door that showed a lighted crack, I found a group bowed around my sister's bed. I stood bewildered. Someone took me by the hand and led me away, sobbing nervously, but not at all knowing what it could mean. I crept back into my bed, and slept and waked to hear confused sounds and steps about the old house. The next morning, one of my aunts told me Sister was dead. I knew of death only as something one reads about. I was not so much moved, as mystified. When that morning my Aunt Eliza came, and walked up the steps with her arms held out, I felt utter dismay to see that kind Olympian, my self-possessed Mother, rush into them with a wild burst of sobbing. I felt that the Judgment

Day that Mary, our cook, talked about must be already at hand, and I fled precipitately to the orchard, where I sat cowering and shivering with apprehension, perched in my favorite tree.

The funeral I do not recall, but as was the custom in the old South, it must have been over and done with as soon as possible. Then at home it was quiet and sad enough. The leaves showered down in great drifts from our oaks, and there were but three of us sitting quiet at breakfast, Father, Mother, and myself. I did not see any more outward show of sorrow, but I sensed very well that we were a family in mourning.

XV

ON HOME LEVELS

THE HARDEST part of beginning to remember rather early is the necessity of growing older so soon and leaving behind that childish Eden, with the inevitable discovery how much less of perfectness there is in this world than we would like to think. Autumn, after Sister's death, was a cold season. The excursions in Father's good company had to cease for the time being. Every experience which has become too blissful must pass away.

In the later part of that same autumn occurred the deaths of two older relatives whose lives belonged to an earlier epoch. Both were very old folk; my father's father and my mother's mother. All these deaths seemed to make severance between my earlier and later childhood, although I did not know anything intimately of either of them. Death always makes changes in atmosphere if not in actual experience. My two aunts, Miss Margaret Mitchell and Mrs. Eliza Grant, had moved rather recently to Statesville, twenty-five miles west of Salisbury, and had there established a school for girls, in the old Simonton College building, which is still in existence under the name of Mitchell College. Because of Mother's repressed grief, the aunts thought it desirable to spend all the time with her that they could manage, and one or the other, usually Aunt Margaret, would come down by the evening train, bringing for luggage a funny square hatbox much deeper and far solider than the modern article. After supper she would open it and take out her knitting, and she and Mother would sit down to an endless talk. I would sit by, with ears pricked, and piece a good deal of information together, before they would remember about me and send me off to bed.

There would be talk about those Yankees who were ever bugbears to frighten southern children with, the people we shouted about in ballads, and were going to "hang on a sour apple tree, As we go marching home." The Yankees, it seemed, were mostly gone back home. Today's oppressors were called "carpetbaggers" and black Radicals, and were not identical with Yankees. Among them actually there were people whom I knew who were not black. One in particular had settled in our town and had planted here a superlative garden. Some of his box borders are still growing, and have come together across the whole width of the garden bed. He was also the owner of rows and rows of new books of the most interesting kind, books which a few years later he most graciously lent to me. I cannot guess what my mental garden would have been without Mr. Blackmer's Dickens and Thackeray, and George Eliot and Bulwer, not in casual volumes now and then, but set in their stalls, side by side, rows of fair coursers on which to ride out into the world. But I gathered that these reprehensible Radicals were accused of stealing—and it had something to do with railroads and with elections. But this election they could not steal, for our side (which is always the right side), had at last come out victorious.

It was intimated that these Radicals had been to blame for the way our Negroes had degenerated, considering themselves to be better than white people, when all the world knew the contrary. And it was bad for the Negroes, who needed some control, although the old ones, our Uncle Harry and our Aunt Mary for example, were not deceived. The young Negroes were saucy and mannerless. White children must no longer play with little Negroes as Father liked to tell of having done when he was a little boy. This took the form of a strict prohibition to me, and I soon found out why I was told it was forbidden.

Coming home from an errand to a neighbor's one day, running along a back street, which after a square or two trailed off into a Negro section at the edge of town, I met four Negro girls walking abreast. Mindful of Father's caution, I spoke not a word to them, but made the mistake of acting a little afraid of them. Seeing this, they took hold of hands, and stopped me. I gave them the whole sidewalk and jumped down into the road-way to pass them. They caught me, pressed round me, and the tallest one—a good deal my senior—attacking me, boxed my ears repeatedly. Then, perhaps a little alarmed at what they had done, they let me run home. Of course I flew in to Mother in a high state of tears and outrage; of course she, too, was filled with indignation, and Father was told. Father said little. He asked a question or two, and went out to make further investigation. He found out that the father of the largest girl who had made the actual attack was a self-respecting Negro, self-supporting at his trade of blacksmith. He told the man of his girl's attack on his little daughter. "You should control your child better, John, and you must punish her for this. As yet I have told nobody, but unless you do something about this yourself, and at once, I shall have to bear witness against you." Instantly, John went in search of his daughter and gave her a sound whipping, and the other colored parents followed suit. No word of this was said to me, but a week later I spied two of my persecutors and started to run. They ran from me instead, one girl calling back to another, "Come on, le's we git away f'm here! My Daddy done half killed me, 'count o' dat white chile!"

Here can be told the story of a fright Mother experienced the year before. She was up, ministering to my sister, who was very ill all that night, and it was the wee, small hours.

I was asleep just inside the nursery door, and Father had been called out to a patient. Suddenly Mother looked up to see a huge and brutish looking Negro man standing in the doorway. He must have seen Father leave the premises and had found the bolt of the door, which opened on the back gallery, left undone.

"What do you want?" Mother asked as casually as she could.

"I wants money" said the visitor gruffly.

"How much money?" asked Mother. "I haven't much change in the house."

"Fifty cents is what I got to git," replied the Negro.

"Well, here's a dollar bill. Take it and bring back the change, and put it on the table outside the door. *Look* at your feet! aren't you ashamed to bring all that mud into a white lady's house?" she cried as she handed him the money.

Instinctively the man stepped back from the doorway, and Mother shut the door and shot the bolt. Then she sat down and trembled for half an hour. But the honest Negro burglar brought back the fifty cents change and put it on the table!

Our fat Mary Woods and our Uncle Harry Cowan were both what used to be called "White-folks Darkies." Mary was highly respected, and her son, who lived on our lot, was a brakeman on the passenger train of the Western North Carolina Railroad, going out of Salisbury. Uncle Harry had been a member of our family with a right to his opinion even longer. Sometimes he complained bitterly of the damage one little girl could work in his vegetable garden, and when Mother heard she would banish me from it on his testimony; but let there be any other child, even my niece my own age, concerned in the business, Harry excused me, and made the other one the culprit. Harry was unable to read or write, but he was a man of thoughtful piety. Mother used to read the New Testament for him as he sat on the back steps after supper. On Sunday he was a preacher, and when he stood before his congregation he wore a long-tailed coat. My niece and I were always required to speak respectfully to him, calling him by the title, "Uncle," which betokened esteem for an elderly Negro of proved worth. Like most of his people, Harry had his sayings.

One morning he reported that one of our neighbors was "drowned." Mother was greatly shocked. "How did it happen?" she cried. "Was anyone with him, or was he found drowned?" "No Mistis, he ain' *drown dead*. He jis went a fishin' down to de River, an' he fell in, an' he got drownded, but he ain' dead yit."

In his official capacity as a colored preacher, Uncle Harry once made the prayer at a hanging, which remains to my mind the model of what such a petition in behalf of a criminal should be. The condemned man was one who had brutally murdered a woman companion of his own race, and in the fear of a riot at his execution, he was to pay the penalty outside his own county, in Salisbury.

Harry prayed, "O Lord, Have mercy on dis po' colored man, 'cause O Lord Thou knowest he didn' never have no chance! He was bo'n in ig'nunce an' raised way out in Davie County, an' O Lord, what You gwine ter 'spect from him!"

However good the Negro race at its best surely is, these could not be made overnight into intelligent voters, but were the tools of party heelers. The recent years had been fraught with a deep sense of discouragement for all minds retaining the older evaluations and with a mocking elation on the part of the untried and unstable elements now seizing their turn at ruling. These last while in power had tossed and tangled our inherited ways of governing and being governed, until every fixed ideal was lost in a sinister confusion. But from now on, the better inheritors of tradition hoped that more stable influences would be in the saddle. Even a child could tell that the drift of expectation had altered, that, in the minds of the grown folk, restoration was taking the place of "reconstruction."

The University, around which so much of the former interest of my family had revolved; the University, which belonged to the days of Grandfather Mitchell, had been closed for years. It was now reopened, and this was due, so Mother and the Aunties joyfully agreed, to the faith and initiative of their friend, Cornelia Spencer, who had built up sentiment and worked for it. That was cause for rejoicing, and Mother had written to congratulate her. She might regret that my brothers had gone to Davidson College instead of to the University, and she might at the same time be grateful that there had been such a good place for them to go while the University was closed. It was by stories I heard and impressions I received then, that I was able to bring back to actuality, the tale of its restoration. Not only from Mrs. Spencer's own papers, but from my recollections as well, I saw what an example of heroism she gave. She was even in my childhood one of my favorite heroines.

It was sometime in these later seventies that Zebulon B. Vance, our former War governor and the beloved leader of the conservative elements of our harassed commonwealth, was reëlected governor of North Carolina. He is conceded by verdict of history to have been a man of great sanity and foresight, and in this decade he resumed the actual leadership. It must have been in the late summer of 1876 that he came to Salisbury and spoke in Boyden's Grove.

Do not look for that grassy enclosure, shaded by venerable trees, near the center of town. It grew up in houses fifty years ago, but as a little girl, sitting beside my father, I heard Vance speak there, heard the rise and fall of his oratory, heard the people cheer him, and laugh, and cheer him again. I was near enough to see him quite plainly. The entire County had turned out—all the men and a good many of the women and older children. John Steele Henderson—a direct descendant of John Steele, Washington's comptroller, and of Archibald Henderson, and a man who was to serve his native district in Congress for years to come—introduced the speaker. Vance the Great thanked him for his eulogy and shook him familiarly by the hand, while all the people cheered. Glory could no farther go. But for myself I am not sure whether this speaking took place in 1876, or in the following year. Vance spoke in Salisbury both times, and on one of those occasions I heard him. When he was safely inaugurated governor, and not until then, as we all steadfastly believed, did reputable history take breath and begin to run its course once more in old North Carolina!

Mother did not need her sisters' or any other creature's admonitions to remind her what she ought to do, but the Aunties must have been asked for advice, must have lent some authority to the ideal, now that they came often to visit Mother, and she found herself steeped anew in the essence in which she had grown her character. It was the Aunties who now helped Mother plan what sort of a prodigy they wished to find in me. It was manifest enough that I was at a loose end. I could read far more than I could understand, had known how to read for years, do not remember learning but that was all it had come to so far. And so, with Aunt Margaret to advise her, Mother decreed an end to the carefree philandering with Father, and set me down to strictly ordained lessons that next spring. I did not relish the change, and yet learning is a pleasant game, once you accept it. Now that Mother had no more nursing duty, she not only taught me my lessons but regulated my goings out and comings in and appointed my habits. The nap-in-the-afternoon was one such ruling, believed invariably to prevent frowardness in children.

At the closed and shuttered end of our low-lying house, was the twilight parlour which I seldom visited unless the day was so hot that Mother said, "You must take a nap this afternoon." A nap was unnecessary, but you never teased Mother. She would make me lie down on the cool, slippery, haircloth sofa which stood opposite the life-size portrait of Father when he was a handsome young man, and would say, "Go to sleep quickly now." The parlour would smell musty behind the close-drawn blinds. On the mantel were two great bouquets of dried grasses, not renewed every year, made up of pampas plumes, with a few immortelles. I would look at these familiar things, and suddenly come awake from a long way off. Mother would declare, "You have had a nice nap." (I did not know I had gone to sleep at all.) "Only look, the clock has gone 'way round, and it is four o'clock."

A Presbyterian child must be taken to church every Sunday. When first I find myself going there, I seem to have been going many times before and to know how to behave. The church was three squares from home, whichever of three ways you took, but the road invariably taken seemed to have a Sunday morning orthodoxy all its own. We went first north to Innes Street, and when we reached the turning at the great oak on the Overman corner, it was obligatory and a settled custom that a child must walk outside, all round it. The sidewalk curbing of granite had been carefully conducted about its wide-spreading root claws, but as the tree had grown it had heaved up the stones until footing was difficult and required careful balancing.

For one block from the Presbyterian Church in all directions, granite stepping-stones had been laid, against muddy seasons. These have been removed long ago, but in the days of my childhood it was very bad luck to miss stepping on a single one as you walked churchwards. You must stride with extreme effort as far as your short legs could reach from one to the middle of the next one, and this must be done even if it were dusty underfoot. Our church might just as well have been a courthouse, so devoid was it of ecclesiastical detail. There was a round belfry over the front and a porch with high Doric columns.

Our pew was close up, near the pulpit, and it was forbidden to turn and look behind you. The church had light walls and a red carpet. Its double range of oblong windows were clear-paned. Galleries went around three sides of the rectangle, forming the organ loft and choir at the north end, but in the south end there was no gallery—only two high windows above the pulpit through which sunshine would stream down in slanting lines of turbid, dusty light.

From the lower window that opened to the right of our pew, little was visible save a green yard, flecked with the broken shadows made by cedar foliage, so that I amused myself by gazing fixedly into these bright bands of indoor sunshine. I would dream the drowsy service away, for I discovered how to widen my eyes and stare into these slanting beams, until they swirled and curdled and became winged shapes weaving along the golden stairways of the light. These visions I could recall at will, almost like playing over a set record on a phonograph. But to enjoy such a dream of wings, I must sit perfectly still. It was uncanny how an abrupt movement or a sudden sound would break the spell.

Often that sharp sound would be a bark from our serious pastor's vociferous white poodle. From our window I could see him, chasing round the flat roof of the back porch at the Manse. It was diverting to watch how he careered round and round, or hung over the extreme edge, longing to leap off. He had to be shut out there because he would insist upon coming to church. Sometimes he made good his escape and did so, and would have to be removed from the pulpit by the scruff of his neck, yelling loud protests the while. "Snowflake" looked like an animated white chrysanthemum. I used to wonder why tall dignified Dr. Rumple wanted such a funny dog, but indeed I found him a very present help in time of a long sermon.

All around us, in the various pews, were large families whom I knew, sitting decorously. Mr. "Bank" Davis, one of the elders, always sat bolt upright with closed eyes, his hands, like Jacob's, folded upon the top of his walking stick. I became firmly convinced that he took naps that way. One Sunday I caught him at it. A large bluebottle fly alighted on his nose, and the rousing start he gave assured me that it was from sleep he awakened and not from meditation. In the "Amen Corner" of the opposite side, there sat a numerous row of McCorkles descended from a famous schoolmaster and pastor of Thyatira, and behind them an equally long series of Marshes. Mr. Murdock, the stone mason and bridge builder was one of the elders, and very deaf. He used to get up and place himself in one of the chairs under the pulpit desk; there he held one hand carefully cupped behind his ear in order to hear better.

At that time all mature women were still wearing bonnets covering the entire crown, and although neither my mother nor Mrs. Bruner were what is called advanced in years, they wore such bonnets, made of straw braid or folds of black silk. Mr. Bruner, another of the elders, and the editor of the *Carolina Watchman*, our paper, sat well back on the opposite side of the church. I always tried to screw around until I caught sight of him, for I was fond of him, and wanted him to be in his place. In cold weather, he would be wrapped in a man's gray shawl, such as was the fashion about 1860.

For a Presbyterian church, not supposed to be concerned with embellishments, we had excellent music. I remember the pretty, frilly, young organist, who has long ago joined the Choir Invisible. I can recall the man who played the cornet, which lead the tune. There were soprano singers and an alto. I cannot recall the tenor. There was also a man of massive frame, bearded like a Confederate general, who would sing out a great booming bass. I have an impression that the rest of the choir persecuted him, perhaps because he made their voices sound pale.

From three-quarters to a full hour was allowed for the sermon, old-fashioned, with all its bones of structure fully visible, its fourthlys and fifthlys in sequence. But when I was very small, Mother always brought me a cooky, wrapped in a handkerchief. I ate it as slowly as I could, and then composed myself to sleep. Some later year, grown older, I had my choice of listening to the sermon, or of committing to memory a hymn, to be recited at home after church. The hymn would have to be learned anyway, and so to have it out of the way seemed practical. I found interesting hymns in the book, by which I mean they made pictures for my childish mind. Mother's favorites did nothing of that sort, but I still remember the shiver of "Lo, on a narrow neck of land, 'Twixt two unbounded seas I stand, And how insensible!" In another hymn I fell to wondering at the strange statements about washing garments in blood, of all things! The hymns which I really enjoyed hearing had lilting tunes to them! "Joy to the World," and "There is a Land of pure delight!" all about green fields and flowers. Up to this time, no Moody and Sanky jingles had been included in formal service. I remember the plaintive old Scotch airs, and the hymn tunes made up of big round notes with or without stems to them—great, solemn "O's" of sound.

When at last the sermon was over, and the last hymn sung, Dr. Rumple would end the final prayer with a warm "Ayemen" in a tone that sounded as if he were glad to have done; and I would be glad with him.

After church, all continued to be wholly decorous. Mother would not linger as long for social greetings by the way as I wished she might. She was always in a hurry to get home, and all too soon our decisive front gate would click against me. For that particular Sunday, there would be no more going out by it, unless indeed I could inveigle Father to take me practicing with him after dinner.

XVI

GOING PLACES AND LEARNING THINGS

It is safe to state that for ten years after the War, northern solicitude had been given wholeheartedly only to teaching Negro children, no help being extended to white schools. By this time the benefactors had grown weary. There were no public schools in North Carolina in 1877, and when we achieved them, we were responsible not only for our own but for the little Negroes and their ABC's.

In September, 1877, the *Carolina Watchman* notes the fact that there were perhaps a dozen schools in town, but none of them, save the Presbyterian Academy, was either large or well attended. Most of these must have been primary schools carried on by anyone who would volunteer to teach the three R's, and I knew of one, taught by a niece of Governor Ellis, which was excellent. The Academy was taught and well taught by a Miss Gilmer, and there was a small classical school for boys, begun about this time. Out in the country were neighborhood schools under itinerant teachers, gathered and disbanded as occasion served, and in Mocksville there long existed an especially good academy.

Considering how very little I have ever gathered of formal education to which I can point as definite distance run, it is strange how my mind dwells on what might be done with sanity and foresight in training the young, but educational methods are held like religious creeds—with all fervor of opinion there's very little proof of anything. I wish there could have been some plan devised in my childhood looking toward the education, even in those lean times, of everybody's children. In our small portion of the world, this was given the scantiest consideration, for economic needs were pressing and our popular ideals did not see how important for all needs was education.

If only our children could have been well taught according to capacity, what matter then, or at any other time, for poverty? In one generation all could have been set going again. As it was, with as much sheer ability as is often found in one small town, with a racial mingling that brought out the good qualities of each element, no development of brains was looked for, very little encouragement given to anyone to make of an aptitude anything significant. There is never more brain power in any one generation than that generation can use.

Mother could pass along what had been taught to herself, and so, in the winter of 1877-78 she began to teach me Latin and drill me in primary branches. Lessons came on Mondays and Saturdays alike, and continued when I was with Mother, through Junes and Decembers without a break. They lasted only three hours a day for both study and recitation, so that I was not confined indoors, but nothing short of an earthquake was permitted to interfere with regular lessons. I was quick, but not over-industrious. For some reason I did not seem able to write legibly. Mother grew skillful at reading my scrawl, but it was a good while before I amended it unbidden.

One day when I was translating Caesar, a mouse ran out of a hole under the brick hearth and took refuge by climbing the ample folds of Mother's long dress-skirt. I drew a breath of relief. I did not know my lesson too well, and here was a blessed interruption! Mother closed her fingers over the mouse as he moved higher towards her waist. She kept the book open with her other hand. "Go on Daughter," she said, and go on I did, blundering, to the very end, and realizing as I seem not to have done before that each day's lessons were as inexorable as fate. A silly little incident, but it serves to show the quality of her determination.

Mother also tried to hold me away from the small-town life around me. The steady growth of the town was by this time easy to see, and the newcomers brought in a mixture of social attributes. Mother discouraged intimacies, keeping me away from other children until with the contrary-mindedness of any healthy child I turned eagerly to the adventure of making friends with the neighbors' children. Some delightful children lived near us. There was one of those seething large families which multiply and swarm and roll about (or used to do so in my young days), at the feet of a mother who is cheerfully unaware of sticky hands, who is deaf to strange noises, who never denies her children what they ask for, because she does not make the effort of withholding what they tease to get. Such a family lived just around the corner. Their cheerful disorder was so different from the decorous quiet of my home, and they as individuals were so interesting, that it filled my soul with joy when I could slip away to them and be called in from their fence. Blithely I would skip through their gate into the clutter of their fascinating, totally untidy back yard and join whatever game was afoot. That family was always doing something! The older ones made up wonderful plays, and the younger ones were only too glad to be actors in them. It might be a make-believe of a wedding or a funeral founded on recent town affairs, or it was a bear's den, dug out of a red clay bank and bedded with dry leaves for a hunting scene; or an arbor, remorselessly sawed off the orchard trees to stage a love story. Without showing me the slightest deference, these children included me in their schemes only if I would play my part.

One day Mother missed me and decided to walk by where she felt sure to find me and call me home. She beheld her child upon the top of that family's woodpile, dressed in a long white nightgown, holding a pasteboard rolled to form a trumpet. On the ground things were swarming confusedly, directed by Beulah, the oldest girl. As Mother looked on, I executed a flying leap into the melee. So intent were all of us on our game, that not one perceived Mother slowly pass by on the street.

That afternoon she asked me, "What on earth were you doing on the Stewart's woodpile today, with a white nightgown on?"

"Oh I was the Angel Gabriel. We were playing Judgment Day, and I had to jump down and blow the trumpet."

"How do you children think up such games?"

"Why, Mother, you heard Dr. Rumple read in the Bible about it last Sunday, and Aunt Mary Woods told us how it ought to be at the Last Day; so Beulah had all her little brothers playing dead until I blew the trumpet, and raised them up. We played it all out three times, and it was fun!"

Sometimes the neighborhood children would return my visits by fives and sixes, and wild runnings and riotings went on from porch to porch, while the fun grew fairly deafening, and Mother endured it until it was time to send the crowd home, munching cookies. After these orgies of shouting and running, I would become strangely quiet. I was not limited to this sort of pastime. I loved to think about people and spell out their characteristics, and this sort of speculation is still my best entertainment.

Poor Uncle Harry came in one day fairly popeyed and gibbering with indignation. "Little Miss," as he called me, had been throwing clods at him in the garden, he said. He had threatened to call Mistis, but I had only laughed at him and thrown another clod. "I ain't gwine to have nobody's chillun throwin' dirt at me!" he concluded. I was called in, and questioned. I gravely acknowledged that I had done this, and on purpose. Uncle Harry was setting out pepper plants. Beulah had told me that if pepper was to grow, the person who set it out must be "mad." So I had "tried to make Uncle Harry mad," and I had succeeded, for he did get very mad. Now I was quite sure the pepper would grow. Mother did not know just where to take hold of this prank, I was so unnaturally grave and serious about it. And Beulah Stewart—was she indeed the instigator?

A few days later, our neighbor, Mrs. Bingham, told Mother rather apologetically of another prank of mine.

"She was over playing with my children, and all at once she said she must go home. They are all so fond of having her, that they got round her, and begged her to stay. They asked why she had to go home just then, and she said she was hungry—hungry, mind you, an hour and a half after dinner. But they believed her and came and begged a piece of pie I had locked up in the pantry safe. She took that pie, and said, 'Goodbye all,' and away she went, stuffing it into her face, and laughing! I did not grudge her the pie, but my children felt pretty huffy about it. She deliberately fooled them, that's sure."

For this Mother lectured me, and as a sort of permanent reminder she decreed that henceforth I must sweep the front porch each day, and always before I went out visiting. A week later I was flourishing away at a house several squares from ours. Here came fat Mary, indignantly, puffing and waddling down the street. She called out, "Yo' Ma say fer you ter come right home."

"What for, Aunt Mary?"

"Yo' Ma tol' me ter tell you jus' what I *is* tole you. She say you come on home, right straight, now!"

I flew home, to be met by Mother with the broom. "Sweep the porch, daughter, you did not do it before you left." When I had run my third quarter of a mile and reappeared out of breath at the Foster's, my friend Alice asked curiously what had been wrong at home. "Nothing wrong, just Mother wanted to see me," I answered and would tell no more.

GOING PLACES

It must have been a year later and in the summer that I made the first visit outside Salisbury that I can remember. It was only to the next town, twenty-five miles west, to the school where Mother's two sisters lived. Before the Civil War this had been planned as a boarding school, but the War had swept away the endowment and my aunts had taken over the building for their boarding and day school for girls. During the summer they lived in one wing of the empty resounding building. This year one of them was away, leaving only Aunt Margaret with the Negro servant. In the letters and journals of the day, fevers and malarias are always spoken of as inevitable. No reason for them had been by that time discovered, and they were considered "dispensations of Providence." When a member of a family pined into typhoid, and had to be nursed day and night for weeks on weeks, there was strong likelihood that some other member of the household might take the infection, and the whole exhausting business need to be gone through a second time. Just now, Aunt Margaret, living by herself that summer, was coming down with typhoid, and Mother was sent for to nurse her. I must go with my mother, because there was nothing else to be done with me. We were established in a room of the inhabited wing of the great school building with pillared façade. Some friends from town might help with the night watching, as was the kindly custom, but the nursing took all Mother's time, and I was left alone for the first time in my life.

Some children would have been oppressed by the silence of the empty building. I did not mind. I rummaged the schoolroom, and found McGuffey's Readers to entertain me, and an old copy-book to scribble in. On all the blackboards I drew elaborate designs—my tastes always have been the same for pastime. Mother praised me for giving so little trouble.

Then I made friends with the family of the local preacher, whose children were as numerous and active as the neighbors I had left behind. Marianna, my new playmate, prided herself on her good looks, while I had never reflected on mine; but we two set about decorating our persons. We made caps, ribbons, and sashes of green leaves, pinned together with tiny twigs broken from the "bridal wreath" spirea: we wove garlands, and linked yards and yards of clover chains, and then dressed ourselves in all this make-believe finery. Then we bridled and preened and patted. We discovered our hair, and rolled it up over rags to curl it, and finally, borrowing two of Mother's full calico skirts to masquerade in, we trailed about simpering and switching our trains, talking for whole afternoons the jargon we called "lady talk."

On my birthday, as if in answer to a prayer for raiment, Father brought me a surprise chosen on his own initiative. It was a wonderful new dress, made by Miss Mollie Wren, the best dressmaker in town. With it came a pair of high, bronze button-boots with tassels. My father had that excellent taste in women's apparel often possessed by very masculine men. My little costume was stylish in cut and material, and had—oh delight and bliss unspeakable—a puffy overskirt with pleatings all around the bottom.

After Aunt Margaret recovered, after we went home, I was so lost without a playmate that Mother decided there must be other children, and she must choose them herself. She undertook to teach a child or two along with me, and let me find my place with companions. Mother was valued in her community and only needed to say she was willing to teach other children to have them sent to her. By that time Father had removed his office to a Main Street drugstore; so there was the old office, with all its cupboards, ready to become the schoolroom. A local carpenter made a rough table or two, and it was furnished. There was a jolly, curly-headed boy with a quick mind, who was one of the new pupils, and soon I found myself floundering after him painfully. He construed Latin far more competently than I did, and little Miss-who-was-proud-of-herself, came in a bad second, or nowhere. There were, besides, two girls, one several years older than I, who was merely putting in the interval until she could "put her hair up, and her dresses down," as the saying went. Her talk was all about *who* was "nice" and *what* was "nice," and the joys of coming young-ladyhood. By-and-by a third girl was added to our number.

My mother always pitied the poorer whites—often people of good English blood who had been so long obliged to live in competition with Negro labor that they had lost their self-confidence and industry, in fact everything save the intense pride of the poor white man, be he highland or lowland. These people, their thriftlessness, their ignorance, lay on her mind. Once she had taught in a sort of ragged Sunday school, held in the courthouse, and had learned somewhat of them. In her class had been a handsome red-haired girl of some imagination, who drank in the Bible stories eagerly. Her given name, she said, was "Queen Esther." One day after telling the parable of the "Ten Virgins," Mother was questioning her class. "What was it that the foolish virgins forgot?" With a simper of superiority, Queen Esther bobbed up, and said, "They forgot their kerosene, Ma'am." Her Majesty learned to read and write in a very short time, and then drifted out of Mother's knowledge. Now and then there was talk of a handsome young dressmaker of the town who had become the common-law wife of a wealthy old bachelor, but Mother did not connect this woman with the old odd name. But it was Queen Esther, nevertheless, who brought her daughter to my mother and begged to have her taught with the rest. This girl was now called by the name of her putative father, who had acknowledged her and settled money on her, and the mother was married to a respectable carpenter.

With a boldness she had not expected from herself, Mother decided to teach this girl. Instantly she was visited by the scandalized mother of each of the other girls, but she took high ground with them. She stated clearly that they might take their children away as soon as they chose, but that she had found the new girl good and intelligent, and intended to give her the chance of learning something. Neither mother removed her child, and the little undesirable was so deferential and anxious to please, that everything settled into harmony. The facts of the case were told me without concealment by my mother.

If it occurs to question why these children were not one and all sent to a public school, the answer is that as yet no public schools had been reëstablished in Salisbury, or in any other town without local resources, since the debacle of the Civil War had destroyed both organization and endowment. They were under discussion. Perhaps at this moment a lot had been purchased and plans were being drawn. While the doubtful experiment was being prepared, there was no place for teaching the daughters of the town. By far the larger number of children were adrift between the old and the new. Although in denominational boarding schools girls of the "best families" might be taught high-school branches with a little music and "art," their numbers bore but a small proportion to those who might have profited by even such lopsided training. People kept saying that girls must not be trained away from the simple home-making, the church, and children, which must become the sum of their interests a little later. A Negro in the kitchen, and everybody could afford one, made a woman indolent. Self-improvement had not come in fashion, and men did not admire a "strong-minded" woman; so little education was bestowed on them.

We spent Christmas that year at the Aunts' school, and made of it a real festival. Money matters were very slowly relaxing their stringency, and there were a few dollars to spare. On Christmas Eve we went, all three, and enjoyed the foolish time-honored ceremonial that goes with Christmas when children bless it and make it a delight. My niece, my own age, was now living with the Aunts, and "Cousin John and his sisters," from another family, made five children of us.

First of all, every single soul must hang up a stocking, and Father, declaring that no little sock could contain all he deserved, hung up a pair of trousers with each leg tied into a bag with string. A great Christmas tree stood trimmed in the sitting room. We had made profuse wreaths of holly and mistletoe, which were abundant a mile out of town if you would but go out and cut what you wanted. Real candles tipped the tree and had to be watched to guard against fire. Much popcorn was strung and looped about it, but there was very little tinsel. After breakfast, everyone from the Doctor to the smaller children filed in and sat in a circle. Then Emma, Aunt Margaret's toothfully smiling black maid, took many trips to bring in the stuffed stockings and other presents heaped on a japanned breakfast tray. Father's trousers were reported empty, save for a switch we children had put into them, for even those could not contain the huge arm-chair, and the thirty-pound turkey which were his portion. After presents were looked over and thanked for, we children went out to shoot off firecrackers. Southern children always mixed up Christmas and Fourth of July like that—nobody has ever told why.

The Presbyterian child was systematically taught the whole Bible, all of it being considered useful, "for doctrine, reproof, correction and instruction in righteousness," and besides this a Presbyterian child must learn the Shorter Catechism. That was the law of our house. I was expected to learn it thoroughly—by question and answer—by pages—by wholes, without one word or one comma misplaced. I was not expected to understand it. It was considered a deposit laid up for the future in the bank vault of my mind. If ever I changed my early beliefs, as everyone is liable to do, it would furnish a comprehensive statement from which honestly to dissent, not a fog bank to fight against, or the ghost of an ancient authority to be exorcised. Such a point was made of my learning this Shorter Catechism that I grew nervous about it. The day came when I was expected to go to Dr. Rumple's study by appointment and recite the whole of it to him. I went with misgiving and half way through reached a question from which a word dropped right out of my memory, not leaving a trace. Dr. Rumple sent me out into his garden to sit in the sun and relax, and after half an hour recalled me, and back I went not yet remembering the word.

"We stopped here," said the Doctor, reading out the elusive phrase containing the word "Now go on." I wondered if he knew what he had done. He made no sign. He sat there, large and dignified, his blue eyes folded down at the corners, and on his knee, older and not so vociferous, sat that absurd white poodle. I finished the Catechism in triumph, and to this day I remember that lost word. Moreover I became sure that I liked Dr. Rumple, trusted him, and found in him a discerning friendliness.

Although there was not the least religious excitement afoot, I calmly and simply joined the church that spring, as quietly as I put on my Sunday clothes. In doing so I spread around myself such an atmosphere of reserve that no one ever tried to discuss the decision with me, and even an autobiographer, although admittedly omniscient, will not force such a confidence.

At the cost of making a long chapter still longer, the story of my second stay away from home should come in here.

It was 1880, and my oldest brother was married, was just now entering the Presbyterian ministry, and was about to take charge of his first church. His wife came from somewhere in the Middle West, and she was beautiful. I was fascinated by the new sister, and she seemed to be amused and entertained by the youngest of her husband's family; so she pressed for an early visit from me at her country manse. In early summer, I went.

The long drive, far from a railroad, and off the main-traveled ways, took all day in a jouncing buggy. The red clay track was dry, but so little worn by wheels that it had dried all lumpy from the last rain. The journey ended in a country still much wooded, where the red earth was sown thick everywhere with snow-white flints.

Long before the American Revolution, a drift of Scotch-Irish settlers had come into the red clay counties both south and west of Salisbury. Leaving Pennsylvania, they had followed the foothills of the Blue Ridge the whole way down. They were Presbyterians and often moved by church units, bringing their pastors and building their log churches as soon as they did their barns. Thyatira, in Rowan County, was one of these, and my brother's church was even a little older, and still called by the name of its first makeshift shelter, "Old Poplar Tent." Both church and manse stood near the "big road" a little way apart; both were roomy, square, and without the slightest pretense to beauty. The Poplar Tent Church I knew was a plain box-like building of brick, the belfry being represented practically by a farm bell on a scaffold outside, to call the congregation into church after they had assembled. Any Sunday morning, innumerable Johnsons, Jacksons, Stevensons, Laffertys, and even some with German names like Phifer and Stirewalt, rumbled churchwards in their wagons; or, if it was too wet, came on horseback along the squelching morasses of the way. Whatever might be the weather, to church they would come. Having arrived, their first care was to unharness their horses and put them under the church sheds, or hitch saddle nags to the long rail beside the church, where they stamped and whinnied. The mothers gathered their small children and went immediately inside the building to exchange gossip over the backs of the pews. The men and bigger boys, dressed in sober Sunday black, seated themselves on the long bench made of puncheons with legs set under them, which extended on each side of the straight gravel walk leading to the vestibule of the church. The first man to arrive seated himself on the extreme outer end of this rough bench. The next comer shook hands with him, and sat down opposite. The later ones filled in solidly to the church door, until, just before the bell began to jangle, the whole double row arose to be greeted, each one, when the minister walked in. Then all of them clomped in behind him, to preaching.

In this church, old-fashioned pews were still in use; and inside these convenient square pens, rolled and squirmed great healthy families of Scotch-Irish. The men and boys sat in the galleries by prerogative, and with them associated themselves the hounds which always made part of the congregation; although now and then a long yellow dog with a black muzzle would stretch down beside a pew where his family was sitting and take up most of the aisle with his legs.

There was no organ. Tom Mack raised the tunes by the help of a tuning fork which he held to his ear, sounding a preliminary humming in unison with it. Then he scooped up or down to the opening note of the hymn tune. Tom was tall and angular, and his Adam's apple worked up and down his skinny throat while, with head thrown back, he gave all his energy to the tune, his rasping, nasal voice sounding above everyone else.

Babies, always numerous, would cry and have to be taken out and pacified. Once I saw a three-year-old escape from a pew and wander down the aisle eating a "jelly piece." A hound got up to take it away from her, whereupon she whacked him with a hymnbook, and, tottering, sat down hard and suddenly. The wailing and ki-yi-ing were ear-splitting, but in Poplar Tent pulpit that day stood a colleague used to country congregations. He said parenthetically, "Will someone kindly remove that dog?" and went straight on with his discussion of original sin.

After morning sermon, Sunday school lasted the next hour. After Sunday school everybody made for the lunch baskets. The older women had tea and coffee for everybody, and neighbors were invited to eat with neighbors, while housewives took the opportunity of tasting somebody's cooking beside their own, and of giving and receiving recipes for outstanding cakes and pies. Some of the congregation who had come in ten or twelve miles to church did not expect to be fobbed off with but one skimpy discourse; so it was the custom to preach a second sermon after dinner. The morning sermon must be doctrinal, but in the afternoon "practical application" of scripture was in order, beginning half an hour or so after the last cake or custard had been consumed. By afternoon sermon, all the children were utterly lethargic, or frankly fractious. The tiny ones napped on the hard wooden pews, their heads in their mother's laps, while in fine weather the larger ones were sent to spend the time in the old graveyard beside the church. Dire threats were made of what would happen if they made a noise, or worse still, fought on the Sabbath day. Glad of a respite, the children poked about the graveyard, and, if it was the right season, might flush a mother partridge with her dainty brood, and could watch them disappear on the ground, right before face and eyes, or, if it was autumn, see a covey whirr up and fly when the dogs snuffled them out. The older children would teach the younger ones their letters from the tombstones, and after a long, dragging hour, the doxology would be sung, the families packed into the wagons, and all would move briskly off. By the time most of them would reach home, evening feeding and milking would be late. Those who lived nearer by, loath to part, would drive leisurely, teams abreast, shouting to each other as they went. Last of all, the Minister and his family would step off the few rods to the Manse, make up fires in the chilly house, if it was cold weather, and go early to bed after a long day's exertion.

The manse stood square and bare in a large yard, with a drive laid out in front in an oval, marked out with a close-set row of white flints. There was no shrub or tree to break the bleakness. Behind the house was a garden, and behind that a grove of large trees shading a downward slope. At the bottom of this slope welled up a spring of purest water, and near by was the washing shed, and the large kettle with legs where the clothes were boiled outdoors. In the background of this picture loomed a hill, one of those bubbles of pure granite, resembling Dunn's Mountain near Salisbury. This hill was about half a mile long, a few hundred feet high, and quite rugged. Its central mass, of close-grained granite, would have furnished building stone for a city. Boulders stuck through its scanty soil at intervals, but the giant hickory trees must have loved their fare of disintegrating granite, for their roots took hold in the crevices, and they stood like primeval forest. Down behind this hill rippled a little stream, frequented by coons and crayfish. It was a friendly wilderness. Among the sunny rocks scampered dozens of tiny gray lizards which matched in color the lichened boulders where they ran. I was fascinated by these lizards, stalked them warily, and one day succeeded in catching one. I pinned it carefully into my apron pocket, and ran back to "Sister Anna" in triumph, telling rapturously of my luck. Sister Anna was a town-bred girl, and anything that looked as reptilian and ran as fast as did these lizards was frightful to her. When I showed my capture, she began to scream, "Take it away! Take it away!" I looked at her with astonishment, and said in reproof, quite seriously, "Sister, they are interesting clean little animals. I had a hard time catching this one, and mean to look at him before I let him go again."

Anna kept right on, crescendo, "Take it away, take it away!" but I let it go instead, upon her dressing-table. The little fellow ran up on one of her big cologne bottles, and sat clutching its round glass stopper, his tiny throat throbbing with terror. I can see now that a genuine natural-history enthusiast was new to my new sister, and was hard upon her. Next day, when she found her pint measuring cup accommodating a couple of crayfish she boiled over again, and again I reproved her. "Sister Anna, I don't think you ought to act so fussy, and call crayfish 'dirty things.' They are quite clean. They live in the spring, and you drink off them every day!"

Old Poplar Tent was a delightful place. All around lived good respectable country folk, in their roomy gray old houses, with a flower stand on every front porch, full of geraniums and Christmas cactus, which had to be brought through the winters in pits, or in the living rooms. These homes were furnished with handmade split-bottom chairs, and had gay rag carpets. The chimneys had strings of red peppers festooned over their wide throats. Now and then an especially promising boy would be sent to Davidson College and would do well there. He might be heard of as a preacher or a successful lawyer in the Southwest.

My mother must have seen the need to detach me from her side and the stay at Poplar Tent taught me many things. With the people, I found myself adaptable; if they were but themselves, I liked them as they were. If old Mrs. Johnson smoked her pipe before the fire, Anna thought it somewhat disreputable, but I was interested in the way she handled it. If Jane Lentz publicly fed her small son four successive slices of rich pound cake to keep him quiet during sermon, Anna said it was "disgusting" but I laughed at her, for I remembered my own church cooky, in rather recent times, and I was very little shocked.

XVII

BREAD AND BUTTER (WITH IMAGINATION)

ALL MY LIFE it has interested me to find out whence the daily bread of animals and people may come, and how they get the simple means of staying alive. From a child, being shown a strange beast in a picture book, my first question was invariable. "What does it eat, how does it get it?" Now that eighteen-eighty has drifted so far back into the used-to-be, when our grandchildren and great-grandchildren separate the now from the then, perhaps somebody would like to know how we ordered our humdrum lives, or even ask what we had for dinner, and how we came by the very few dollars which, added in with the well-tilled garden plot, and the family home built before the War, furnished forth our simple living.

This sort of detail is what this chapter is made of, and it has cost me a deal of pains. Let me try to prove it.

Money was needed to make the mare go, and precious little money was in circulation in Salisbury at just this period. Well I remember the first quarter of a dollar I ever possessed. It was a birthday gift from Aunt Margaret, when I was ten, and as it lay in my palm it looked as large as the full moon!

Salisbury had somewhat revived in the seventies, but now after manufacturing had begun in a small way in other towns of the Piedmont, workers were moving away again. The unattached young men, seeing no prospect at home, were seeking fortunes in the Southwest. In January, 1879, the *Carolina Watchman* chronicles the fact that "Fifty people have left for Texas from the Depot in Salisbury in the past year." Like the weary old man's wish for his first hundred years of

BREAD AND BUTTER

Paradise, old Salisbury "just sat still" for much more than the first decade of my life.

Cotton fell lower and lower in price, and along with it the value of farm lands grew always less. Times closed down harder and harder in our corner, just as they did in the marts of trade in the United States, which was just now repenting its orgy of postwar expansion. We had felt none of the prosperity, but we were feeling the regression.

Out in the country, for every two barns which might be burned down by one agency or another, only one would ever be built back. Moving to town gave no relief, for there was nothing new in the way of business, of getting a living, to be done after coming there. By the advertisements regularly inserted in the *Carolina Watchman*, the weekly paper which Mr. Bruner had bought back in 1872 and edited afterwards, there existed the same three or four law firms, the same physicians, the identical merchants, dry goods and commission, the necessary drug store, the usual livery stable. These businesses had their stands in the same buildings, which were shabby holdovers, some from forty years previous. One butcher, baker, saddler, shoemaker, and tinner satisfied the needs of this town of less than two thousand inhabitants. It is needless to say there were no rich, and indeed few who were more comfortably off than the rest. Equally it is true that not many were so poor that they did not have food and clothing of the plainer kind.

A new hotel was built with somebody's money, and after it was ready the old Mansion House was torn away. In the few years before cotton had fallen to its final disastrous level, a few homes were built in Salisbury. Of these the Knox house and the Bingham house on Bank Street are still kept up. I have heard Father say that for some years after the War, money was easier and collections freer than they became after 1880.

Late in the seventies, an editorial in the *Watchman* urged

everyone to take advantage of the bankruptcy law and save his homestead, compromise his debts, and start again. "Now is the time, the sooner the better." This shows as could not be done otherwise the lessening productivity of our County. About this time, commercial fertilizers began to be advertised in every state paper, because the chemical formulas were taking the place of, and increasingly required for supplementing, other methods of restoring fertility. In Rowan, the yield per acre of grain and cotton kept lessening, and tobacco was not much produced there. No important tobacco factory was ever built in Salisbury, and other manufacturing did not exist for some time to come.

All through the County survived the ancient water mills wherever there was a creek capable of turning one. There was a steam sawmill or two—one of these last, operated quite within the residence portion of the town. I remember being on the street near our church, and seeing a great comet-like missile fly over my head with a heavy report. It broke against a tree in the yard of the Manse, and buried itself in the turf. No one was hurt, and Mr. Marsh installed a new boiler and continued business as before. Afterwards, when I passed that way, I used to run by as fast as I could, imagining myself being pursued by pieces of machinery hurtling through the air.

We had a local tannery, and some skillful old-time boot and shoe makers had survived. Boots were still worn, and not being easy to purchase ready-made were hand-sewed and very durable. A bootjack was part of everyone's home equipment. My father's looked like a huge black iron beetle, whose mandibles gripped the boot heel and helped him to slip it off.

While recalling Salisbury of eighteen-eighty and a few years later, I must not forget our remarkable town paper, the *Carolina Watchman*, which, since great syndicated news-blankets have come in, could not be matched today in our whole land. It was in size but one large folded sheet, and its four pages included, besides general news and editorial comment, a careful selection from exchanges, notes on agricultural topics, and a local column noticing all the incidents which gave color to the passing show, made up with good taste and good humor. Its items ranged all the way from the weather and the crops, including that most important crop of new babies, to minor accidents and accounts of occasional entertainments and festivities. Descriptions were expected of the remarkable vegetables which our inveterate gardening public brought around to astonish the editor. There could be read the story of how the few who had learned to read among the congregation of the Colored Baptist Church had renounced our Uncle Harry Cowan as their pastor, and how he in his turn had renounced them, walking out with two-thirds of his members at his heels, to return a little later, and repossess his pulpit in triumph. All the accretion of homely detail of life can be rescued from oblivion by conning such a well made column of "locals" with an understanding heart.

Mr. Bruner's political comment is striking in the calmness and justice he maintained even in those irritating and abusive times. Always he is conservative, but he also commends good public service by whomsoever rendered.

Our County was entirely supported by agriculture, and extremely unremunerative agriculture. Cotton brought ten cents a pound; pork, four or five; beef, from five to ten cents according to cut. The local supply was tough and stringy. The very best butter brought from twenty to twenty-five cents. Food in general was quite plentiful. Chicken was cheaper than either beef or mutton, full grown chickens costing the householder about two dollars and a half a dozen. I have eaten my full share of fryers at ten cents apiece.

From six to ten cents was the regular price for eggs, and when they went to twelve and a half, everybody said they were too costly to eat.

The census report for 1880 gives ample confirmation of this. There was but one farm in Rowan County selling, in one year, as much as seventeen hundred dollars worth of produce, including beef and mutton. This report comes from a man I remember from my childhood as the best farmer we had—a man thrifty and industrious, who rotated his crops and farmed five hundred acres at least. From this largest sum, down to the hundred and fifty dollars cash which was produced by one-horse farms, the incomes varied. Three-fourths of the farms were owned by those who worked them, and a good many belonged to widows. Cotton was the money crop. Corn was raised to feed pigs and people, wheat for the farmer's bread, rye for the local distillery, oats for the horses—and all these crops were grown generally in the County.

Our farm women raised chickens, made butter, and tried to feed their families and have a surplus with which to trade in town. They needed to buy only coffee, sugar, and salt. Black molasses called "black-strap," so tasty and thick in those days, and a little golden New Orleans syrup was not too dear. Sorghum was boiled as a neighborhood project, and freely used.

For clothing, the women kept up for a time their revived weaving industries until, one after another, the wartime weavers dropped away. "Alamance" gingham, and unbleached "domestic" and calico were the fabrics they made into their children's clothes, and every woman knew how to tailor her husband's trousers out of the cheaper heavy materials such as "Salem Jeans" for his suits, and for his underclothes white drilling which had to be bought at the store. About 1880, my father must have collected as much as fifteen hundred dollars a year, but by no means all in cash, for his country patients paid him in firewood, corn, oats, hay, chickens, dried apples, and fence posts. I have seen the accounts. Dr. Rumple had a salary of a thousand dollars a year, regularly paid, and was provided beside with a good house and a large garden. According to our standards he was well off. While cotton brought so little money, cash must be earned in some way. Salisbury became a market for dried fruit of every kind. Thousands of pounds were prepared and shipped out, but those orchards set before the War never seem to have been replaced. By no means is there as much orchard in Rowan now as used to exist in my childhood. Dried fruit, unsweetened, was used as a vegetable and was a regular article of food before canning became common.

At our house, we ate the proverbial "hog and hominy" and could always depend upon eggs, chickens, and both sorts of potatoes. Like most natives today, we enjoyed a good many different kinds of cooked greens. Perhaps things were made too greasy, as was universal in southern cookery. Our table was abundant, but we did not use frozen desserts, save on state occasions, owing to the high price of ice. We did have all the standard varieties of pies, "kivered, unkivered, and barred." Mother was celebrated for her custards and cakes, especially her rich pound cake.

At Christmas, no one was too poor for a fruitcake and a roast turkey, no one in town at least, for if kind friends heard of such a deficit they supplied it. Town and country were alike in raising food. The large, well cultivated town lots produced quantities of vegetables, and although it might be called unsanitary today, we were blessedly ignorant, and kept a cow in the back lot, and had plenty of milk, and also might keep a pen of pigs as well, to take the kitchen leavings and the buttermilk left over. Such doings sound as archaic now as the ancient Assyrians.

About this time, in Piedmont towns not far from Salisbury, there was a noteworthy beginning of manufacturing, but we had no share in it. Again it was the gold mines which came in a small way to our economic rescue. For years, Gold Hill Mine had been allowed to fill with water. Now and then we heard of a new "pocket," or the discovery somewhere of a fair-sized nugget aroused interest. Our ores were of a kind hard to reduce by methods then understood, but the great California lodes being by this time pretty well worked out, and Alaska gold fields not yet discovered, North Carolina gold became of speculative importance.

In all the references to negotiations for and sales of mines to this northern company or that, our own people are not mentioned as acquiring stocks. Of course they had no money to risk, but also they knew how expensive a little gold can become and preferred to sell outright to the stranger. There must have been a dozen so-called gold mines in the County, and the reopening of the more promising brought more work and more wages and contributed some picturesque additions to our static social order. When the mine superintendents came to live among us, they brought in a whiff of strangeness from outside. Salisbury, as you may suppose, had become a self-centered, self-sufficient community, knowing no more about Charlotte, or Greensboro—that is, about the personality of those towns—than we might surmise about Jacksonville, Florida, or Lancaster, Pennsylvania. There could be none of the sociable running up and down the road, which is so pleasant in these motoring days. No one made extensive trips save on business. Merchants might have to go North to buy goods now and then, but when they did other merchants sent lists by them. All the millinery necessary to excite the feminine taste of the town could be bought on the side, by some merchant laying in a stock of substantial shoes or hardware on his own account.

But how we did love clothes! We tucked and trimmed our underclothing, we furbelowed our innumerable petticoats with tucks and laces ("store-bought" and handmade), tatting and crochet. Stockings were woven of cotton, white or black. I was grown before I had ever seen a silk stocking.

For best we wore all white in summer, with "sprigged" lawns and calicoes at home. All of it was washable clothing, easily laundered. Such a "doing up," such a fluting of our ruffles as was the regular prelude to a visit to a near-by town! We could seldom buy anything new, save perhaps a new sash of broad ribbon, but we freshened all we had. Coats and wraps might come ready-made, but all the rest of our wear was home made. Girls had to learn very early how to sew for themselves.

My mother's idea of the way a well-bred girl should be dressed, included plenty of clean convenient clothing, but style did not matter to her. Once she had an entire dozen of white dress-aprons of "cross-bar" constructed for me, all cut from the same bolt of goods, all trimmed with the exact same pattern of "Hamburg" embroidery! These were like sleeveless dresses, and to be worn over a plain-colored woolen frock. Father, man as he was, could never have done a thing so inhuman and unimaginative, for he, too, loved pretty clothes.

For everybody there remained the two greatest of human interests, the two which never grow stale—the love game, then played on a more restricted plan and by old-fashioned rules, and the absorbing and disquieting certitude of death with all its pageantry. A courtship must be maintained as secretly as possible and was shamefacedly but delightfully surreptitious. The interest in a wedding might last, for the whole town, from three weeks before to as long after the event. The thought of death, however, was not put aside in that day as something too terrible to contemplate. The firm belief in immortality, then implicit, made dying an interesting departure for a bourne unknown but to be surmised. It was poignant, sorrowful, but not regarded as the vestibule to nothingness. A funeral was a subject of intense and general if very sober interest.

Since there was no daily paper to make announcements, a white-haired old Negro would be entrusted with the "Funeral notice" to carry around. When you saw him coming, you might be at once sure who had died, because if the person was old, the ribbon drawn through the folded sheet would be black, if middle-aged, lavender, if a child, white grosgrain. And because no regular florists existed, and whether one knew the family or not, all the treasures of each garden as far as white or purple flowers might be in bloom, would instantly be sent to the house of bereavement.

There was one interest followed in Salisbury with almost the fervor of a religious cult, because there existed a real and fervent taste for music. Mrs. Rumple taught pupils in piano, whom she drilled inexorably, and with success. With great initiative she devoted the proceeds to sending her daughter to Boston to the Conservatory. Wonderful results were obtained by her self-denial, for on her return, this daughter played classical music so well that she taught all the community to appreciate it and has always been a musician of taste and distinction.

There was another music school besides (this before any public schools existed), and because "harmony, heavenly harmony" is seldom promoted by two such establishments in competition, there were heartburnings, slighting remarks, and strict partizanship—each person upholding his favorite music school. The Neaves, who maintained the second, were an unexpected and interesting couple. Mr. Neave was a Scotsman, one of the dark knurly ones. He was entwined, obsessed, immersed in music, as determined in the pursuit of it as only a Scot could be. How nearly he attained the excellence he claimed is beside the question. He had been a well known bandmaster in the Confederate Army, could play many instruments, and understood orchestration. He was the leader of a cornet band which was summoned from place to place to play for commencements and fairs, and he arranged music for his band. Mrs. Spencer mentions their playing at the reopening of the University in 1876.

Mrs. Neave was a German lady who had been well trained in Europe. She had come South before the War as a teacher of piano, and she married her husband late in life. Having no children, their music and their music school became their sole interest. Mrs. Neave was a charming person, kindly, cultivated, but naïve, speaking in a high sweet voice with a delicious accent. She was tall and very nearsighted, and would bend suddenly from the waist for the closer inspection of things. She was given to making the most whimsical remarks, in pure innocence as it seemed, although one guessed that sometimes she joked thus for her own refreshment.

All public concerts were held in the only auditorium, "Meroney's Hall," and once at a musical there Mrs. Neave's clothing became entangled in the clumsy old curtain as it rolled up, exposing her white stockings nearly to the knee. Describing to us her embarrassment afterwards, she said plaintively: "And I would not have felt so aba-a-shed if I had not b-e-e-n so the-e-n!" And when we went off into gales of merriment, she looked at us deprecatingly. For so thorough a musician, Mrs. Neave's artistic nervousness was but slight. She made the discipline of music no harder by the rapping of childish knuckles or sharp admonition. Sometimes she would give lessons in the German language to evening classes, and from her I gained early an interest in the classics of her fatherland.

But there were some who did not care for music, and for us there were no pictures, no drawing, save illustrated magazines and an old portrait here and there. Highly colored advertising cards were kept in boxes by us children, treasured, discussed, and exchanged. Mrs. Stewart, Mr. Bruner's daughter, by simple inborn ability could draw from nature, making paintings of actual flowers which had an odd Japanese quality and are still lovely to eyes which have seen many such things since then. And it was her daughter and my friend Beulah who was the very first to awake to the summons, to break away and immerse herself in the new art world of America just a-borning. That happened years later, and we others, who loved pictures best, went about hungering, and hoping for the substance of things not seen.

Social gatherings, except those sponsored by the churches, were few, although occasionally there would be an evening party, now and then a picnic for the children. The older young folk of the dancing coterie went to semioccasional "hops" at the Boyden House, or took part in some small-town dramatic effort. The picture of a town as quiet as country, without dinner parties, without card parties, with no moving pictures, no radio, no automobiles, is scarcely to be imagined by modern young folk, making them wonder why we did not go crazy from want of variety.

In the town lived a family, not of our own people but coming to spend their lives with us, who were made significant by the contribution they gave to us. We were sadly stingy in our return for what they brought us, for their talents and abilities gave them an only meager subsistance.

We knew this family collectively as "the Wrens," and especially talented was the son, "Jimmy," as we called him, half affectionately, half in patronage. These people represented among us the adornments of social life, so lacking in our scheme—the art of interior decoration, the planning of tasteful dresses, the setting of beautiful tables, the arrangement of weddings and festival occasions. Mr. Wren was a rather short man, with a kindly wistful face and a drooping mustache. Neither he nor his clients knew that he was indispensable, but he could teach dancing, stage an amateur play, decorate a wedding cake after his mother had baked it exquisitely, plan a trousseau; and after his sister, Miss Mollie, had made the bride's and the bridesmaids' gowns he could pass all in review and see all the arrangements perfect for the ceremony. Had he been born a Frenchman, in Paris, he might have attained world reputation as a dress designer. Miss Mollie's gowns, a little too ornate, a little too placed, perhaps (although again this was a time which fancied such clothing), never disarranged their lovely folds, never came apart, never wore out of shape, until they were threadbare and fit for the rag bag. Mrs. Wren's cakes were such as have never since existed. The innate taste of these people seems to me now the reason that from old days Salisbury has always had good taste in dress and in the art of arranging simple homes graciously.

Miss Mollie sewed her eyes almost out, because she never could employ anyone to set stitches as daintily as she wanted them. It is a question how much, or rather how little of all his wonderful expert advice James Wren was ever paid in money for, or how much he simply gave away, just because he loved to do such things.

I am glad to remember that my father was their physician for many years, never sending them a bill, and only now and then consenting to their independent protest by saying, "Well, Miss Mollie, if you must feel like that about it, suppose you make a dress for Hope." And these occasional dresses Miss Mollie made me live in my memory like poems. The result was rather too enchanting, too unlike the plain things I wore at other times.

Finally, we younger ones maintained a great habit of reading, although magazines were scarce, and books were mostly old ones. We conned a little good poetry, and perhaps after all the list was not so very short! As Beulah has said to me, "We were not so narrow after all. We knew in some degree the civilization of the Old World. We were the physical and mental descendants of our parents, and heirs of all that has gone before since the beginning of time; we had sunshine, we had hope, and imagination."

What we did not actually see before us, we could picture by this imagination, and some pictures were so fascinating that they persist after the reality is known to be commonplace. An example of this pictorial imagination was the old Chilson House. Those who built it must have felt the same craving for romance. They had put a wooden tower with sawed-out battlements on top of their plain, two-story country home. The outline of this house against the sky suggested to us youngsters all the romances we had ever read—chateaux in France, castles on the Rhine—all of Walter Scott. All this belonged in our childish fancy to the odd, silly old house on the hill.

Such books and magazines as we did possess went the long rounds. After we had sampled Scott and Dickens, however, we youngsters desired something more sensational. We read the novels of Augusta Evans Wilson and John Esten Cooke and greatly preferred them to such housekeeping stories as Miss Alcott wrote. *Saint Elmo*, devoured of a summer's afternoon, along with many soft peaches, in a convenient crotch of a tree, was indeed a glorious feast. A reasonable amount of trash is very good for the growing imagination. It was dime novels which first awakened the fancy of O. Henry, but these were by no means easy for a girl to come by, unless she had a brother from whom to purloin them.

Sunday school books, so easy to borrow, were read by me in dozens, but have left not an image on my memory, and they must have been insipid things indeed. But my semi-occasional quarter of a dollar could buy copies from a collection of cheap novels called "The Seaside Library." These were reprints, very poor in type, and among them we found such stuff as Mrs. Braddon, *The Duchess* and *Ouida* along with some translations of Dumas and Victor Hugo. With these we were entranced. We knew also who in town owned stray copies of Mark Twain's first books, and who would lend them. These were all too few to keep pace with our desire, but when you add to these Shakespeare, which we read like a story book, leaving unquestioned everything we did not at once understand, we must have found in the weird mixture a stimulation and an interest that a more regular training sometimes misses.

XVIII

TWO MORE YEARS IN OLD SALISBURY

AFTER THE LONG summer at Poplar Tent, when I came back to my mother I was received with a joy which was concealed from me by the comment that I had been running wild and would have to be brought into bounds again. I was sunburned, which was too bad for a girl. I had become lazy and must make up my studies. Looking back, I know that Mother just said all this so that I should not feel myself too important in perceiving how she ached to have me again beside her. Subconsciously I knew she doted on me. I said to myself that my mother was taking great pains to make a fine person of me, but I sighed to think how fervently I loathed the greater part of the process! One experiment after another was tried during this interval, but the education I acquired was more by reading and by observation, a pursuit of my own bent rather than a subjection to my mother's fluctuating ideas.

Mother was trapped and restricted by the turn her life had taken. She had wished to have something worth doing for the underprivileged, but now there seemed no outlet for her save the very narrow one measured by her little daughter's scanty ability and resistant mood. To Mother I was a last opportunity to incarnate her potential self, and I withstood her firmly in this, as children do resist such management. Mother must have known that her cherished culture was beginning to date, that it came from a past now growing so remote as to be sterile. Her Greek and Latin classics, her older Victorian authors, her French belles-lettres, as she antiquatedly called them, interested herself alone. The reference books were out of date, the popular science pre-Darwinian. The only new volumes on the shelf were a few child's books bought for me.

Mother did not mean to give her mind into the keeping of the victors. She was convinced that their well trumpeted ideas were not sound, but her breadth of thought was scarcely any better contented with the drift of southern ideas since the Civil War, and so she found herself one of a despised, a scarcely considered minority, and no longer a part of the progressive thought of the world. There had been casualty after casualty among the young men of the northern kin during the War, and these graves were built into a Chinese Wall which separated my mother from her own people. All her children save the youngest were by this time gone about errands of their own. The stringency of the times had set all the world desperately to grubbing for a living, with no desire that reached an inch further, but we three were, as regarded subsistence, removed from the pinch of poverty and comfortable enough. Mother had her old friends, but made it a point to be on visiting terms with almost everybody in the town. This seems to have been her one change in the habit of her living since my sister's death had set her free.

There was one of Mother's friends who managed to see how the art of living with simple gladness and a contented mind was both goodness and beauty. She practiced this art, whatever it may have cost. Her distinction as a great gentlewoman is perhaps forgotten in the many years since then. Let me recall her memory.

Not far from Main Street, in our quarter of the square old town, there stood on one of the original lots a pleasant rectangular house on whose expanse of gray weatherboarding no paint had ever been used, while many seasons had toned it down to the mellowness of unpainted wood. Set flush with the sidewalk, in front, at the eastern corner, was a bachelor "office" with a history. It had once been the lodging of young Andrew Jackson, come from upper South Carolina to learn what Spruce McCay could teach him of legal terminology. Jackson rioted and raced horses on our streets, studied some little law, and with his license went away to live his real life in Tennessee. When Judge McCay sold the house, Mrs. Jane Boyden, born a Henderson, bought it and lived there until her second marriage, and after her second widowhood.

Judge Nathaniel Boyden, her second husband, was a great lawyer and a determined Union man. It has been said with authority that had Lincoln lived, he would have been appointed provisional governor of North Carolina. In that case, Wilkes Booth changed history for Salisbury as well as for the rest of the land.

When I was a child, Mrs. Boyden was already a widow. All that was kindly and hospitable drew both friend and stranger to her door. Her house had polished floors and dark cupboarded walls, and was altogether a dusky shady place with gleams here and there of glass, of satiny old silver on the sideboard, or polished brass fender reflecting fire-flame. The lady who sat by the fire, who jumped up and welcomed her guests so gaily, was quick-motioned, gray-eyed, and vivacious. I can see her, dressed in crisp black silk, or well ironed lawn. She always wore an elaborate cap, exquisitely fluted, white as snow, perched above her face like a crest. She would move about the room, with gestures of welcome, handing a fire-screen in winter, bringing a palmleaf fan in summer, with laughing friendly comment. When Mother and I went to see her, she would serve us dainty wafers with raspberry acid. If Henderson relatives called, she would have a mint julep brought in on the silver tray, with frost smoking the sides of the glass.

She was a charitable woman as she was friendly, pious but never bigoted—a devoted Episcopalian.

There were two sorts of mild bigotry rife in Salisbury: that of the Puritans and that of the predetermined never to allow themselves to be so classed. A new Episcopal rector had come in about this time, one who was to give good account of himself in the town, but very zealous at first with a youthful fervor, which was going to turn everything over at once. I could tell stories of what the Presbyterians and Methodists sincerely thought of him at first! He was Anglican in his devotion to ritual, and a man of genuine piety. He tightened up the slackness which had long been allowed in his parish, and he once gave Mrs. Boyden to understand that he expected her to be in her place for morning worship, at the appointed moment, and that the latch of the church door would be drawn against all late comers.

"Then I will have to enter through the vestry," said Mrs. Boyden placidly.

I am afraid the "Dissenters" laughed derisively at first, and then became annoyed over the things he thought important, for the Rev. Frank Murdoch was as Scotch as his name, and brought a truly John-Knoxian fervor into his Anglican convictions. When a first heir to the Hendersons was born, the young rector and his leading parishioner put their heads together to think of a distinctive way to dedicate him in baptism. Why not administer the rite by the triune immersion, on the eighth day, as was practiced in England before 1700? The child's mother besought the two young enthusiasts to be careful with her precious baby, and the family doctor was asked to be present to see that they did not injure it in their zeal. So a font was improvised, the water warmed to the proper temperature, and the Doctor gave the young Priest lessons in how to hold the tender infant, how to close its mouth and nose effectively as he immersed it the three times.

At first all went well. "In the name of the Father," "In the name of the Son"—but the third time the Rector's technique failed him. Somehow he allowed the baby to swallow water, and it was choked on the name of the Third Person in the Trinity. The mother cried out from her bedroom, the doctor, seizing the heir of the Hendersons, administered first aid, while the prayers worked on to a conclusion.

After that, when the rest of the Hendersons came along rather regularly, it was a joke when the Doctor would solemnly inquire, "John, is this child going to be christened by the old English Triune Immersion?"

Mrs. Boyden regarded the town life about her with friendly interest, not disdaining kindly gossip. She was apt to grow enthusiastic and emphatic, as she talked, and would gesticulate, until "Aunt Evaline," her maid, who was always hovering about her and whose voice was tuned so identically with her mistress's that from the next room you could not tell which was talking, came in to look. Invariably from behind, she would have to adjust the great cap because by that time its top-heavy edifice would be bobbing over her mistress's ear.

Mrs. Boyden was a great reader, having fine literary discrimination, but her chief hobby and recreation was her garden. Almost any morning she could be seen there, clad in a deep black sunbonnet and a cape, digging vigorously in her enormous garden. There she planted flowers as if they were vegetables, in bulk, in long rows, making a crop of them. All down the long plot would extend perfect hedges of narcissus, of daffodils, of tulips and hyacinths, with "flags," as we called the white and purple iris, in their succession. All summer there would bloom a "prolixity of roses" with gay annuals between. The flowers she loved she took care to share with her friends, sending trays loaded well. Her old servitor would appear, balancing this mound of fragrance on the palm of his hand held shoulder-high. With the other he would salute—"Mrs. Boyden's compliments, Ma'am," and then—such a marshaling of the tall vases and the small, such exclamations!

The excitement of living, the practicing of that art with eager interest, can be carried on just as well in quiet surroundings as in crowded ones, and even better perhaps, more absorbingly. An instance of this is found in the carefully, the passionately tended gardens of old Salisbury. It was a neighborly contest in beauty, carried on by "saints" and "sinners" alike. The production of flowers for delight, as well as the growing of a few distinguished plants hard to bring to perfection, for interest, was the regular pastime. With the left hand, casually so to speak, a productive vegetable garden added variety to the family's food. People had flower pits, crude holes in the ground covered in with window sash, to keep alive through the winter delicate plants. Then there were greenhouses. I can think of a dozen. Some were mere bay windows filled with greenery, some were quite large.

Very near Mrs. Boyden lived Mr. Murdoch, who was a master mason, and who, having finished all the railroad bridges on the Western North Carolina Railroad, had now retired to busy leisure. He controlled a large greenhouse and an extensive garden. He used to give midnight parties to witness, by invitation, the unfolding of his night-blooming cereus. He and his sturdy Negro helper toiled side by side in all weathers, adding to the beauty of what was once the Maxwell Chambers garden, where was still growing an ancient square of box border set long before Cornwallis made the old house his headquarters. Mr. Murdoch loved to give away slips and roots to his friends, which means that he supplied the entire town.

Mrs. Moses Holmes lived in that pleasant "Judge Caldwell" house well out on Fulton Street. In a grove close beside it stood her husband's gin and cotton press, but her home was spacious, the greenhouse as good as any. She was a plain practical woman, and was none the less esteemed, but rather more enjoyed because of her latest Malaprop-ism and the smiles it brought. She too was a flower lover, and flowers loved her, for every slip which she stuck in the ground grew with abandon. The long borders leading to her home were riotous with "Polunias," "Sweet-Melissey," and "Highphlox," as well as the low, and her shady porch was covered with "My-deary" vines. As good a cook as a gardener, her house in the green yard was a pleasant place to visit, and her fried chicken and cream biscuits can never be effaced from the memory of one of her grateful guests.

As has been said, Rowan County had the heritage of a double tradition, and its patronymics covered a mixed inheritance. Easter is a great festival among the German people, and we followed the pleasant Easter customs they brought us. Before the day came, eggs in dozens or even in bushels, were hoarded, were boiled hard and dyed bright colors, so that at Easter the boys could "fight eggs," pecking the small ends together, the broken one going to the breaker. If a small turkey egg was dyed and foisted in, and a single boy bagged too many eggs, he was thrown out of fellowship. This wholesale play was one of the customs. "Easter Monday" was another. I had to leave home to learn that this familiar holiday was not universal. But in my mind Easter used especially to be connected with two ladies who lived far out on Main Street northward. To visit them you must go past the courthouse, past a row of disreputable groggeries, and almost as far as the wall of the ancient Lutheran Graveyard. There, in an unpainted house, whose front door opened directly on the sidewalk (as the Germans liked to build them), lived two maiden ladies, Miss Christine and Miss Julia Beard. They were oracles deeply versed in the old stories of Salisbury, and their memories were seldom at fault. When Dr. Rumple wrote that excellent *History of Rowan County*, finished in the eighties, he went continually, so I have heard him say, to these ladies for his data, and while in justice to them, he investigated what they told him, he never discovered any important inaccuracy. But it is because of their Easter eggs that I revere their memory. Using black and white wax, they applied lovely designs upon the surface of colored eggs, using a single simple form like a comma, turning this in every possible way, to make with it a spiral, a fern-like spray, or a rosette, put on in relief with a pen dipped in melted wax. There were never any two of the hand-decorated eggs alike. A nestful of them was glory enough for any child's Easter, the one trouble being that we wished to keep them to look at, and this could not be done.

These ladies lived in the old house where Tarleton spent a night or two during the Revolution. Over and over again did the name of "Beard" appear in the history of Rowan County. Their kinship enters into almost any family tree of the elder, more established folk. The elder Charles Fisher married a Beard. The younger Charles Fisher, Colonel Fisher, killed at Manassas, married a Caldwell, whose mother was a Henderson. Here are varied elements, English, Scotch-Irish, German, combining in a new race which, in this instance, produced something akin to genius.

The Fisher house—just across Innes Street from the Overman House, it used to stand—was a well built dignified home with square porch-posts to its double veranda; and, like all of our older houses, it was shaded by fine old oaks never planted by man, but remaining from the time when the squirrels set the forest. In this home lived our novelist, our romance writer, well known and much admired—Miss Frances Fisher—whose many books were in their day "best sellers." Her pen name was "Christian Reid."

The sister of Colonel Fisher, Miss Christine, had gone in her girlhood to New Orleans for a long stay, and there she encountered and fell in love with the romance and ritual of Catholicism. When after her brother's death she took charge of his orphaned children, she did not rest until they also were converted. Thus she tried to immunize them from the deadening drabness of the after-the-War. They did not care for the commonplace of dull old Salisbury and never mixed much with its people in my day, although the town had a settled habit of revering the Fisher name, and they were not criticized for this. Mother knew, or had once known, these ladies well. She shared with them the few new books she might have to lend. I remember the only time I ever saw the inside of their house was, when carrying a book from Mother, I waited in their sitting room to give my message, noting its portraits, its fine mahogany, and its frayed carpets.

After the surrender, along with many another gentlewoman, they had stark penury to face. It was then that Miss Frances developed her gifts as a writer. I have heard that it was her aunt who first recognized and encouraged her. The first long novel was published in 1870, and pretty regularly after, published first as serials in magazines, they were reprinted in volumes which sold widely. Romances such as she wrote were but dreams of escape from the sordid difficulties of the time. Mrs. Boyden, who was her kinswoman, would groan to my mother over the successive volumes, and say, "Why doesn't Fannie with her good sense and her fine literary style, write about something that could happen?" But people paid for high-flown novels in those days, whether or not they bought any other books, and Miss Fannie's stories must be, first of all, salable.

Once she finished a novel that was different. On a slender thread of love interest and incident, she strung the exquisite descriptive journal of a trip through the mountain country of Western North Carolina, then a thinly populated and unfrequented country, and unvisited and unvexed by tourists. Because the clouds come down to rest so lovingly on the blue dreaming highlands of our West, she called her book by an inspired title, *The Land of the Sky*. Today this book, which was beautifully illustrated with line drawings, is still delightful, and has been prized by collectors. It gave a poetic name to the section it describes which is still remembered. This book was a lovely and sincere thing, but no more such stories came from her pen. To gain a livelihood by imaginative writing in this time and place was in itself a great achievement. Patrician ladies, suffering saints, and wooden cavaliers prevailed again over the scene, because of the money they would bring.

Mingling streams of inheritance liberated the talent of Miss Frances Fisher, as such a condition is apt to do, where abilities are combined that have grown strong apart. In Rowan, distinctively German traits were coming more to ascendancy, for while the Germans and Scotch-Irish were about equal in numbers at first, the former remained, while the latter were always a restless race. This German flavor was more in the turn of thinking than in any other quality, for the language had passed save in the mouths of a few oldest folk, fifty years ago; and excepting Luther's Bible, there had been no literature to consider. The Germans were materialists, eager to be safe from want, safe from adventure. The look of solid prosperity was what the German or "Dutch" farmer desired you to see when in passing you identified his home. He did not leave trees where he found them. They shaded the ground which he needed for crops. In the barnyard every atom of compost would be saved and heaped together, and the manure pile reeked to heaven, while the space in front of his family home would be in burning sunshine, and swept bare of every spear of green. The barn would be larger and better built than the house, and the fields carefully tilled. In my childhood, there was another infallible indication of a "Dutch" farmer's place. On the top of that mountain of compost I mentioned there would slither and coil a slender black-snake. He might have beside him a dish of milk, into which to plunge his lipless mouth. He would be tame and fearless, respected by all, the sacred mouser. Far more efficiently than any cat he could scrape through the burrows made by rats beneath the barn, driving all in terror before him. But when he had grown so large that he liked eggs and chickens better than rats and mice, the farmer would kill him one day, in a time of drouth, and the farmer's children, following an old superstition, would hang his body across the fence to "draw rain."

As the intermarriage and the amalgamation continued, the keenness of the Scotch-Irish desire for classical learning became dulled by the more stolid practical German ways. In the country districts it was the Lutheran Church that drew the larger congregations. Of each family, one of the sons would be named Martin Luther, and a daughter would be Katherine Von Bora. Many a blonde Kitty or Cathy of today takes her name from a sturdy, plainly clad grandmother in some German farmstead.

The passing of the years since my parents came to live there had not so altered the town of Salisbury that its temper was much changed. It was still vivid with elemental urges, full of combative ways, and a place where partizanship ran high and ginger was hot in the mouth. Sins were generally condoned there, and oddities found interesting. The few residents who possessed real culture, would have this refinement counted to them as *their way*, as a sort of pardonable queerness.

The few fiery old Revolutionary families might hold their heads high and send their sons off to the University so that they might know how to rule the political roost. They were too long established to abide question. But the primitive and the crude made up the large majority. Besides, all agreed on one universal custom which had prevailed from the first, and, whatever else might alter, this remained. The distilling, the testing and tasting, and the full approval of strong drink had always been a thing unquestioned in Rowan.

In a small town, there is not much that escapes the eyes

of an observing child. When I was what is called "a frying size girl," drunken men on the street were far more common than horses have come to be of late, in automotive times. In fact each one of us was warned how to avoid a drunk, how to slip into the nearest dooryard gate if we saw an especially vociferous one coming. We knew all the signs, we took great interest in the subject, we children. We would say, "Is his face awfully red?" "Do you think he's very drunk?" "Does he wabble funny when he walks?"—and we were not deceived.

One of the locals in the *Watchman* in the year 1880 reads, "Drink, Drank, Drunk. That is what they did last Saturday afternoon, without regard to race, color or previous condition of servitude." Ladies and children never went to shop on Main Street on a Saturday. The farmers would rumble in from the country in their wagons, trade their produce, talk their politics, and start home late in the afternoon, with a jug between their feet, whaling their horses. Of course not every single one would do this, but enough to make a rule and to make Saturday afternoons apprehensive and perilous to a peaceful wayfarer. I have seen them and heard them so often; have watched them hurl countrywards along our street, wheels and hoofs banging, scores, nay many hundreds of times!

How much treating, how much youthful spreeing, how much sodden, determined soaking went on in the sordid barrooms that lined Main Street, on below the courthouse, it was not for a girl child to know. On the few occasions when we must pass these places, we would quicken our steps as we neared them. We actually knew nothing of the grossness concentrated there; but, knowing nothing in reality, it is wonderful how we children guessed aright at almost all. Nobody in his right mind in old Salisbury could have thought unlimited whiskey a boon to society, but most of them used it. Some drank and went to church, and were prayed over.

Some were denounced as hypocrites who concealed the habit and "took a little for their stomach's sake." Some deceived the very elect, but the doctors knew. Some got drunk and stayed away. But nobody stood any higher in public esteem because he was reputed to have true independence of mind and drank all the liquor he wanted at any time.

XIX

MOUNTAIN TRAILS OF BLOWING ROCK

JUST TO GIVE a little variety, just to look at what existed outside our corner at this time, we made a journey one June, and the eyes which have served me so well for seeing were filled with the newness of the scenes we passed. Mother had not been well for some time. Father wished her to have something pleasant to think of. There had been so pitifully little travel in her life. So we made a round of Father's kinsfolk, in the blazing summer time, and I added to my gallery of landscape a level country, fringed with a horizon line of pine forest, all steaming in the humid low-country heat and seeming to be beaten flat by the impact of the strong sunshine. Cypress trees grew there, soaking their swollen feet in coffee-brown swamp water. Curious pitcher plants grew plentifully beside the roads. We visited Norfolk, looking sad and down at heel after its recent yellow-fever epidemic. We boarded a little river-steamer up the James to the capital of the Confederacy, going there over historic water. The cutting-across at City Point still showed how recent it was. The story of the *Merrimac* and the *Monitor*, retold as we passed the place, was an experience not to be repeated, for there were a couple of Confederate "colonels" who talked to Father, pointing out the localities and reviewing the whole. In Richmond we spent two days with Father's half sister, and the city was full of poignant memories still fresh; pervaded by the sorrows of a recent past.

Mother was not benefited, only fatigued. The winter of 1883-1884 came early and was a bitter one. Often it happens in North Carolina that we pass a whole year, or maybe two, with the least possible snow and no hard freezes at all. Then another year the cold moves far south again. The habits of open-air folk, living in homes not too closely built, make these extreme winters as miserable as possible. This time the cold had set its teeth in, long before Christmas, and in January it was bleak enough. Eggs were freezing in the pantry egg basket, and the new milk went solid and cracked the stoneware crock in which it was set for cream. Open fires, usually sufficient in the daytime, and regularly allowed to go out by night, now left the house to the mercy of the freezing cold, oozing in through all the dark hours under loose-fitting door and window frames. Negroes, with their tropical antecedents, suffered most severely. For weeks, Father traveled in his buggy placed on improvised runners, shod with iron by the blacksmith; and sleighing would have been general if there had been sleighs. When the deep thaw came in early spring, he had to take to horseback and saddle-bags as he had begun. "Old Wat" could not carry the Doctor's two hundred pounds of weight and his length of limb, and a tall, bony, fox-hunter was hired from the livery stable. Later in the spring, the deep frozen clay spewed up its frost and the bare ground would every morning be covered with ice crystals in serried ranks, which by noon had thawed to a muddy, slippery surface.

I did not mind all this, for my blood ran warm, but Mother became depleted by the continued cold. One of her sisters, Aunt Eliza, died that winter, and the loss worked havoc with her mind and spirits, for all her sorrows were stoically borne, and ingrowing. In early spring she was taken with a sudden chill while working in her garden, and it threw her into pneumonia. She was a very sick woman, and I had care, such as I had not taken before, dropped upon my childish shoulders. Very slowly recovering, she had only partially regained her strength before warm weather. Father

AT BLOWING ROCK

decided that what she needed was change and a rest in bracing air; so he planned for her a summer in the mountains taking me as her companion.

A trip to the mountains today, means jumping into your motor car, and making a short day's pleasant run. Tomorrow it may mean climbing into your plane and alighting in an hour or so. Then the western mountains were a wilderness, and not lightly undertaken.

A new railroad had its eastern terminus in Salisbury and was being pushed westward as fast as possible, but to surmount the wall-like Blue Ridge, a ticklish piece of engineering was necessary. The methods, the progress, the mishaps in the building of this our own pet railroad, made the stock of endless conversation in Salisbury. Young men's hopes dwelt on some day being employed on it. For some of us, just to stand on "Shober's Bridge" over a deep cut in the western edge of town, and see the shining rails of the Western North Carolina Railroad converge in the distance, was a thrill. It was by this railroad that Mother and I began our first journey to the mountains. Resorts there were less frequented and habitations far sparser than can be imagined today. Transportation was slow and difficult. We would have to stay the summer where we were going, and rainy-day employment for us both must be taken along, paints, sewing, and a few books.

The first miles were not distinguishable from our own County, but after a few hours the train began to labor and to climb. Faint blue clouds could be seen on the western horizon, clouds which had definite form and did not change. These were the mountains, and when I knew this, I could not have told why, but my eyes grew moist and my throat tightened at their significance. We stopped at a station, where we waited for a narrow gauge to come and take us farther. That last twenty miles was heavy work for the small engine, going up by a steep and always rising grade.

At our arrival it was nightfall in a sleepy, old-time country town. The open square in the midst was occupied by a small square courthouse and around it were ranged the stores, the tavern, and the inevitable livery stable. Next morning we travelers hired a spring wagon with a wabbling canopy, drawn by rawboned horses. The driver, as lank and sinewy as his team, was dressed in homespun jeans, and, like a grasshopper, he copiously exuded tobacco juice at the corners of the gash of his mouth, continually at work in chewing the weed. The trunks were tied on behind, and there was room for us both on the front seat beside the driver.

We were starting this morning, as he declared, "pretty darned late," but we jogged off over roads fairly dry. Here and there might be a great mudhole neglected for months, so that we must careen through it with great wrenching of harness, but why should we care for rough ways when there was so glorious a blue sky, such dewy wayside flowers? There abounded thimbleberry and jewelweed, mixed with luxuriant lady fern, while all the shrubbery undergrowth was rhododendron and kalmia, and it was the season of their bloom, less and less advanced as the road steadily mounted. In the near distance we came toward a shadowy wall, seen by glimpses through nearer forest growth—a green rampart it seemed, reaching halfway to the sky. A few miles farther, and the abruptness and rocky sides of this steep barrier, clothed in spruce and balsam, were easily perceived. A cool breath of air blew from it against our faces.

Just at the foot of the steeper track, the driver stopped and watered his team, holding up to each a pail filled from a wayside spring—and then taking it quickly away. We too dismounted, rested, drank, and ate a bite. The driver contended himself with an enormous chew, which he bit off a plug and thrust into his cheek. Soon he gathered the reins and cried "Giddap, horses!" and clucked to them as they made a sudden turn and entered the windings of a ravine. The track now became far narrower and steeper, so that if two teams had met between the turnouts (the places where the road was somewhat widened around the sharpest curves), one would have been forced back to the turnout just behind. But because the start had been so late that morning the down-going teams had passed us already, and there would be scanty time to go through before dark; we had the mountain to ourselves.

Frequently the horses must be stopped to breathe, and the driver put great stones behind the wheels to ease the drag upon the resting team. Miles seemed thrice as long in this laboring ascent. Pure mountain air, laden with wisps of fog, blew among the trees, then suddenly would thicken until we might seem to be the only living beings in a narrow world of mountain road, for we could see but a few feet before us, and the horses' ears bobbed dim and pale; and in the abyss beside the track we could hear a soft sound of going, which might be wind in the trees or falling water deep in the gorge. Twilight came down, dull and formless, a good while before we reached the summit of the gap.

Suddenly our road grew level, even sloped a little downhill, and the horses pricked up their ears and began to trot. A sharp breeze took us by the throat; the fog was gone, and the stars shone bright above us. "Come, Giddap!—Here we be!" said the driver, and he set us down a few rods farther on, in front of a cottage barely visible, where the only glint of light to guide us in was a yellow shining through window and door from the lamp upon the supper table. We were expected, and ate our supper in this pool of light, surrounded with shadows—the shadows of the stout landlady, of her peering children, of a dim interior half-guessed. Bread and milk and baked apples are good, whether or not you add to them bacon, eggs, and coffee.

Now to find our proper sleeping room Mother and I must

be lighted out of doors, the landlady carrying the candle before us, shaded by her hand, for we were to lodge in a separate cottage. We found our unpainted bedroom very bare. What could be seen by the dim light was simply a bed piled with comfortables, a table and two chairs. A couple of tin basins, and a pail of water were all the bathing facilities. It seemed rather scant comfort to Mother in her fatigue, and after the solicitude she had left behind, but the bed was soft and feathery, and I cuddled down close at her back. The fog had drifted back again to muffle the few sounds. That hushed lisping must mean running water close at hand. A night bird gave a far off cry—and it was morning!

In our detached cottage, standing on its grassy slope, at the foot of which tinkled a "branch" among its ferns, we woke to look about us. Outside the rail fence ran the turnpike. Mrs. Ingle was near it, feeding her chickens and shooing away the Muscovy ducks that tried to gobble their cornmeal dough. All the land we could see was set on a tilt. Just across the road, down a narrow ravine, our brook escaped in a thin trickle to undreamed-of-depths. Down there it was all misty and pearly this morning, with fir trees darting through, but the bottom could not be seen. Behind us a hill went towering, bare of trees but waving with grass and daisies. Only one other building could be seen beside our cottage and the Ingle's three-roomed dwelling—Mr. Ingle's carpenter shop directly on the roadway. These were the first habitations after reaching the plateau at the top of the steep ascent of Blowing Rock Gap.

Mother and I lived here all summer, and it is strange to recall how little of what is called amusement sufficed us. The school books, and the water-color paints were of use on rainy days, but on the fine ones there were so many wonders to behold that the house could not keep me very long. Half a mile farther along the dusty "pike," there began a straggling village of two wooden boardinghouses with double porches above and below, a store, a post office and a livery stable. Mother soon grew stronger and was able to walk the short distance to the village, where she found friends staying. But as for her daughter—the whole horizon round could not confine one so intoxicated with youth and mountain air, who was so in love with this new world and all that grew there, and whose heartbeat quickened when a blue distance unrolled to view.

When groveling under a laurel thicket in search of the waxy Indian pipe, I felt the poignant interest of this new country, and just so was I uplifted by the color of a cardinal flower flaming in a damp spot. My soul went out to meet each azure morning.

The first comers to this rural resort were elderly folk who sat and played cards all day, or who rocked and knitted and prosed about their families. They did not interest me, for I was thinking only of mountain intervals, slipping each behind the other, of sweet, keen mountain air, of the smell of trodden fern, of the wild unhackneyed freshness of things outdoors, beckoning to me. I felt myself a child, and yet a part of the everlastingness of the hills. If, as has been fancied possible, after we have shaken off this flesh, we may be allowed to revisit the scenes of our mortal life, I should like to go back some summer morning. I should like to leave the dwellings along the crest of the Blue Ridge, and waft out toward the mighty profile of the Grandfather Mountain jutting against the sky. I should love to trace the sheer descent of those massive granite cliffs which drop two thousand feet to the valley below. In the bottom of that valley, there used to be a clearing with only one cabin, the only visible break in a sea of forest. This deep cleft was called "The Globe," and with a spyglass could be seen the old woman of the place hoeing her cabbages. Each of us is like that, set adrift in a universe we can never explore in this short life, and busy about our tiny concerns in a circle of wonder.

The wildness and remoteness of the country disquieted Mother; she thought of danger and tried to restrain me from wandering too far. She objected to my eager explorations, talking of rattlesnakes and lonely unfrequented hillsides, until one day the controversy was settled by the coming of the "Professor."

That is what everybody called him, "the Professor that boards at the postmaster's." It was said that he came from some indeterminate and far-off college, perhaps from Minnesota, or somewhere else "out west." Tall he was, athletic, russet-bearded, with a kindly, serious face. I thought of him then as quite elderly, but looking back across the years I have wondered how much he was past thirty. He wore a knapsack on his back and carried a botanist's collecting case and a butterfly net. He was shod with heavy hobnailed shoes and wore stout gaiters. He said he was studying the insects of the region.

One day he stopped to chat and spend an hour with Mother, making friends with her. He asked if she would permit me to accompany him on some of his collecting tramps, which did not go too far afield. Although nobody seemed really to know him, he carried with him an atmosphere which made people instinctively trust him. Mother saw in his offer the solution of her difficulty and the way to give me more of the freedom I desired, without allowing me to wander too far into the woods alone. Whenever after that time he would shout to me in passing, I would be up and away, in his companionship, into the fascinating world of minor mountain ranges flung pell-mell about the plateau behind the Ridge—those ranges which divide the water of their little streams between the rivers of the East and the great Mississippi Valley.

The Professor was a taciturn fellow. Here and there he would sweep an insect into his net, or would gather some herb or flower. I would draw near to see what he had, or to question him about it. He always explained so simply and kindly that it was plain he liked my interest, but he never enlarged into many words. Much of this man's careful quartering of the whole region adjacent must have been done in a delight like my own in the untraveled country and its luxuriant growth. Finding me a good walker, the Professor took me almost daily on his favorite tramps.

It was he who introduced me to that mystery of the laurel thicket, the old Indian Trail, and guided me the length of its green tunnel. The thrill, the romance of this secret path were a keen delight to my imagination. It ended as suddenly as it had begun, on a hillside, with no marked footpath to show the way into it, and this after perhaps two miles of blind traverse.

Another favorite walk ended in a little dingle, a narrow green valley where the grass grew thick and fine. The stone chimney of a cabin still stood, a monument to show where a hearth had once burned. Apple trees, bristling with scions, still dropped a few knotty fruits to show that the pioneer had intended to make a permanent home there. A stream (and this whole country was whispering with tiny waterchannels), flowed along the lowest part of the meadow, and stones were laid up to show where once the dairy house had been.

Whatever of remoteness I felt in this kindly man, I can never forget the smiling taciturnity, the simplicity, the companionable patience of a mature spirit dealing with a youthful mind just awakening, which, in this association, I enjoyed but a few weeks. At my youthful age I had known very few men. Never have I encountered another like this one. It was good fortune that the first young man I ever sat down and talked with impressed me with intrinsic qualities of calm, sunny friendliness and tolerance.

Midsummer was now past. Rhododendron and kalmia had faded. The Grandfather Mountain had put on his white cowl. It was blue sky for days together. Young folk began to come in to the boardinghouses, and I was included in their picnics and trampings. We sang and rollicked so loudly on the "pike" that the Professor did not care to explore with a whole party of bushwhacking youngsters at his heels, and I stayed with my younger associates. Only once more did we see him; that was when he came to say good-bye the day before he meant to leave. The next morning, when the teams made their early start down the mountain, Mother and I overslept. The postmaster gave us a message, and a period was put to an idyllic association.

In a few weeks more, Mother and I started back to the low country. I had hitherto been a home-taught child and had never been for a single day in a real school with set classes. I could not read aloud without confusion; I did not have a proper handwriting but used a personal, imperfect speed-writing as it might be called, legible only to Mother and me, and far indeed from that "Spenserian" penmanship just then expected of all young ladies. Mother well knew how badly I needed the discipline she could not enforce. All during this summer, therefore, she had been corresponding about a school for me. A too-remote or too-expensive one was out of the question. She could not have her youngest-born too far removed from her this first year. The matter was brought to a decision with Aunt Margaret's help and counsel.

When the coolness of the mountain air was exchanged for the heavy stuff they breathe on the lower levels, I did not regret the change so much, because I was busy imagining other changes. Youth goes out to meet a change halfway.

Almost immediately upon our arrival at home, Miss Matilda Brown, the family helper in sewing, was sent for, and muslin underwear with many tucks was devised. Mother pretended to be very cheerful, but really she felt very blue. I tried to seem becomingly sorrowful, but inwardly I was quite jubilant. In a few weeks my childhood was going to be over, definitely, and for always. How glad I was of that!

XX

AN OLD-TIME GIRL'S SCHOOL IN HILLSBORO

HILLSBORO STILL exists, but sadly altered. A stranger could never recognize it from this description, but those who once have known it may recall the old conditions. The usual succession of filling stations and road signs may be seen along a highway good enough to entice one quickly away from a dull little town.

The old "Nash and Kollock" school building is still standing, or lately was, a poor, dun-colored shell of a house. The superb avenue of cedars, which once led to it, attained the extreme age limit of such trees and were cut down. Even the stumps have been grubbed up and forgotten this long time.

Hillsboro was once the capital of the state—before the Revolution. Still visible in the belfry of its Georgian courthouse is that old English town clock which was ticking off the minutes while the Regulators were assembling, which timed the weeks of their imprisonment, and which struck the hour of their execution.

In Hillsboro in the eighteen-eighties, there still survived a boarding school, advertised in a tiny square in local papers as for "Little Girls and Young Ladies." It was a private school, dating from long before the War, and one which had lived on by its merits, and because there were so pitifully few schools for girls in our state. "Misses Nash and Miss Kollock's" was indeed a survival. It was a home school after the pattern of those described in Miss Austen's novels. It made no pretense of being up to date. Its branches were the ones usually taught in high schools today, only not so comprehensive. The instruction, however, was as thorough as the principals knew how to make it, with infinite pains. The manners and ideals held up to the pupils were entirely of the past, but those who conducted the school knew perfectly what their ideals were. It was a good safe place to which to commit a young daughter.

And so I, of whom my aunts would often say, "That child will die of old age before she is grown," was being sent there, avowedly to "learn to read and write." I was to be held down to a strict curriculum. I was fourteen and well grown. My brother was going that way and was given charge of me to hand me over—to plump me down as he passed on his journey.

A brand-new epoch is able to produce a thrill with small show of novelty, but the appearance of this new experience was entirely commonplace. A shabby, wabbling old omnibus turned sharply from the railroad station and went down a narrow street dusty with such a depth of September drouth that one could easily picture the mud that would come of it under the first autumn rain. A gate in a stout picket fence, with a stiff hedge inside of it, opened into a front yard filled with shrubbery. The house stood high, with a good many windows. It had never been painted. All along the long piazza was set a series of orange and lemon trees in tubs, the topmost boughs of which touched the eaves and made the porch a leafy arcade. We were met at the door by Miss Maria Nash herself, the younger of the Nash sisters. She was both impressive and dignified, but, after all, she could best be described by negatives. She was not cordial, but reserved, and although she possessed the keenest gray eyes in the world, they were almost colorless. She looked at me with an appraising glance full of sagacity. Her prim clothing and her smooth hair were all of the same neutral grayness. My brother gave her the letter from my mother, planted a hasty kiss on my lips, hoped I would not be homesick, and took his leave at once.

I was not attending to him; I was busy looking about me, observing the parlour and its pictures, glimpsing the wide hall with its row of wraps hung on pegs at the end, and eagerly wondering about the comrades who must wear them. Immediately Miss Maria led me in to be introduced to her elder sister, Miss Sally Nash, a benign, gentle old lady who was lame. Next, there pounced into the room a quick-moving little, eager woman, dressed very modishly in all the bustles, knife-pleatings, and overskirts then in vogue. Her hair was frizzed out all around her forehead, while Miss Maria's and Miss Sally's was drawn smoothly down in shining gray bands at each side of the parting. On the top of her head she wore a heap of rolls of false hair, which resembled little sausages, and about her neck was a tinkling necklace worn over a series of bows of lace. This little lady was Miss Sarah Kollock. She had a quick jerky movement, and a sudden glance. Her eyes were not calm and judicial like Miss Maria's, but fiery, and she seemed to be smiling grimly, and against her will. Her whole atmosphere vibrated with restlessness and tension.

Afterward I came to know Miss Kollock very well! Just now, I was further presented to a stout cordial teacher who looked kindly and spoke with good nature. So I had met them all—the brain, the heart, the energy, and the good soft buffer between the school girls and trouble.

The room assigned to me was at the top of the house, all the space of which was occupied by a good-sized attic room with dormer windows, arranged for accommodating six girls. My roommates were already come, I having arrived late. There were two cousins, from Wilmington, by-the-sea— bright, petulant, dominating—and a girl of my own age, a kind blunt sort. She had the most amusing way of turning every hindrance and every difficulty into a comic fatality.

"This had to happen!" This girl was to be my bedfellow. In the third bed were two girls from South Carolina. One was rather dull looking, the daughter of the rich man of her village, so I discovered later. Paired with her, and from the same town, was a gentle brown-eyed girl name *María* (with the Spanish accent), which is the same name as Mary. She was the daughter of a minister who held a Bible Society's translator's job. She had been born and had lived most of her life in a South American capital. She was now being sent to school by the people of her father's denomination. She was thin, even to meagerness, but had sweet liquid eyes like a fawn, long lashes, and a pretty, retroussé nose, but she could not be called beautiful in a regular way, for there was a disfiguring scar on one cheek from an old burn. Her manner was nervous and uneasy, but as I came to know her this passed, and she was sympathetic, and often very witty.

To the left, as the stairway came down to the first floor, were the sitting rooms of Miss Maria and Miss Sally. To the right opened the big schoolroom, opposite the parlour into which I had first come. The dining room was in the basement, reached by a headlong stair and a dark passage, but at the end it was well lighted and cosy, a place for the dispensing of the best of substantial fare. We boarders were given good milk, well-cooked meat and vegetables, and all the bread and butter we cared to consume. Nobody could have been more decently served or better fed at home.

This old school building had been adapted from an antiquated residence, and had been added to here and built out there. As at this date no plumbing whatever was either found or expected, all water for bathing had to be carried to the second and third stories in pails. But, withal, how daintily clean the twenty-odd girls were expected to be! Bathe in cold water to the waist we must each morning, while great tubs of warm water were prepared laboriously for us twice a week, for "the altogether." It was a regular requirement to have the hair shampooed often, and for this purpose an old Negro woman came each Saturday. She did half the heads in the school each week (there was no bobbed hair then), and for her really expert service she must be paid a big round *dime* every time she did you up! But here I am, describing the hygienic arrangements of the old house when I have not yet introduced the persons more than casually, or given any account of our routine of study and play.

The studies were, as I have said, what we should now call high-school courses, but they were not without their vicissitudes. Miss Kollock taught the mathematics, and in her classes one learned self-possession and tested it; for, joined to a very real talent for instructing, she had a temper which hurried and impelled her restless personality like steam from a boiler without safety-valve or governor. Instead of being mistress of it, her temper mastered her and drove her, apparently against her will, into frequent excesses. One mistake at the blackboard set her fidgeting; two errors, and her eyes flashed, her feet shuffled, while her pencil beat an accelerating tattoo: at a pupil's third mistake, thunder and lightning flew about, and the sky fell! Nobody knew just when she was going to explode or whom the pieces would strike. Everyone sat agog in Miss Kollock's class: attention there was well-nigh perfect, and one would study a good deal, even of algebra, to prevent her raising the voice of condemnation. And yet in spite of her passions, I found her quite likable. She had a fierce, brusque, good will, and I was not afraid of her, but found her exhilarating. Poor gentle María, the Spanish American, would be frightened almost into hysterics when Miss Kollock pounced upon her to worry her like a terrier about French verbs or the binomial theorem. When she did this, I should have liked to put Miss Kollock to death by slow torture; because it was so unfair—the way she tormented poor faithful María, who held constantly before herself the thought that her expenses were being donated to her and that on this account she must be extra diligent. María tried the dangerous experiment of attempting to satisfy Miss Kollock, who never intended to be pleased. A bit of mud, left on a practice-room was a mountain of iniquity; a mistake in a French verb, the same as a profane oath. She could not have made more turmoil about either. I refused to care. I would stand at the blackboard stating a problem (and my mathematics to this day is a hole in the ground), while behind me Miss Kollock would be fidgeting, twisting, frowning, and suddenly would begin to rave. Then I would lay down the chalk and face her, quietly, and she would catch herself up and probably finish by explaining the whole till it was as plain as day. She must be fairly faced, for she loved to bully those who trembled before her.

A large day school was connected with the boarding school, and to this a number of sons of select families were permitted to come with their sisters until they should reach the age of twelve. Delightful urchins these were. Miss Goodrich, the fat kindly assistant, had charge of them, and was sweetly unaware of their pranks. Young Robin Webb had the habit of warming himself by bestriding the stove pipe, and one morning in November a foggy emanation poured out of her schoolroom smelling like burnt feathers. It was Miss Kollock who whipped hastily into the room and collared young Robin and sent him home to put on a proper pair of breeches. Robin's brother Thomas was a member of the famous algebra class, and on one occasion he so angered Miss Kollock that she spelled his name. She spelled it quite loudly, "Thomas Webb, you are one great big g-double o-*c*-e—goose!" and not one of the class even dared to laugh.

In the jolly companionship of this home school I expanded happily, and because of my abiding interest in the novelties of a world so full of things and people, I found not a moment's homesickness. The two girls from Wilmington damned me black by saying I could not be really "nice" because I liked so many sorts of girls. "That María, now"—leaving the sentence unfinished. But I took their comment as a continuation of the war between the East and the West, of which I had often heard, and I was sarcastic to them. My bedmate and I were the best of chums and quarreled happily all the while. May would plunge at me to choke me, and all the wrestling and pummelling would have to be done in an undertone so that Miss Maria Nash's sharp ears could not detect it. Neither did the teachers ever find out the perpetrator of our excruciatingly funny caricatures. They could be traced by the waves of merriment they produced. I did study. I could be noticed as determinedly studious whatever the currents of suppressed giggling that flowed around. My best friend was always María. She was sincerely patient and good, endlessly kind to the girl with whom she had to live, who could scarcely have been congenial. She was as true and sweet as a violet is fragrant. I measured my critical, epicurean, self-sufficiency against her character of real love and unselfishness, and I saw myself as the less worthy. I learned deep lessons from her, for so do we educate each other.

Being a family school, it was managed by the Nash and Kollock ladies according to their respective religious traditions. Miss Maria and Miss Sally were blue Presbyterians. Miss Kollock, their own cousin, was a high-church Episcopalian. All three were agreed that the girls placed under their care should have thorough religious training, should learn psalms by heart, and must have the Bible read to them and explained. Besides this, there was a set time, twenty minutes before going to bed each night, when each girl was supposed to read the Bible for herself. On Sundays, all must attend church. Two out of four Sundays the Presbyterian girls went to their own. The other Sundays, they bestowed alternately on Episcopal and Methodist worship. But if parents so directed, Miss Kollock took the Episcopal girls every Sunday to the lovely little Episcopal Church, where, in the rector's absences, a lay reader filled out. It was here that I learned to follow and admire the prayer-book service so filled with the aroma of ancient pieties.

The Presbyterian minister was not one who managed to convey much meaning to his young critics. Every Sunday afternoon, Miss Sally catechised all the boarders. The Presbyterians recited their catechism (if they knew it); the Episcopalians began theirs with "What is your name?" and it was much shorter, and the Methodists appeared to have no catechism at all—unfair of them, so it was considered. After this, Miss Sally would ask about the sermon. The text having been carefully noted, it became my especial task to arrange enough heads and subheads to satisfy Miss Sally, who, on account of her lameness, never went to Church. Sometimes she would say that it was "a most excellent discourse" and our minister was "praised for labors not his own."

The most enlightening influence of all came from the old town and its people. Hillsboro, although poor enough—and everybody in those days was "so happy and so pore"—still retained a flavor of real aristocracy. Sundry homes still remained which were indeed good to visit, good also to think back upon, with their portraits, their old mahogany, placed in balanced arrangement along their walls, and their pierced silver baskets shining on the sideboard. These homes opened their hospitable doors wide to the Nash and Kollock girls on the slightest pretext of acquaintanceship or cousinship. The old town itself, with its pre-Revolutionary traditions, with its turbid little river winding through, then possessed a picturesqueness which has long been lost in the ragged development of so-called progress. The town is set in an intimate bit of broken country, and near it there are abrupt hills, then densely wooded, between which the river slipped, and which could give within the limits of one afternoon's stroll, slopes with differing exposures which severally displayed the flora normally spread along hundreds of miles of slowly rising altitude. Yellow jessamine grew on a southern bank, mountain shrubs (such as rhododendron and kalmia), on a northward slope, while arbutus nestled in many coverts of the woods.

There was another walk, ending at the white-pillared home of one of my family's friends, a rustic pathway so overarched with great oaks, so canopied from view by vines which festooned them, that sunshine only casually flecked the water flowing by, and it was called the "Dark Walk." Do not look for this romantic lane today. The river is flowing, the bank is there, but the real estate agent has let in regularity and ruin.

Mother wrote in November that I was expected to remain at Christmas. This decision must have cost her a good deal, but I never questioned it. The winter was cold again this year. Little parties were given at many homes for the leftovers. Miss Kollock unbent and became quite human, and my María and I were inseparable. In January came another freeze, and on one day school was dismissed to permit of enjoying the winter sports which seldom come so far south. From bank to bank the river was frozen, and young men of the town invited the girls to be drawn over the ice on sleds. Thus we followed the winding river for miles never before penetrated.

At Easter there was a picnic at "Joe's Garden," the site of an old home down the river. This was a high rocky knoll, overlooking the stream, not far from where the Duke quarries now are. It was a home site grown wild, but still sweet with the remaining shrubs of an old flower garden. Walking home a part of the way, María and I gathered a sheaf of those lovely, slender, pink-tipped lilies which come up with never a leaf and star the meadows in the North Carolina April.

Roses of later April faded in May. June brought flowers to overflow the boxes on the lawn of the old school. After the simple commencement, I went joyfully home. I had learned to read and write as Mother had bidden me, and I had learned by association with comrades, and had gained memories of old gardens, old homes, and happy playtimes. Even Miss Kollock's temper had pointed for me a solemn lesson. I had made one friend whom I unselfishly loved, and never saw again. And, last of all, I have a shrine decorated with meadow lilies, those my friend and I gathered in that long-vanished spring, which seem somehow to be a suggestion and a symbol of her sweet life and our friendship.

XXI

A YEAR AT "MISS BALDWIN'S"

THE NEXT AUTUMN, my brother, now in the way of earning his own living and a little over, offered to send me to what he called a real school, and not the old dame's affair he considered Nash and Kollock to be. This time it was to be a school which has gone on, and prospered, and is today a college well patronized. I cannot remember the argument he used against one of the three or four schools for girls in North Carolina to which I might have been consigned, but that September, in care of a friend of ours who taught there, I was sent away to a boarding school in the mountainous part of Virginia, "Miss Baldwin's," as it was then familiarly called.

I tried to sleep doubled up in the car seat, for pullmans were not commonly demanded, and all night long the train rumbled northward. In the morning, the prospect showed hill country, with a range of blue mountains on the left. We arrived at the close-built town of Staunton, with some streets so narrow that a mountain wagon must go all around the square to turn. After a bit of breakfast, we beckoned a rickety hack, and it twisted around one or two corners and then stopped in front of a steep-tilted square filled with a miscellany of buildings all interconnected with covered ways. From the street, stone steps led up to a large residence with the conventional white pillars in front, but close beside this stood an old brick church building, steeple removed, and three stories made of it for school use, while other and varied structures were flung pell-mell against the hillside.

The Principal, whom next we interviewed, was in that day a woman celebrated all over the South for the faith and intrepidity with which, against every difficulty, she had built up an excellent school for girls. She was by that time an elderly woman and was disfigured with facial paralysis, but was the same dynamic person. While my studies were being discussed and my room assigned, my mind as usual was taken up, my whole being fairly squirming with interest in my new surroundings. I was shown my room, not far from the entrance and a few doors from Miss Mattoon's, who had brought me. It was one of a row, and my huge round-topped trunk (called a Saratoga), already sat beside the door. My roommate was in the room already, and appeared about my own age, a stout pudgy girl. Without a greeting, she began to chatter. Said she—

"Yes, I was wondering how long I was going to stay here all alone, getting homesicker and homesicker every minute! Isn't this the awfullest hole you ever got into? You must be my roommate. My folks haven't left town yet, and if you are, I'm asking you, right now, to go driving with us this afternoon. My mother—she's not my real mother, you know, my own mother's dead, and this one's step—She's my father's wife and she brought me, and she'll be glad to have you. I live with my grannie when I'm home. Where are you from?"

And without waiting for an answer she began to sing, "The sun shines bright in my old K. Y. Ky Home!"

I managed to stem the torrent and contribute my name and home and ask my roommate's name.

"Berry's my name, short for Barbara. Isn't Barbara awful? It was my dear mother's name, or else I'd have it changed to Opal or Maude. My last name is Amis. My grannie is Mrs. Carwell, and lots of folks call me Berry Carwell, but that is only my middle name. Did you ever go to school before? I never did, and I'm most sure I am not going to like it. My grannie's awful good to me, and about everything they try to have me do, she'll say, 'Poor little girl, she has no mother. Don't make her do it!' and when I write and tell her I am crying my eyes out for her, she'll come by the next train and take me home."

I stood laughing at this flood of information. I was asking myself how I could tell it so as to sound funniest, for I loved to dramatize things. I giggled and replied, "I don't want to go home yet; I've just come, and I want to see what it's like. Please come tell me which is my bureau and which bed is mine."

Three wooden chests of drawers with mirrors stood in the room, which was a good large one. There was a single bed and a double one.

"This room is for three," said Berry. "You and I have got to sleep in the double bed together, and there's another girl coming in today, who gets the single bed. That awful, fat, old woman—she's the housekeeper, or something—came in here and made me take my sheets right off that single bed."

"Where's our roommate coming from?" I asked.

"From down south somewhere, Mississippi, or Louisiana, and her name's Emma something-or-other. Your side of the closet is next the window, if you want to unpack."

The closet was a huge square one, lighted, whose three interior walls were fitted with hooks and shoe racks. There was one large washstand with bowl and two pitchers; and a plain study table with three straight chairs completed the furniture. The floor was bare and splintery, made of pine boards oiled dark.

Berry's stepmother came at noon and took us to the hotel for dinner. She was nice looking although not young, but she was evidently unused to controlling her stepdaughter. Berry was good-natured when things went to suit her, but her chubby face clouded at the first hint of her will being crossed. She could squeeze out tears when she wished.

After dinner we three drove in state through the streets, in an old-fashioned barouche, a carriage cut low at the sides, in which the occupants faced each other, and the driver sat on a high perch in front. I was deeply impressed by the grandeur of our progress. Soon we went a short way into rich, green country walled with mountains. Then we came back and drove twice around the city reservoir, then a novelty and a wonder of itself. Finally we went to the station to bid Mrs. Amis good-bye.

Berry snuffled busily into her handkerchief as we went to the school, not because she felt so very desolate, but because she considered it the proper thing to do.

We had supper that evening, the first meal in the big dining room. The school numbered a hundred and fifty boarders, besides day-pupils. Tables each held twelve or sixteen girls and were presided over by teachers. There was, that year, a fashion of wearing long scarves or shawls of cashmere, in all possible bright colors. The girls wore these to supper and let them trail over the backs of their chairs, so that the great bare room was full of splashes of color. The new girls looked about them curiously, many seeming as strange as we felt. Berry tried to get acquainted with the girl next her, who screwed up her pretty face and looked disdainful.

"She's awful pretty, don't you think?" said Berry to me in a stage whisper.

"Pretty stuck up!" I formed the words behind my hand.

"You certainly are find-faulty," said Berry out loud. "I think she's a perfectly lovely girl, and I would like to know her!"

The girl in question sat stiff and stolid like a wooden Indian and pretended not to hear.

After supper, we scurried back to our room, to find there the expected roommate. She must have been at least two

A YEAR AT MISS BALDWIN'S

years older than either of us, and she sat sorting her effects into her bureau drawers.

"I am so glad to see our new roommate," I cried.

The girl replied without cordiality, looking us up and down, each in turn. Emma Wolff, for that was her name, was medium tall and quite well-rounded without being fat. Her hair was the color of a scoured copper basin; her eyes, large and brilliant, were light chestnut brown. Her skin was pallid, with the texture of white kid. She would have been beautiful save for a mouth too large and red as a pomegranate. Her dress was reddish-brown, and contrary to the prevailing fashion, she wore her long, heavy, red-gold hair plainly braided without a "crimp" or a "bang," tied at the nape of her neck with a bow of orange ribbon. She sat composedly, as one who intends to dominate, who is confident that she is wiser and more significant than other people. She told us that she came from a river town in Mississippi, where she lived with her mother; her father, who had been German-born, had died some years before. She may have derived her remarkable coloring from him, but the pallor of the Deep South could be seen in her magnolia-petal skin.

Presently she said, "By the way, I wanted that side of the closet next the window, and one of you had already hung her dresses there, so I had to change them."

I ran to the closet to find all my cherished new dresses flung down pell-mell upon the floor.

"Who said I wanted to change?" I cried.

"I do not ask any more than my share," said Emma, "but I must have the side of the closet next the window." Then with a naughty gleam in her eye, and as though addressing an infant, she added, "Better keep on my good side, child, then we will be friends."

Berry was much impressed with this masterful beginning. She offered to help fold Emma's things away, admiring each article as it came to light. I saw I would have to swallow my wrath this once. I looked over the pile of new books sent up for me, and, to make conversation, asked the new roommate what she meant to study. Emma replied,

"German, in the first place, for that is like my native language: then English, History, and Math. Enough for anybody, although I hear they give great importance here to the writing of English. I want to join one of the composition classes."

I remarked then that I had been assigned to one of those classes under a Miss Wright. As I said it, I fervently hoped that Emma would not sit next me there.

Just then, girls came in from the next room to make acquaintance—girls from the upper valley of Virginia. I asked them about their limestone grottoes, recently explored, but of these they were unwilling to talk because they cared nothing for them. They were interested only in personal attributes, in this one's curly hair, and that one's tiny feet.

Emma Wolff made a far greater appeal to their interest when she began discoursing about the ways of society in her home town. From her account it seemed quite as raffish and as self-complacent as small-town life near a large and naughty one readily becomes. She began to explain to these girls somewhat of the customs of New Orleans and of the underworld society there.

"You know the men who come down the river on business want to see the whole show, and I've heard"—Here the talk became too intimate for outspoken statement, and itself went under cover, being whispered with secret gusto into the ears of the next girl.

"O Emma!" they cried, "How do you know about such things? Did your mother tell you?"

"Mother thinks I ought to know," answered Emma. "She thinks it is better for girls to know facts as they are. If I should ever marry, of course I should expect my husband to reform for my sake, but about beforehand, girls should not be so fussy. All young men sow wild oats, only some of them are hypocrites and deny it, and some are truthful, like Dart, and own up to it honestly."

"Then did your *Dart*, as you call him, tell you all the things he did in New Orleans that he should not have done?" I demanded indignantly.

"He didn't go into detail of course," said Emma impatiently. "He said 'You know those up-river country merchants, how they are; and so I had to go 'round with them, and I showed them the whole Quarter'—and I knew what he meant!"

I had the sensation of being soiled. It seemed to me that the great world must be a furtive, slimy place, wickeder than I in my small-town isolation had ever guessed. The facts of sex I had been honestly told. My ideas of the world were derived mostly from Dickens and Thackeray and other novelists of manners. I had read many things in Shakespeare which, as I well knew, no one openly discussed—but this was different. This was schoolgirls talking for fun. The meeting in our bedroom had taken quite a turn for speculation. Emma was retailing all she remembered which was salacious, some of her stories being adaptations of the time-honored, gamey ones of Boccaccio. Her audience huddled together on the side of the bed, giggling convulsively. Finally I burst out:

"I don't believe girls ought to talk about such things for fun, even if people *are* that way, and I am not going to listen to any more of your ugly stories. I just ought to go and tell Miss Mattoon, and have her tell the Principal the kind of stuff you like to talk about. It's nasty, and it's vulgar and you know it!"

Emma slowly turned her beautiful head with disdain, and her whole face flattened into a superb sneer. She said,

"W-e-e-ll, Miss Prue, I suppose you will be calling us down for mentioning 'legs' next! I want you to know that I shall talk of what I please, in this room or out of it. But I'll do you this favor: I'll never part my lips to YOU again, for good or bad!"

Berry laughed. Her sympathies were entirely with Emma. The other girls were flustered, and said good night hastily. They said it to Emma, and to me they scarcely nodded as they went out. I felt myself put in the wrong, I could scarcely tell why. "I suppose I sounded a prig," I thought to myself, "but I do hate to be crowded out of my room with all this filthy talk, and not say what I think of it." Emma kept her word; she utterly ignored me, and I was a bit lonely when I went to bed that night. Sleep and rest brought morning, and the new day's interests in the school and the classes.

A letter I received a few days later can be anticipated here and will set the exact date of my first day and night at this school. It may be found in the files of the nineteenth-century newspapers which tell of the "Charleston earthquake." Far into that first night when I had gone homesick to bed, hand trucks rolled from hall to hall, placing Saratoga trunks from all over the Southeast; and slight earth tremors which might have been perceptible even so near the backbone of the Blue Ridge, were not felt. My letter told me the details in Salisbury, how the old house shivered in all its sturdy timbers, how the brass candlestick had been shaken off the high mantel, and was broken upon the hearth; how Mr. Bruner, wakeful and alert as usual, had danced out into the street at the first trembling, clad in his nightshirt and slippers and wrapped in his shawl. How not much behind him, all the neighbors in that part of town had burst open front doors and gates and spilled out into the street, highly excited and sketchily clothed. Munroe who was, it seemed, nodding in Uncle Harry's old corner in the kitchen-across-the-yard, came knocking and calling to the Doctor that Judgment Day had come. Aunt Fanny, Aunt Mary's successor, declared next morning that in her opinion it must have been "one of them whirling harrycanes, what used to be down wha' I come from, when I was a little bitty girl, an' my Mammy done los' me plum outen de cradle!"

This land slip, near the low-lying coast, serves to date my first night at Miss Baldwin's. Later on that first school day, I found myself in Miss Wright's English class, which gave a course thorough and full of interest. Miss Wright was a woman in middle age, plain with an extraordinary homeliness. One of the girls, after a first look at her that morning, wrote a note to me which described her as "like a bulldog and a billygoat scrambled together with hairpins." It sounded like a naughty, witty description at the time, but after surrendering to the fascination of Miss Wright's teaching, I never again thought of her as grotesque.

On Saturday mornings, this English class became "Miss Wright's Composition." Two subjects had been given out, one fanciful and one connected with the week's lessons. The best themes were read before the class and criticized. After a year of such sifting, at the school commencement there would be awarded one of those gold medals suspended upon a blue ribbon, which fluttered the hearts of schoolgirls in that dear, simple old time. No one ever had the least certainty of the winner, until the Principal had her called down from the circular ranges of seats in Chapel, and laid the ribbon about her neck. This was the only medal the school awarded, and naturally it was the most coveted and prized honor of the school year. All this I heard talked of, and I resolved to try for this glory, although I assured myself there was little hope of my gaining it. Miss Wright's class was so comprehensive and so much reading was required, that only enthusiastic students could keep standing in it, and many had to be dropped into the class below. I did manage to keep my place there, but this is anticipating.

The afternoon of this first Sunday, Emma told Berry, for my benefit, that she had seen both Miss Wright and Miss Drew, the two teachers of English. Said she—

"I would not be obliged to look at that hideous Miss Wright every day, for any consideration. Besides, she is a Northern woman. No true Southerner, certainly no person brought up as I have been, would willingly have anything to do with a Yankee. I have not signed up for Composition Class yet, but Miss Drew is the teacher I shall ask for." And Emma went to class several times under her affinity, pretty Miss Drew, before she found out there was no medal attached to her class. She chose to consider me the author of her mistake. I should have set her right—ought to have done so, even if we were not on speaking terms—would have done so if I had not been afraid she would take the medal!

When I returned to my room at night, Berry would be rolled up like a pudgy little animal, in most of the bedcover, her face to the wall; and at the turning up of the gas, Emma would lift her head and glare at me. If my clean clothes came in and I was not there, Emma threw them on the floor and trampled them. Finally Aunt Sidney, the old colored housemaid on our hall, finding it out, took them away, pressed them, and directed my washerwoman to deliver my laundry to herself in future.

One afternoon I came into the room to find Emma there alone, reading. I thought perhaps I had not done all that could be done in the interest of peace. Thought is free, but it seemed so stupid to be running a feud, when a small amount of decency would make all smooth outwardly. So I said, "Emma, why are you still angry with me? Let's be sensible, and make up our minds to be at least outwardly civil to each other." Emma whirled upon me, and said with emphasis—

"You deceitful girl, I would never *look* at you again unless I was forced to do it, much less speak to you!" And resolutely she turned back to her book, while I, being somewhat dashed when my olive branch was thus snapped in two under my nose, said "Very well," lamely enough, and drifted out of the room. I went into the room of the teacher with whom I had come, Miss Mattoon, who lived on that same hall, and asked leave to study in her window seat.

"You are are as welcome as the sunshine my dear, but pray why is my window seat better than your own?"

"I am in a three-girl room, Miss Mattoon. Two is company, three is trumpery, as you know, and I reckon I am the odd one."

"Tell me the rest of the story," said Miss Mattoon.

"I think I would rather not, I'm no tattletale." I answered.

"Then give me leave to find out the rest of the story for myself," said Miss Mattoon smiling. "Sometimes, my dear, it is necessary to take one's own part." I simply looked at her, saying not a word more, but I am afraid I was entirely willing she should investigate! It must have been a month later, during which time I had been working well, but never going to my room unless there was no other place to go, when one day I ran in to prepare for supper. I found Berry alone there, prostrate upon the bed, weeping loudly. Thinking this must mean bad news from her home, I put my hand on her shoulder with a "What is it, Berry?" The hand was promptly shaken off. Berry sat up with a distorted angry face.

"Oh, you snake in the grass, you did it!"

"Did what?"

"You told."

"Told what?"

"Told the old teachers that Emma was not treating you right! And what you never told was how you insulted her the very first night she came! Oh, you despisable tattletale!"

"I do not know what in the world you are talking about," I said.

"Then I'll tell you, even if you do know, and even if you did manage to drive Emma out. She's got to move over into Number Nine, and nobody has told her a single real reason for it—just Miss Mattoon called her in immediately after dinner, and said she must go down and see Principal. She came back, and she moved. Emma has written to her mother about it, but Principal told her she would have to move to-day, or leave school. Oh how I hate you and your underhand ways!"

"All right, hate away," I exclaimed joyfully, "and while you are hating, I will give you something more to hate me for. I am so glad Emma has to go, I could laugh and sing. She has persecuted me all the fall, trying to drive me out of this room. I did not tell on her, but I made up my mind she should never drive me away, and from now on I'll have some peace from you both, while you are over in her room, visiting her. She is full of meanness and dirty talk, and you lap up every word she says and do everything she wants done, until the two of you have made this room like Hell on earth for me. I have as good a right here as you. What are you going to do about that?"

Berry found the wrath of the patient so surprising that she sat up and wiped her eyes in pure bewilderment. Her tears had not come from very deep; she looked at me and felt an admiration for a girl who, as she believed, had managed this affair so skillfully. She gave a gulp and replied: "I think you were mean to Emma, and I always shall think so, but perhaps that is not any of my business. Let's go down to supper." And we went out together with arms wreathed around!

Emma had not played all her cards yet. I acted a bit self-conscious when my friends asked the cause of Emma's moving from the room, and refused to discuss the matter. She had no such inhibitions. She constructed an elaborate tale of the reasons, the lies I had told, the pressure I had used through my teacher-friend, Miss Mattoon, and all this she retailed to anyone who would listen. By necessity I had been absorbed in my studies, and had not yet become what is called a good mixer, but I saw a difference. Acquaintances spoke to me more briefly, or even avoided me, until the atmosphere of being sent to Coventry was unmistakable. Finally Addie Hood, one of my few actual intimates, came to me with a troubled air. She said,

"Do you know what Emma Wolff is telling everybody about you? She says you worked against her because you are jealous of her, that you influenced Miss Mattoon to get her moved out, because she reproved you for using profane language and cursing in the room. She says she had to stop speaking to you, because you were so abusive, and she insists that she is very fond of Berry and has been separated from her against her will."

"I have been sure she must have been telling something pretty awful," I answered. "It will not do to deny what she says, for you know it's only my word against hers, and nobody knows which to believe. If anyone asks you, do not go into detail, but just say they are mistaken in Emma, and let it go at that."

"One thing is sure," I said to myself about this time, "all this is good for my scholarship. I've got few friends, no 'crushes,' no company in my room, no parties, nothing in the world to do but study." Aunt Sidney, the old housemaid, was more outspoken. She was delighted that Emma had been moved. She told of the remarks she had heard her make and finished by saying, "Give her a plenty of rope, Honey, give her a plenty of rope, an' she gwine to hang herself higher'n Haman!"

All through the darkening days of December I kept at work, for I had found out for myself the restfulness of study. I did not go home for Christmas, but instead was sent to Baltimore to have glasses fitted that I must have been needing for years. As I passed Washington, electric lights, the first used to light a whole city, cast their defined, wavering, shadows about the station. There were innumerable interests and incidents which my memory brings back in drifts, and which would make a book out of my school year, rather than the simple chapter to which I am trying to condense it. Last year I had met with warm affection from one my own age. This year I had encountered hatred from a similar source, and it is with the idea of showing education in human values that I have given this schoolgirl tempest in a puddle so much time in the telling. But even schoolgirls, with their wholly conventional ethical views, are bored to hear one person singled out and abused constantly. Emma had to subside at last, while a number who had been on the verge of liking me, felt impelled to find out what I was really made of, and some of the leading girls of the school began to notice me. I became so engrossed in the life of the place that I began to reproach myself with disloyalty to the house under the oaks. I wondered how I was going to crawl back into my chrysalis for the summer and was loath even to imagine doing without my fine new comrades whom I had invested with all manner of ideal perfections. In my weekly letters, I felt now as if I were writing as a stranger to strangers.

With my favorite teacher, Miss Wright, I was learning appreciation of the portion of English literature which we studied, and which, although not so minutely analyzed as in modern days, was more imagined and more savored.

Each morning Berry would count the passing of another day on our large calendar, marking off yesterday with many flourishes and diggings-in of her pencil. Then she would chant loudly, giving the proper number of days,

> "A few more days and I'll be free,
> From this old hole of misery
> A little more beefsteak, a little more hash,
> A few more country dudes to mash!"

The rather lingering spring of this mountain country came at last, with baby oak leaves and blossoming shrubs. Class work was intensified, for textbooks must be finished, and time was afoot with increase of urgency. I passed all my examinations, while Berry serenely flunked most of hers. There remained but one matter pending, and that was the award of the medal for English Composition. I felt entirely uncertain where I stood, for one of my best friends, a brilliant girl, highly educated during long country leisures by a learned uncle, could have taken it away from anyone. If Kitty chose, she could turn her hand over and win. She had the gifts and only needed to make the effort. But although she was so apt, Kitty was lazy!

The last of my themes was one in which I set myself to describe the summer in the mountains of two years before—the summer when I climbed the cliffs, when I penetrated the ancient Indian trail, when I had come so close that I felt the soul of the Great Blue Ridge—in short, the summer of my roaming with the Professor. I put in a little of what he told me of the Alps, so much grander but, I could not help maintaining, not a whit more beautiful than the green-forested mountains we explored together. Prudently, I reflected that in view of the way the school estimated friendships with young men, I might as well lay a few more years on the head of my Professor. He would have been surprised to find himself grown gray, and his stalwart shoulders bent, though the story was the wanderings we made, the shimmer of morning on dewy roadsides, and blue sweet distances folded each behind other. Although I did not know it, this theme was the deciding effort which gained my distance in this contest.

Commencement was upon us. Each white-clad girl sat in her regular place upon the semicircular ranges of seats which mounted at the sides and back of the large stage of the auditorium, holding up the "whole bouquet of maidenhood," as the Commencement speakers liked to say, to the view of the assembled parents and townspeople. Sometimes among these last would sit a worthy youth who was also wise, who had worked his way through a maze of red tape and was sitting well out in front where his sweetheart could see him. On the floor of the stage were assembled the faculty, sitting in front of the snowbank of white dresses. Certificates were given out, sheaves of them, asserting proficiency or improvement in this or that. Excitement mounted; whispering went round in waves. When the diplomas were given next, there was some speechmaking to which nobody listened. Then another four-handed piece was beaten out on the piano, followed by a last chorus. When the final sustained note had died away, Professor Masters, one of the elderly duffers who was permitted to teach girls, rose in behalf of the Principal. Had her face not been paralyzed, she could have spoken far more to the point than he, but in this epoch, at the South, she would have thought it improper to do so. Only the shameless Suffrage sisterhood would appear so, for in those days no womanly woman ever addressed a mixed assembly. The Principal sat still, and "Daddy Masters" spoke her piece for her.

He told of the growing need for careful and correct English, of the greater attention the educated woman should pay to writing. He referred to distinguished "female" writers, mentioning Miss Edgeworth, Miss Brontë, Miss Austen, but saying no word of Mrs. Stowe or Miss Alcott. He spoke of the emulation always astir in the school when there was question of the "First Honor in English Composition." It was, as he stated, the supreme prize of the whole student body, and attainable by anyone who was able to win it. It was always announced last, because after it all other award would be an anticlimax. It was a gold medal, and this year it had been awarded—and Daddy Masters looked all around the tense rows of panting girls, licked his lips, and hesitated long enough to work up all the excitement he thought the occasion demanded. It had been awarded to Miss—and the name was not Kitty's. The girls pushed me forward. I caught my breath and stumbled from stage to stage of the circular seats. I came forward, and the blue ribbon which was part of the decoration of this yearly drama, carrying its dangling pendant, was placed about my neck by the Principal. She patted my shoulder and turned me about to face the audience. Daddy Masters gravely bowed and shook my hand. As the clapping began, I turned back to ascend to my seat near the top of the stage, grasped at and kissed by the girls as I went. I stumbled over somebody's slipper, set well out in front as if to intercept me. Recovering, I turned to apologize, and found myself looking into the pale golden eyes of Emma Wolff. I felt that in so rosy and right a world no resentment or ill feeling should find place. Without thinking, I spoke Emma's name. I received, from eyes narrowed and keen under lowered lids, a most intense look of bitter hatred. It dashed me through as if it had been a real dagger—struck me like a vicious blow. I flushed, and then shivered, as I took my place, with the laughing girls reaching out from both sides to handle and inspect my golden bauble as it swung from its loop of ribbon. As I sat down, I closed my eyes for a second. I felt cold, and almost gray.

XXII

NO THOROUGHFARE

IMPORTANT PASSENGER trains from the North were apt to arrive in Salisbury in the dead of night, so that if anyone came that way he must be met at the station. When I returned home this year it was the middle of a warm June night, and our factotum, trusty Munroe, and no one else, stood on the platform to welcome me. Out of the circle of light at the station he carried my hand baggage toward a shadow across the street, which was the horse and buggy; then, driving slowly back across town, he gave me the home news. The hour was very late, and black velvet shadows brooded on familiar lawns. When I reached home, a single lamp shone from the sitting room window, and Mother was waiting for me in her long gray dressing gown. The house was full of the spell of sleep, but I wanted to sit and talk awhile. Mother would not allow this; kissing me, she said, "Tomorrow, Daughter," and sent me straight to bed. Suddenly the full fatigue of commencement week flowed over me, and I went to sleep to the sound of the breeze in the oaks above the roof. Next morning I slept late.

Now I would tell my wonderful story! I took the box containing the medal to the breakfast table and laid it down by Father's place. He casually said, "Very pretty," twice in an absent fashion. Mother took more notice, but seemed to consider it a pleasant recognition of her child's well known ability. Neither of them perceived the dust of battle about the thing. Father was far more concerned with the state of my eyes, and of my headaches, than he was with my school triumphs.

After the good home-tasting breakfast, Mother went out to see the cook, father took his departure to his patients, and I, being left alone, perceived how warm stillness and lassitude settled upon the old house, and felt the summer monotony even now begin. I went as far as the front gate and looked over it along a dazzlingly sunny and deserted street. I had come back to my old level; there was not going to be anything whatever worth thinking about or doing. My dearly loved father and mother were, I knew, glad to see me, but I believed they did not recognize that I was not in all respects the girl who had gone away. While my ideas had been developing, no change at all had appeared at home. This surprised me, as it has many another, to see the furniture not a hairsbreadth shifted from its regular place, and not one new volume added to the old familiar shelves. Tedium and relaxation enveloped me like an atmosphere, and after putting my clothes away into the drawers and closets of my room I could scarcely conceive that I had been a year away.

One change was discussed. My sister who lived in Texas was coming in a few days to make us a visit. My niece, nearly as old as I, would come to stay with her mother here, and there was a little nephew whom none of us had seen.

The headaches from eye strain remained with me, and became a daily visitation. Great wavering coils of light would circle before my inner vision, and then the pain would drop like a curtain. Father, fearing that my glasses were not perfectly adjusted, sent me to an oculist in a neighboring town, who declared that the vision was corrected, but that the extreme nerve fatigue would take longer to overcome. I was forbidden to use my eyes at all either for reading or sewing. To a person of my temperament, life became a penance on these terms. I worried for fear my eyes would not be recovered enough to let me go back to school, and the summer, first thought of as very long, became cruelly short.

Just at this time, Aunt Margaret Mitchell, who lived in Statesville, wrote for me to come and pay her a visit. At Aunt Margaret's, there was even less to do than at home, but there was much uninterrupted leisure when she could read to me for long hours, and we could discuss books and characters together. Aunt Margaret proposed a small alleviation for my enforced idleness. She was a great knitter, and she advised me to learn to knit by touch as the blind do. She provided the material and instruction, and I would bandage my eyes and, at first, tangle hopelessly; but soon I began to heed the messages of the sensitive cushions of my finger-tips. I soon could manage simple garter-stitch. "Knitting will not fill your mind," said Aunt Margaret, "but it sets a rhythm to your thoughts which is a comfort." Soon she cast on a piece of "real knitting" for me, and we went on to finish Boswell's Johnson.

When after a few weeks I went home, I heard that my sister had taken a teaching position in the old Presbyterian Academy, and that she and her children would be with us for the whole winter. She arrived, a quick, wiry, dark-eyed woman, browned with Texas winds. I had not remembered her very well, and she seemed a stranger. She and Mother sat and talked long and earnestly, and I was not expected to listen. I grew still more depressed, because I knew it was time for me to apply for my place in school. Then Father told me one day, what I already knew perfectly well, that my eyes would need to rest perhaps a year before I could go back to books again. That if I could go back in a year he would send me, but I must stay at home for the present. He said he had wanted Mother to tell me but had decided to tell me himself. This situation must be faced.

We, as a family, were resolutely undemonstrative people, but do not gain the impression that we seemed unfeeling.

I told Mother. "I know now, Father told me," which was all I could just then articulate. "Try and be reasonable," answered Mother, "and whatever you do, do not begin crying. Nothing could be worse for you—for your eyes I mean."

No use detailing the agony of the disappointment as I felt it then. The wall I had looked over last year had now been built right across my path. I felt that I was being buried alive behind its barrier. I do not like to remember that first night when I knew my best hopes were to be deferred indefinitely, but when I awoke in the morning and looked for the sharp heartbreaking pain which had been so keen the night before, it had passed. I did not want to weep and wail any more. The emotion had become a thing lived through. I got out my little medal, which I had been childish enough to consider a sort of key to the future, dropped it down into a corner of the clothes chest at the foot of my bed, and resolved to forget its existence. But I wagered against fate, "I will not give up. There are days coming, and always more days, and I am going to make things come my way at last."

I was at a loss for a private gesture which would from that time forward defy the future. One came to my mind. That morning I initiated a habit which has held all my life long. "A hard night implies a hearty breakfast," I said to myself. "How can anyone think things through on an empty stomach?" So I set myself doggedly to eat my meal, slowly, calmly, and made it as plentiful as I could manage.

Then it dawned on me that I had not been so eager to help Mother with her household tasks, doubled in the last fortnight, as I ought to be. Such work was no strain on the eyesight. So I surprised her by asking what she meant to do with all the peaches which were bending down a tree in the orchard. These were what are called "press peaches"—clingstones—fit only for cooking. So she proposed that I make preserves of them. "We will be more of a household this winter to be eating such things," said Mother. So I got out the big brass kettle, and the smaller one, and scoured them both carefully with fine salt and vinegar. Munroe picked the peaches, and I peeled and cooked them over the charcoal brazier in the back gallery. That day, and the next, and the next, I sat a picture of industry, with dark glasses over my eyes, knitting, and skimming my preserves at intervals. My jars soon filled a long row on the pantry shelf, and I was fretting less.

The third week in September had been set for the opening of the Academy, but the week before, the associate teacher sickened with that "run of fever" still regarded by the doctors as well as by the common folk as a mysterious visitation of Providence. My sister was frantic. Her livelihood depended on this school. Forty-five or fifty pupils were enrolled, far too many for one teacher.

In despair she called me in where Mother sat. "Don't you think, Dear, that your eyes are getting a good deal better?"

"Yes, improving all the time. Father is sure now that it was only overstrain, and when they are rested they will be well."

"Then I wonder if I could ask your help with the little children, until Miss Jennie is well? You could teach them mostly by the blackboard, for they are tiny tots, just learning to read. That would not strain your eyes."

"Why, Sister, if Father thinks it is reasonable, I will be more than glad to try it out," and I smiled to think that after all there was going to be something new and unexpected this winter.

With the consent of Miss Jennie and the patrons, the matter was so arranged, for in those days primary teachers were not the highly trained specialists they have since become. People thought that any kindly female could teach little children their A.B.C. I took charge of my dozen beginners, and led them through the alphabet and into short words and sentences. I made up stories about the queer shapes of letters, and I could draw enough to interest them. My eyes grew better as I forgot about them.

Autumn wore away, cold weather drew on, and it was only a matter of weeks until Christmas. Crisping weather with bright days helped Miss Jennie to recuperate, and I learned that after the holidays there would be no further need of my services at the Academy. I taught my little people to read, and I was paid a little money for it, the first real money I ever had earned, and the last I felt sure of gaining. I resolved not to squander it at Christmas, but hold it entire for a purchase. Purely for sentiment, I wanted to buy a bit of land at the top of the Blue Ridge, on the turnpike, near that place where Mother and I had spent the pleasantest of all summers. Talking to Mother about this made her recall something she had forgotten. Hurriedly she went through her desk and found a letter from the Professor, enclosing a sprig of edelweiss. It accounted for his life during the two-year interval and announced his early return to the United States. It asked straightforwardly and formally whether his young companion, as he called me, would be permitted to answer his letter and say for herself whether she cared to remember him as her friend. The letter had been addressed to Mother, who had laid it aside. She seemed greatly surprised at my disappointment and chagrin at not having been told of it sooner. Immediately I wrote to the address he gave, but in a few weeks my letter was returned undelivered, not greatly to my surprise but to my vexation. I did not know of any further step proper under the circumstances, and now my friend had passed finally out of my knowledge. The manner of it, as well as the fact, galled me. "As if I were about six years old," as I often found occasion to exclaim, and as is so often said by the youth of all ages!

That year I helped with the Christmas cakes, under Mother's direction. She and I baked them one Saturday, in the old plantation way—in the hearth ovens with legs and lids to them, before the dining room fire. On Monday, Mother was not feeling well, as was frequently the case this season. She pulled herself together, however, and spent the whole morning in the smokehouse with Munroe, assorting and packing in chaff the store of hams and bacon recently taken out of the smoke. They placed the meat in its customary half-tierces, a whole year's supply, and when Mother came in she was exhausted and went to bed immediately after supper. Next day, she had the huge feather bed brought down and set across the clothes line to air, but before she knew it, the wind had whipped into the north and it was bitter cold. She hovered over her open fire until the afternoon, and then she had that thoroughly chilled feather bed brought in and made up for herself. When I returned from school I found her lying in it, and because she complained of chill, I heated bricks and wrapped them to place around her. It was of little use, and by the time Father came in that evening she was in a hard chill. By morning it was her old enemy, pneumonia.

Trained nurses were not available, and the same old kindly Negro woman was called in, who had nursed her before but was far too apt to obey the whims of the sick woman, whose strong will remained, although her good judgment was relaxed.

There came a morning when she lay slack and exhausted upon her pillows. For the moment the terrible wrench of her breathing and the pain of it was somewhat lessened. She was fully conscious, her mind clear, and she smiled at Aunt Margaret, who sat beside her bed.

"Mag," she whispered panting, "I am all exhausted; very hungry. See tomorrow I get some food, real food. I need it so! But first I will sleep awhile. Mag, do you remember, when we were little girls, we read the *Vicar of Wakefield* together? Do you remember how we laughed when we read how Miss Arabella, Araminta, Amelia Skeggs said, 'by the living Jingo, I'm all of a muck of sweat?' Tell the Doctor to stop giving me things to make me drip so, for I feel just like that today!"

Almost instantly she sank into a heavy stertorous lethargy, from which she only once more roused for a moment. Aunt Margaret went to tell Father how naturally she had been talking a few moments ago. He shook his head sadly. He knew the death hunger and the cold sweat.

That night we all stood watching by her bed at the very end. We saw a tremor from head to foot, a few shallow gasping breaths came last, and Mother died on the day after Christmas, 1887.

After the funeral, many things were to be talked over. Aunt Margaret, always consulted in family conclave, thought I should keep house for the family, and indeed I thought so too. My sister must teach, but would be always at hand to refer to if necessary. The first weeks after Mother's death brought a grief more personal, more devastating than a rather youthful person often feels. We had been such comrades in spirit! It was only by the elapse of some time that I arrived at the sober analysis of what I must expect, and the readjustment to present facts.

During the whole course of my life, I have been given to white nights—sleepless, lucid, aware of detailed, consecutive remembrance of things past, when I would lie and watch with the inner eye event chained to event like a moving film. Then also the implications of the future would unroll like a scroll. Following such a night of vision, I would grasp with both hands for the courage needed, and would start forward, former plans having fallen into ruin. There was to be no more schooling for me, nor did I mean to insist upon any more. Nobody even remembered that I wanted it, now that Mother, who cared about it, was gone; they had simply forgotten all about the matter. I had, so I perceived, come back forever to the old home town, back where I could not just then remember that anything interesting had ever happened. I thought of the blind traverse of the Indian trail through the laurel; nobody could tell where I was going, or what would appear outside when the opening came. Life, I had heard somebody say, was mostly second choices. I decided that I must learn housekeeping. The detail of a home like ours included many things not now thought about. I would be kept so busy that there would not be too much time for brooding.

The tobacco-brown Munroe, who had succeeded Uncle Harry, under Father's teaching had developed into the best gardener in town. It was the custom to have upon the table at the one o'clock family dinner one meat dish and five or six vegetables, and our Aunt Fanny could not be expected to attend to the bedrooms, the porches, the milk and butter, and the preparation of all this food for cooking, as well as get the meals. I had to help her, remembering all Mother had taught me in the past year. I sewed, too. I learned to make my own dresses, as girls had to do who wanted to have any, in those times. I helped with other sewing, as was needful. My eyes were strong enough for ordinary purposes by this time.

Living in a small town is a difficult art, discovering both virtues and flaws in the character, and now I lacked the refuge of Mother's larger spirit. But I wanted to feel myself a part of the old town, to believe that I liked it, to be happy in it.

Because of my strict Presbyterian upbringing, I could not share the amusements of the young people who were making an effort at a social life. I knew besides that they would have none of me. How about the older people?

My old friend Beulah was already married. While she was my friend and frequently my instigation, I never cared to imitate her, for she was, herself, inimitable. I was planning a pedestrian attack on society.

First, last, and always, the social life of the church was of necessity the key to social acceptance of a limited kind. The Presbyterians were the most numerous; the Episcopal church, old and well established, included the socially ambitious element and was the most liberal in criticism of life-patterns. At this time the Lutheran and Methodist groups were smaller and composed of simpler folk. Salisbury was not now, and never had been, like Charlotte, a pious town.

I began by asking for a Sunday school class. I had not gone much to Sunday school for Mother held me out of it. Now I took a dozen small boys of the age when, as the old saying goes, they should be "headed up in a barrel and fed through the bung." I made great friends with these urchins, and with their families. I had influence with them, entertained them. They came storming out of the separate class-corner in my wake, not pulling quite so much hair, or throwing quite so many paper wads as they had done before my day.

Then a class was organized in German, with Mrs. Neave as the teacher. Some of the students kept on, and I came to know them as one knows only the people with whom one has worked to an end.

There was the reading club, when other resources failed. This sort of organization, the thin wedge of a good deal of mild *culturine*, developed by way of the Chautauqua, and ran later into women's book clubs, giving a homespun self-education. Such organizations were becoming prevalent even so far south as this. It was a peace-offering to a stay-at-home hungry mind. Some who did not feel called to work in the missionary society, or had no urgent responsibility for their neighbor's moral regulation, found in this some outlet for the imagination. It was customary to choose some preacher or lawyer who might be induced to address the meeting on a literary topic. All the members (mostly women), looked up and were fed by his wisdom. The subject was ordinarily chosen from some well quoted and familiar poet—Tennyson or Scott, for instance, whose works many people owned. Byron was risqué and Browning incomprehensible, while more modern authors had not yet appeared in many collections. It must have been later, by more than a dozen years, that I was told by a nice conventional old politician, who would have stolen votes from his opponent by any method whatever short of murder, what was his conscientious opinion, as a man of decent feeling, of the woman so lost to the realization of what was proper as to read Ibsen!

Returning to our reading club. Dr. Rumple was tried out and found to be so inordinately thorough that his preliminaries were never done. Next, the Reverend Frank Murdoch was tried and found to be the best of teachers, making his subjects of living interest. Sometimes there would be as many as thirty attending his meetings. The reading club was rather a success.

When, that spring, I decided to restore Mother's garden, neglected of late, I found I knew very little about the actuality of such work. I consulted Father, who washed his hands of the whole matter, saying he knew nothing of flowers. Munroe had his cue when he was called in to dig the beds for my annuals. He was as utterly grumpy as only a good servant can be, evidently not considering work in a flower garden a manly occupation. But Father's friend, old Mr. Murdoch, was living in Salisbury then, retired from his stonemason business. He raised flowers as well as vegetables in his garden, and he was an enthusiast, reverting in his deafness to the broadest of Scotch dialects. He cultivated his garden, missed no service at church, prayed prayers in prayer meeting so burred with Scotch that nobody could understand them but the Almighty, and every open night he played checkers with old cronies to any late hour: so Mr. Murdoch was quite at leisure and delighted at being consulted. He was with difficulty restrained from stocking my entire garden offhand. He would thrust his grizzled head across the fence and explain methods, but as he said,

"Hope, ye can nivver do all the wurruck by yersell!"

One day, as I was doggedly excavating near the front gate, a velvety *black* voice said near by: "Now dar you is, Miss Hopey, a diggin' in de yearth an' a devillin' in de groun'! Ah could come in an' help you."

It was Joe Ballard, a huge black fellow who "jobbed 'round," as the saying was. He was said to be an "Affikin Nigger," and the nursemaids frightened their charges with him, saying that he was a "blue gum Nigger wid a mouf rank pisen, same as a rattlesnake." I found him a harmless, kindly old fellow who would sing at his work in a chesty bass which could be heard half a mile. Like most Negroes, he scorned to discriminate flowers from weeds and had to be watched. He was great at deep digging and pulverizing the soil, and my garden prospered.

While I was seeking some outlet for my energy, like an animal circling inside a fence, there was one neighbor who understood and sympathized with me.

Kerr Craige, son of Burton, lived across Fulton Street in front of us. He was one of the best of those excellent lawyers Salisbury has always bred. First he gave me the freedom of his general library of rather serious history books. Then one day he suggested to me that I should "try reading a little law." This was before the days of elementary introduction to legal lore, but I found the books he lent me fascinating.

Why I did not persevere I cannot imagine, for here was a notable opportunity for one looking for a way out. Mr. Craige was not one to draw back from a promise. He would have seen me through. But they laughed at me. I was used to that. But this time the idea of a girl's studying law was too new and too bold. It is doubtful if there were half a dozen women lawyers in the whole United States!

I was like the Negro who was asked to change a ten-dollar

bill. I could not do it, but I was grateful for the compliment paid me. My friend did give me the idea—the feeling of the Law in its antiquity of human wisdom gained by long experience, and this has remained with me ever since. And he gave me more of the confidence which has made me try many new things since then.

These were some of my doors. Others were not wanting. But first of all, my entrance was ministered by the lives my parents had lived so many years and so near the pulse of the community.

XXIII

DOING THE NEXT THING

It is a temptation, in chronicles like this, to treat one's own doings too minutely. Nobody has seen just what you are trying to show. There are not many alive, for instance, who remember the kind of clothes I wore, clearly enough to describe them. They were in the fashion of the day, James Wren planned them, Miss Mollie made them, and I believe that if necessary I could reproduce them today to fit some slim granddaughter. I must be circumstantial if I tell at all how I made myself at home in my home town. I want to make you see the dear old place as I came to know it, both personally and objectively.

Mourning, at the South, was a convention we all rigidly observed. After Mother's death, my sister and I had our mourning exactly alike. There were English crape bonnets with long crape veils, the bonnets being tied demurely under the chin with black grosgrain ribbon. The black cashmere dresses that we wore had tight-fitted "basques" and were elaborately hooped and plated with wide bands of crepe. Another plainer black dress gave a rainy-day costume. Dresses in that day were gradually contracting from the wide crinolines of Civil War times, and the skirts now had become a round rolling-pin sort of shape with a protuberance behind called a "bustle." These were at their largest the year I was at Miss Baldwin's. One Sunday Berry had laid her red hymnbook on the shelf afforded by our Principal's bunched-up rear, and it rode to church there, attended by giggles from all the decorous procession of young ladies.

By this time we wore a special petticoat which held out our wash dresses, but hoops were built into our heavy dresses. These were difficult to sit down in, without disarranging the loopings of the dress or locating painfully on a gridiron made of sharp-edged hoops collapsed crisscross on the seat.

Besides acquaintanceship renewed with the good friends in Salisbury, besides the responsibility, of which more later, of servants, meals, desserts, and the routine of housekeeping, I found I had to spend uncounted hours in sewing and mending. I could take neat stitches, but never had cut or fitted anything. That summer fifty years ago, after school was over, my sister moved her sewing machine out on the back gallery to make up the year's supply of cotton things. My sister was an expert. She could have made a living as a dressmaker anywhere, and she had an eager pupil. But before the ruffles and tucks could be set going, I had to make a whole set of underthings of fine white drilling, such as he wore in summer, for my father. He was as fastidious as any modern miss with his frequent changes, and the care of his clothing was another responsibility taken over from Mother. The pearl buttons used on his white shirts were always getting ironed off by the laundress, and woe be to me if I did not sew them on before he took out that single shirt from a whole drawer-full all fully buttoned, for that was a faculty he had. Then he would say, "All the buttons are off all my shirts!" And now these underclothes! The tailor cut them to his measure, and all that June I labored and perspired over them. One day a neighbor came in and sat with us on the back gallery. I was lamenting loudly because I had just had to pick out a carefully sewed closing which I had made on the "lady" side. She settled the matter for me forever, saying, "Why daughter, don't you know women *lead over*, and menfolks *grab across?*"

After that we put in a long busy summer, and autumn came on with a better feeling of adjustment. My niece was

DOING THE NEXT THING

sent off to school, and I saw her go with less feeling of disappointment. I was becoming interested in those myriad things which cannot be learned out of books.

I do not remember just when Livingstone College was established in Salisbury. It was a sore spot with most of us, being an institution for Negroes, supported by the Northern Methodists. It was first opened in a large house to the west of town, which was added to year by year as the students multiplied. My father was the physician employed there. Our dislike of Negro schools was founded more on the thought of what we had to do without than on envy of what they had been freely given. Father was quite arbitrary with them; he commanded the respect they paid him, showed them much toleration and understanding, and I know that his fees were never left unsettled.

I was the one who remained on hand in this year, when Father was out in the evening, sitting up until he returned or I knew that he would not return. Accordingly we sat waiting for bedtime one evening, and there came a messenger from Livingstone. Father returned in a very short space of time, slumped into his chair, and gave a disgusted snort.

"Anybody very sick?" I asked.

"Humph!" said Father. "Things are coming to a pretty pass when Negro girls get the hysterics!"

"What did you find to do for them, Father?"

"Gave them an emetic, and a compound cathartic pill apiece. Gave them something else to think about. Humph!"

At the head of this school was a remarkable Negro whose name was Price. He was well educated, and the most finished orator I ever listened to. Once he was asked to speak before the Methodist Conference of North Carolina. At the end of a magnificent effort, outlining the proper relations of the races, he said in conclusion:

"My white brethren, what we need is more educated Negroes, better educated Negroes, and *blacker* Negroes!" He himself was the large, intelligent, coal-black type, and my father used to call him a "Gentleman in Ebony." The difference between the manners of young Negro students, so much better in Salisbury than in other towns, was due, as we were convinced, to the good judgment of Price.

Towards Christmas that same year, my school friend, Addie Hood, who lived in Georgia and who had never lost track of me, wrote an urgent invitation to come and spend three weeks at her home near Atlanta. Father, although he had not commented upon it, was pleased by the way in which I had tried to adapt myself to my new tasks. He was not only willing, but eager to have me enjoy the change thus offered. Aunt Margaret came to us to be a sort of rallying point for the household at Christmas. My niece was coming home, the Doctor was always busy. I "lightened my mourning" after the first year and added white accessories. The visit seemed so desirable that I could not sleep for several nights anticipating it.

The bitter winters of several years preceding had given way in 1888 to very mild temperature. It was like a sunny bracing spring day, scarcely cold at all, when Addie met me in the great "car shed" then considered one of the wonders of Atlanta. That afternoon we went shopping and took a train going west, reaching the small town where Addie lived, in time for supper. Immediately I could feel the difference in the atmosphere of things. At home we were so sober, so busy, so earnest; here in Georgia people had plenty of time to be genial and enjoy life, plenty of time for a good time. A large group of young folk gathered that evening around the open fire in Mrs. Hood's plain sitting room. They had come to welcome the newcomer, to chatter and gossip, but mainly because they were in the habit of gathering there. Over near the lamp, a game of old-fashioned whist was begun; somebody passed around a box of candy, and one of Addie's cousins cornered me on the sofa at the fireside and began preliminaries for a red-hot flirtation. Mrs. Hood, elderly and genial, sat knitting and throwing in a word now and then, showing she knew the thoughts of this crowd as well as her daughter did.

Next morning we had our breakfast in bed, and Mrs. Hood sat down to see us eat it: then we dressed and started down the street. Two of the young fellows of the night before joined us. By the time we had reached the postoffice we had accumulated quite an escort. The young man who had attached himself to me the night before was on hand to make directly for my side and keep me laughing at his nonsense.

Three weeks of jolly comradeship followed, and I took to it mightily. I had to warn off my devoted swain when he tried to put his arms 'round me, helping me on with my cloak in the hall. Once I laid my hand out from under the table with his clasped over it where he had been squeezing it vigorously, but after I had convinced him I didn't like to be "pawed," we understood each other, and went in for a glorious time with no end to the chaffing and daffing. Together we all went to Atlanta and saw and heard Gilbert and Sullivan's *Mikado*, the first stage play of any kind I ever had attended.

Our last merrymaking was a picnic on Kennesaw Mountain, by moonlight, in that abnormally warm January. It gave nobody a cold, not even a shiver. The local paper, bidding me good-bye, cited me as that "charming visiting young lady," and when all was over, and I found Munroe, and nobody else, to meet me when I returned home, I gave a sigh for the passing of the jolliest holiday I had ever known.

That was not all. It is wonderful the effect produced on a young girl when she establishes her right to choose an admirer, to be preferred by someone, to hold her own in the give and take of social intercourse. She is like the boy who has been accepted by his gang and is a regular fellow. The feeling of belonging to my generation, formerly so deficient in me, rose on my finding myself called in the slang of the day, "such a sweet girl, and awfully popular with the men." It was not sticky or self-conscious, as I remember it, only that I had learned to play a jolly game and could hold my own at it. In the over-serious atmosphere of my home, this could not be done, but it was good to know that where I did not have this handicap I could begin offhand and be recognized as a social asset.

Back home again and taking up the routine, I found that our cook, Aunt Fanny, intended to leave us at the beginning of spring and go back "Down wha I come from." She was acting with consideration and honesty in telling us, and not going traipsing off at the moment she took the notion, as Negroes dearly loved to do. She would give no particular reason for going, and because we were used to her unforeseen vagaries and respected her industry, we were sorry to lose her.

Servants, as I have somewhere remarked, were our only luxury, if you may call that a luxury which is a daily study in adjustment. What the guidance and control of two grown people does to the inner reactions of a young girl, the psychologists must tell us. I fear it is something far too stimulating.

Our southern Negro is a person whose qualities, and they are very good in many ways, are so different from those of the white man near whom he lives, that the more you are sure you understand him, the more you are certain to meet some quirk or quibble that sets all your expectations awry. Aunt Fanny was, it seemed, afflicted by the fact that I "waren't nothin' but a girl chile," who was yet in authority and she had to take my orders, and have me give out the meals for her. As long as my sister kept her hand on the reins ahead of mine, all was well, but now I was growing too confident and executive.

This "giving out" system was one which had been perfected in long years of dealing with the Negroes, who considered all eatables as much their own property as their master's. They could be trusted with money uncounted, but they were not proof against a stray chunk of bacon or a quadrant of pie. So pantries must be locked, and each meal must have its constituent parts measured and placed in the bowls and trays for the cook. This the mistress must do herself, because if she looked away, even for a second, the maid would take a lightning scoop of flour or sugar and have a little treat. Aunt Fanny used to enjoy muddling me up in my inexperience. Then she loved to appear at the parlour door when I had afternoon callers, wearing a dirty gingham apron and looking her *cookyest*.

"Miss-Sope," she would say, "You ain't gimme dat lard I needs to fry dem fish wid." But I was growing too competent, and Aunt Fanny decided to take her departure.

She was easily replaced by a slim, elegantly formed, and too smooth-spoken woman named Charlotte, who, being a mulatto, was more quick-witted. Charlotte's seasoning was excellent, her kitchen always tidy, but I had been told by some former employer of hers that she was "light-fingered." Very carefully, then, I watched and carried my keys, gave out the supplies and locked up the pantry. I must have been over-zealous and attracted the attention of Charlotte, but all that summer she made no sign, and we congratulated ourselves that we had come by so good a servant so easily.

When November nights had grown cool and frosty and the meat would be properly chilled, hog-killing time came, when Munroe's pride and delight, the six fine porkers, had to be slaughtered. There was much for her mistress, as well as for Charlotte, to do. I was working along with her, cutting up lard for rendering, without any perception of wastage, when suddenly she turned, and, lifting a large dishpan pushed back on the kitchen table, she showed me, piled beneath it, a peck or more of neatly cut squares of fat pork ready for the rendering kettle.

"I put dem dere right under yo' face an' eyes, Miss Hope, jus' to show you how easy I could do it any other time. I ain' dishones', but somebody done tole you I is! Effn I wan' ter steal, I sho' is smart enough ter do it. Jus' look at all dem pounds o' good meat I could er took dis mornin' and you would'n er known!"

I was so taken aback that I did not know what answer to make to Charlotte's lesson. She had that day taught me something worth learning for the proper management of servants, and of fellow mortals in general. I resolved never again to watch pinches, but to concede what is needful in time and material and then look to results. Moreover, all those not wholly reprobate can be appealed to by the desire of doing right which is innate in everyone.

This chapter is taken up with the narrow things of home, even as I said it must be. During the time of it, I had been growing interested in many of the things which the town outside of four walls could show. I like to take a walk now and then, and point out our celebrities, and that must come in the next chapter. School had receded from my desires, and I was no longer fretting because I could not leave old Salisbury and become book-learned. When the news struck town amidships that my friend Beulah's husband had done the very unexpected and very indulgent, and, the gray gossips said, the very foolish thing of sending his beautiful young wife to study art in New York City, in the studio of Elliott Daingerfield and among the first coterie of truly American artists who had gathered in association there, I could only rejoice with her.

"Art, indeed, when she doesn't know how to keep house yet! Her mother has to go and untangle her and clean up her house every week!" So it was said on our street rather ill-naturedly, and quite untruthfully, for Beulah could do anything she chose, and do it better than most people. I was delighted that she was going to have her chance. She accepted her limitations far less equably than I did, and she was a gifted person. The Beulah Moore who danced and who flirted, who talked witty nonsense and who always managed to give the old ladies of her neighborhood the titillation of an unexpected shock, was not the real Beulah at all! But the town would be duller than ever without her. Some of those I liked as companions were at school, at Peace Institute, or Saint Mary's in Raleigh. There was very little to do about persons one's own age to play with.

XXIV

VARIETIES IN SALISBURY

THIS CHAPTER heading could be the title of the whole collection, save the trips and stays in other places now and then. So much of the recent space has been used for the house under the oaks, that we will walk abroad and see what has been happening in Salisbury, the town proper, outside my home.

While we sat under our oaks on the one hand, and the Bruners lived under their grapevines on the other, tenants came, lived, bought, sold out, moved away from the house between. These alternations had commenced in Mother's time. The house in question seemed a pleasant sort of place, but it was just one of those houses. Since the reopening of the mines out in the county at Gold Hill and other places, a succession of those who came to manage them rented the house between. They were not seldom people with adventurous pasts, and would be gamblers at heart, as all gold miners are obliged to be.

First that I remember was Mr. Cady, fat, middle-aged, with tidy New England ways—he who had the pretty young wife and used the Company's funds to keep her happy in sleepy old Salisbury. Then his ill-doing came to light, and his wife eloped with her "cousin," while her doting husband drifted away, giving us, as he left, a great rattan reclining chair, which would creak and groan like a ghost, in its corner, every time the weather changed suddenly.

After him came the Australian miner, who showed me the various colors of gold from all the mining regions round the world. After him again came the man who married one of Mr. Bruner's daughters. When I was returned from school, the Eames family were settled in the house between. He was a Jewish gentleman, who resembled the pictures of Disraeli, and he had an English wife. She was a Gentile, a super-quiet person. As a family they seemed entirely harmonious, although he announced that he adhered to no belief, religious or atheistic. His wife and daughters belonged to the Reverend Frank Murdoch's flock.

Dr. Eames used to come over and argue with Mother, and one after another would demolish all the soul houses she could build for herself. Finally she would laugh at him, and say, "Dr. Eames, you feel that you haven't left me a shred! But in spite of all you say, I feel as confident as ever I did." He was a charming gentleman; he would laugh genially and they would change the subject. The day Mother died, Dr. Eames came over to inquire, and being told there was no longer any hope, he went away, openly and unrestrainedly weeping.

The Eames family owned a red and yellow macaw, a superb great bird, which would climb the elm beside the house, hang upside down from the topmost branches and shriek and shriek. This bird loved viciously to bite any living thing upon which it could pinch up flesh enough to fill its murderous beak, a beak which had the fine bold curve of Disraeli's nose. Errand boy, Negro, dog—all feared it equally, but its master it would not bite. Sitting upon his shoulder and murmuring endearments in his ear, the macaw would ride about the place, punctuating its utterances with an occasional snap of its great mandibles. The Eames moved away in their turn, and the macaw went with them, leaving a scarlet and yellow memory threading the branches of the elm like a flickering flame.

Small-town folk such as we, accustomed to much yard space, lived the year long in the same frame of streets and houses, but the lights of time and season varied infinitely about us. We became friendly with the neighbors' pets, we knew intimately a hundred trees in our own and near-by lots. For instance, there might stand near the street a certain cedar, symmetrical, stiff, and pointed. One summer afternoon a storm, lashing it, bends it double. In winter it stands under the moon cased in ice, or snow powders it white, or in the rain it drips on your umbrella as you pass. One's neighbors' row of daffodils can give as much pleasure as your own. Nothing is so ingratiating as the flowering shrubs that poke their fingers between the pickets of the fence as one walks by. And so, in long acquaintance, I came to love Mrs. Wilson's double-flowering cherry tree.

Down Fulton Street, past Mr. Bruner's, stood three houses which my parents knew occupied by three sisters, married early, settled almost in their childhood as was the early custom. The first of these, a widow, lived with her sons in a little brown dwelling shaded by magnificent trees, and one of these was a poem. It was an enormous, symmetrically growing, double cherry, and if there was no late frost it flowered into drifting whiteness of bloom like the garments of Heaven. After the blooms were shattered, the tree was, for the rest of the year, just a huge cherry tree. On the porch of that same house hung a large cage where lived a mockingbird, which seemed happy in captivity. Not only did Dicky sing over and over the song of every bird in the bush, and sing them better, but he was able to imitate all manner of shrill sounds, the creaking of the windlass on Mr. Bruner's well, the squeak of his own front gate; also he could whistle like any boy in the neighborhood calling his own particular dog. The dogs would come and paw the fence and act sorely puzzled. It almost seemed that Mrs. Wilson's Dicky understood the nature of a joke. He was a well known character in the neighborhood, to whom the children paid homage in grasshoppers.

Next to the Wilsons lived the John D. Browns. The husband, traveling for a great store in New York City, took too good care of his family. They cuddled down into their nest and had nerves. When you visited there, you were told absorbing details of the headache of last week, told with gestures, with blue-eyed confidence. Truly you became just as interested in that headache as in an active adventure, a victory over desperate odds. Miss Alice, the eldest daughter, had apparently never been touched by one little ray of outdoor sunshine. She lay like a white cocoon, in a little snowy room adjoining her mother's, her complexion like a pale rose-petal, her face framed in dark hair reposing upon an unwrinkled pillow. Her body was motionless, covered with the spotless white coverlid, her coquettish nightgown ruffles entirely undishevelled.

Miss Alice was a chronic invalid, suffering from what old Miss Betsy Julian once defined as "A powerful weakness in the spine of her back." She had worse headaches than her mother's and she would "marvel sweetly upon her ills" to those who came to visit her. What was unusual, she was just as deeply interested in, and sympathetic with the aches and ills of other people. If I came in and said, "I've a fresh cold, Miss Alice; maybe I'd better not come too near you," she would answer:

"Do you hear that, Ma? Hope has a cold. I hope it soon gets better. I saw you, Hope, running home in the rain. I could see that it was raining quite hard, and I said to Ma, 'Hope will be having a cold next time she comes to see us,' and sure enough so you have!"

Miss Alice was given every item of neighborhood news, which was brought to her in her cage much as the grasshoppers were given to Dicky; and she transmitted all that was told her to the next caller, quite impartially, and without exaggeration or cattiness. When Miss Alice was told about an event, it was the same as putting it into the paper, for her prim room was the clearing house of all the personal intelligence of the town. Even when she had on her head-handkerchief, when she was immersed in the endurance of "terrible suffering," she would come to the surface and comment in a faint voice upon the fresh gossip her sisters might bring her.

Mary, the third of the neighbor-sisters, was a very different woman. Married in her middle teens to a man twice her age, she had borne him a large family of sons. Her husband was lately become an invalid, and the sons and wives of the married ones, lived there all together in her large house. The brothers agreed well enough, but their young wives constantly contended among themselves—among themselves, but never with the knowledge of the mother-in-law. How she controlled their warring egos was her secret, but she made all these self-assertive daughters-in-law respect her living and mourn her dead. As for the sons, they adored their mother. Although they were made of clay not too uncommon, she lived to see one of them a United States senator. The others, if not so conspicuous, made good citizens.

Strong, capable, lovely in face and serene in temperament—what more of worth could a woman of her day manifest? She seldom left her home except to go to church. Her progress, of a Sunday morning, to Methodist worship, in her plain black dress with its broad white collar, wearing her poke bonnet which showed silvery curls at the sides of her unwrinkled cheeks tinted like a sea-shell: who that has seen her and admired her can forget her!

When her aged husband lay a-dying, Dr. Summerell said to him, "You should be thanking God for this good wife who nurses you so tenderly." Even on his deathbed this was a genial soul. He answered, "Yes, Doctor, and haven't I raised her well, from fifteen years old, to be a comfort to me!"

It was across the street from the Overman home that the Fisher house stood, in my day densely shaded, and with a great neglected garden, in part of which the little Catholic Church was built. This old house held much mystery for us. Its inmates did not fit into the scheme of things in everyday Salisbury, but we were very proud of them. We loved to show strangers where the elder Charles Fisher, the friend of Calhoun, had lived, and his son, Charles Frederick, who rode away among the first, at the head of a regiment he had himself equipped for the Confederacy, to be shot from his horse at Manassas. After the War, his two daughters lived on in the old house. They lived in the closest seclusion there, with their remarkable aunt, Miss Christine. It was said that the latter lady was the critic and the inspiration of Christian Reid's novels, and that she in her turn drew on the keen judgment of many a learned Catholic priest. Each manuscript was copied for publication in her exquisite handwriting.

A little further along this same street stood a great, square colonial home, which never had been painted. It, too, possessed stately mahogany furniture upon which the haircloth was beginning to fray. Over the drawing room mantel hung the portrait of a young beauty in a hooped dress, made low off the shoulders. She was holding a fan of feathers to shade her lovely face as she looked out directly at you from the canvas. The frame was not the conventional gilded moulding, but was made of oak leaves cut out of russet leather and lapped to form a continuous border. The fire would play lights over the brasses of the fireplace beneath this portrait, while the same face, grown older, was smiling to welcome her guests. She had a voice like a harpstring, and said always pleasant things. She was a notable beauty, who had married, as beauties will, the quiet man among her many suitors. But never on that account did she abate her own airyness, or lose her love of admiration.

Like anyone with aspiration, like my own simple self I could say, Mrs. Shober felt smothered by the small-town stillness and the need of pinching, every day. She was formed for something more distinguished, and she tried in her own fashion to win to it. She sent out her sons and daughters, advancing them like pieces in her game. She trusted that she would see them reach the king row some day. One of her girls was so utterly lovely to behold, so radiant, so vivacious, and possessed such great violet eyes, that she was certain to find a fortune at the end of the rainbow. Her generous smile, her perfect teeth were as beautiful as her eyes. It was said of her that she was beautiful just as far as you could see when she opened her mouth and laughed at you her opulent lazy laugh. But when her mother sent her out to bring back the something the War had stolen away, she failed utterly. She refused successively all her wealthy Northern suitors, and, as her mother had done, she came home and married a pleasant, honest, home-town gentleman, Mrs. Boyden's son, a man whom she had played with when they were little folks.

We used to have one set of visitors—thank Heaven they did not come very often—who were very high and choosy. They were greatly contemptuous of the small-town atmosphere of Salisbury. They used to say, "The Hendersons, and the Boydens, and the Shobers, they are all the real people who live in this one-horse town." This used to enrage me, not on account of those they mentioned, for I esteemed them all, but for those they left out.

That would leave out, for instance, all those with whom I sat in church on Sunday. That would leave out Mr. Bruner, than whom no person of the old life lives so clearly today, and none more worthily. I have always thought the better of my penetration, because of the esteem, dating from my early childhood, I felt for this man, and now, looking backward, I wonder how I judged him so clearly. His face was not one to allure a little girl's idealism. His brows were deeply lined, like cooled lava, and the blue eyes under, stirred the certainty that fire still glowed somewhere within. I do not think he knew I admired him. If he had, he was so used to children and their whims that he would have given it no undue importance. But I found in him, as well as in my father, a certitude and a stability that counted.

Being a printer by trade, he had gained for himself a liberal education from his calling. Well do I remember the old secretary with green silk glass curtains, behind which he kept his choice books. I remember his opening it to give me the best volumes in print regarding the American Indian. He was the head of a large clan of descendants, and my friend Beulah was his oldest grandchild.

Mr. Bruner always made the communion wine from his own grapes. The color and the fragrance of it sufficed him, for no one ever heard that he more than tasted it; but what an aroma of richness and of grapes well ripened in the sunshine would spread abroad in the old church when Mr. Bruner, as a senior elder, removed the covers from the silver goblets and, with a cup in each hand, began his round among the congregation.

It was easy to see the insufferable prig I had been when I began to keep my father's house, and how I ended by esteeming very humbly my thin aspirations, comparing them with the warm pulsing human qualities in the people I was coming really to know. I felt the deepest interest in my fellow towns-folk, eccentric, frivolous, petty, pathetic, great-hearted, wise, and loving—all by turns. Every society must so manifest if understood by sympathy, whether it be the old predatory "Four Hundred" in their wigwams of stone, or the ancient and honorable order of tramps and wayfarers under the sky, by the spacious roadside and countryside.

City improvements began to come to Salisbury in this decade, and of these the waterworks were most obviously needed. The huge old wells, dug deep into a sort of rotten friable granite, had grateful coolness of water that was delightful, but open barrel-drains, such as they, were dangerous. Besides, they were unprotected. When Dr. Rumple's pet cat Victor pursued amatory urges and fell into our well, we did not find it out for a week or two. Then, although it was cold winter time, we sent for the well-cleaner, and he had our whole back yard a-slop for a week, getting the bottom clear so that he could salt it. After the new standpipe held up the finger of scorn to the old-fashioned wells, some of the younger married folks put in bathrooms. We girls called them "The Bath-tub Aristocracy." Perhaps cleanliness, which John Wesley has assured us comes next to godliness, is not, after all, such a poor foundation for self-congratulation, but conversations would always be prefaced, "Just as I was stepping into my b-a-wth yesterday,"—or—"I wasn't dressed yet, I had just finished bathing—" with infinite gusto. This irked us, we who had not yet graduated from the class with the tin-tub-on-the-back-fence, to be brought in with cold water and warm, in pails, for the semi-weekly rite.

Perhaps this is as good a place as any to bring in a very special kind of a party, given by one of the young married set, always, then and now, in the forefront of the quest for polite novelty. Cocktail parties are considered the most ultra-modern festivity that is perpetrated, but only listen to the description of the cocktail party in Salisbury in the late eighteen-eighties!

Written in that studied, perpendicular, handwriting we used to call "hickory splint," the invitations, sent pretty generally, were scarcely legible. Of those who received them, nobody was altogether certain as to the exact nature of the entertainment offered. The notes seemed to say, "Luncheon" but the time set was half-past three in the afternoon. "That must be Virginia style," everybody said, and repeated. We all dressed up in our best and went, maidens and matrons, flocking down the street in the early afternoon of autumn.

It was a new home (and there were not many brand-new homes in Salisbury), papered very dark inside, as was the style, furnished with the knobbed walnut furniture then in fashion and, with the few who had any money, just beginning to replace the inherited mahogany which most of us were keeping because we must. In the front parlour, our hostess had placed a gleaming punch bowl with decorative grapes and apples heaped about it. Several of the social set, for this was their party, stood about in decolletage, and served the guests. This formal dress was in itself a daring innovation. They handed the beverage around in small cups. Of course in those pre-prohibition days whatever their opinions were, the most sedate and pious owned to knowing the taste of fruit punch properly "laced." All the ladies sipped and praised, and sipped and chatted with each other:

"The word we couldn't read must have been 'puncheon' and not 'luncheon.' How original! Now, of course, she will give us something to eat, and indeed we'll need it to hold this down."

But in the sitting room, on the other side of the folding door appeared more of the same sort of thing. A highly spiced brandy-punch was the beverage there, the spice of which would set anybody hiccoughing. The minister's wives and the matrons of the graver sort set their glasses down after tasting them, and looked embarrassed. The company sidled about and drifted into a third room.

There, in the great bay-window stood a third bowl, this time of apple-toddy; as a man afterwards declared, "fit to put a head on a brass monkey." Over this last bowl presided the hostess. Flushed and boasting how she had induced the leading saloonkeeper of the town to come to her home, and compound this old southern drink so it should be exactly right, she ladled it out.

Hurriedly the sedater, more wary guests scuttled away. The sober matrons left with indignant waggles of their full-bustled backs. The daring, rushing in where angels would have feared to tread, soon were gurgling, hiccoughing, weaving to and fro, and giving little idiotic squeaks. A few girls sipped, and deliberately listened for the effect, but most women knew this to be no place for them. Two young women escaped and found a seat in the garden, whence they could watch the rest of the show from behind the shrubbery.

At about five, the men began to arrive. They had been better edited than the ladies, and soon hilarity resounded in peals behind the lighted windows. Some of the gentlemen came out pretty promptly, pulling their vests down with the ineffable smugness of a man who has just had a toddy—or a kiss! But when at last the satirical observers were driven home by the gathering night, more than one pair of young men had preceded them, clinging together, lurching down the street—"United we stand, divided we fall."

XXV

THE SEAMY SIDE OF THE HOME TOWN

IN THIS LAST decade of my chronicle, the impression comes, the farms of the County were being tilled more skillfully, and more was produced, more sold. I have mentioned the revival of a problematic search after gold, a thing Salisbury let alone for itself, although glad to sell needed supplies to those who reopened the old mines. Really and actually, the thing that maintained and supported Salisbury at the time was wholesale and retail whiskey. There were by this time small tobacco factories. There was a railroad junction, a ginhouse, and a huge tobacco warehouse. The stores needed to supply the retail trade stood up and down Main Street; but whiskey was the chief concern of the place. This was so well understood that when I gave a black kitten to a friend in Charlotte, she promptly named it "Boozey" to indicate its birthplace.

When the farmers came to town on Saturday, they usually brought their sunbonneted wives with them. They would unhitch in the lot behind the tobacco warehouse, not far from the center of town, and there feed their horses and mules. The women returned thither after their trading was done and awaited their husbands. I can shut my eyes and see that bare enclosure, with its trampled clay, and its swarming flies in summer. I can remember that perched on the high wagon seats there would usually be a few droopy, tired, country women, waiting for the men who when they came were sure to be in liquor. This made one of the unforgetable pictures to be seen in Salisbury on any Saturday afternoon. These were not riffraff, not poor whites. These people were likely to be good farmers, respectable family men. They considered this weekly orgy as the inalienable right and the proper indulgence of a hard-working man who had little diversion, while their wives accepted it as part of the contrariety of life. The day of a political meeting, or a circus, brought the whole population of the County, men with their wives and children, to town at once. The circus was a treat which gave them wonders to relate for a whole year. The man was poor indeed who could not scrape money enough together to take his "ole 'ooman, and the young uns" to the circus, but at least he could bring them to the parade even if they rode in somebody else's wagon. As to politics, in this time they were so one-sided that a rally became simply a festival of self-congratulation upon knowing all there was to know regarding candidates, policies, and platforms. The fun of feeling so entirely convinced might be punctuated by a few fights regarding minor questions, mostly about candidates to be nominated. A man worth voting for was worth fighting for.

Politics indeed was to my girlish mind the puzzle of all puzzles. I did not wonder that it was thought far too intricate for women's comprehension. When I was a half-grown girl, and an election was in progress, two boys of the neighborhood stopped at our front gate to talk; I could not imagine why. They had not been accustomed to do so, but later I recognized that they noticed me because they thought they had done something significant and needed the adulation of the female.

They told me how they had been "voting niggers" all day, placing in the hands of men who could not read, a ballot which they would not have cast if they had known what was on it, and hustling the ignorant fellows into the line along the front of the ballot boxes, with somebody to urge them on from behind. Before this day I had never considered the question of practical politics.

"Don't you think that was not fair?" I asked.

"No indeed I don't. Who gave the niggers the vote in the first place? Good enough joke on the Yankees, that's what I think!" and the boys went off laughing.

I brought this story in to Father. He "tut-tutted" about it; then said, "It's bad and it's sinful, I reckon, but everybody does that way." He went on to describe how, when he was a young doctor just come to town, he used to see the rival political parties of that day, Whig and Democrat, collect all the "sorry" white men and pen them up in rival doggeries at the foot of Main Street, where such places had always been. Sometimes they kept them there for a whole week before election day. Sometimes they stole them from each other, but they kept them too drunk to know much, and they would vote them and then let them go.

"That was bad," I said.

"Yes, Daughter, it *was* bad, and in this world, such doings have to be paid for. But about everybody is tarred with the same stick!"

In after life, I found a good deal of this same tar could be smelled. Sometimes they called it fragrant patriotism, sometimes practical politics, sometimes economics, or self-preservation, or something high-flown, but, as my father said, it all was tar, all off the same old stick.

There was not much limit to the revenge taken, as occasion served, on those who had the temerity to think differently from the ruling majority. There was Mr. Boyden, for instance, who was born in Massachusetts, and who, North or South, was undeniably a crotchety disagreeable old fellow. Town hoodlums hanged this man in effigy in front of his own house one night, for some political reason, while a crowd of better citizens, as they would have called themselves, looked on and guffawed. Such doings do not make for sweetness and light.

And then, of course, beneath the surface of society, slimy

deeds crawled, as they have always done in dark places since the beginning.

There was a pretty girl whom I had been used to seeing in church for many a Sunday, who suddenly stopped coming. When asked the reason, my sister, true to her conviction that eighteen was no older than ten, pursed her lips, shook her head, and refused to say anything definite. On a morning, I met this girl in the street, just opposite the Manse, and she made as though she did not recognize or see me. I must have looked conscious, or doubtful, or embarrassed in some way, for she wheeled in her tracks suddenly and cried out in a strange, uncontrolled voice,

"Why don't you speak to me, Hope?"

"I am speaking. Good morning, Annie," I answered. Annie now stood barring the way.

"I am just as good as you, just as good, you saintly little pussy-cat," she screamed out. "You need not think you can ignore me!" and she burst out into hysterical crying. I turned and fled ignominiously from the scene. I did not know what to do. I knew myself to be in touch with something sinister. When I asked her, my sister refused to tell me, but I guessed. I had uncovered a deal in the old trade which makes a woman a thing and traffics with her, a deal which had reached out and made merchandise of poor, pretty Annie. I never saw her again. Her shamed, distressed face has remained always in my mind to keep me questioning the way of a man with a maid, which is evil and the cause of nameless horror. And if I may be personal, I have done more; I have helped on a cause, helped form an institution which handles many cases. I owe that effort to Annie.

Three of the five churches of Salisbury then organized, joined together one spring to have and to hold what was then called a "protracted meeting." It was the era of revivalism, the day of the Gospel hymns, of Moody and Sankey. The preacher must be invited in from outside. The one chosen was a man of acknowledged piety, a Bible student of the literalistic sort, one who took that great collection of ancient religious aspiration and devoutness, and welded it into one mighty battle-axe instead of seeing in it the varied spiritual arsenal of many thousand years.

This man would not come to preach to us unless a specified number of prayer meetings should be held beforehand, and an auditorium, the largest obtainable, be prepared. In spring, the large, centrally-located tobacco warehouse was not in use; so it was cleared, fitted with benches, and a platform built across one end. Then all the good people of the town went to prayers. There were public prayer meetings, and cottage prayer meetings. Choirs were organized. Pious old maids—people not usually considered of any importance —went around with that expression of joyful exaltation which means the knowing of some blessed secret. Dr. Rumple ceased expounding doctrines and began to talk about conduct, a change he well might make, for there were sheep of varied fleeces in his flock. By these means, a strong current of religious anticipation was turned in the direction of the expected revival. When the tall, ascetic corpse-candle of a preacher came and began his impassioned appeals, the people bowed to his eloquence like fields of ripe grain. No one would consent to stay away from evening service at the great warehouse. Large as it was, it was nightly full to the doors. Church people were asked to give room for sinners by remaining at home, spending the time in prayer, but no one was willing to miss the thrill of these meetings. It was too absorbing. The preacher was a sincere man who did not work for self-advertisement, although he thoroughly knew the psychology by which a great revival must be worked up, managed, and guided. By the lever of his burning zeal, he moved our self-centered, sordid old town as it had never been moved before, and has never been since.

Human emotion, after it is dead, does not make a handsome corpse. No one should try to estimate living aspiration by dissecting the dead shell it leaves behind it. Religion seems, in our time, to have somewhat passed out of the revival stage of its development into something not so readily defined; perhaps this change is permanent—we do not know —but there is no use in our vaunting ourselves, and boasting that we are more enlightened and more worthy. Instead, we should regret that we no longer have access to a reservoir of power, once so easily tapped. Religious enthusiasm nowadays gets a buffet from every hand, and there is much concerning the significant history of religion in our country which has been forgotten, and its influence discounted. This will be for the future to estimate more fairly.

This revival, a historic event if ever one occurred in Salisbury, continued for many weeks. It became intense, earnest, desperate. The easy emotionalism of the Methodists of that day did not carry them. They had to take the things as quietly as if they had been Quakers. The Presbyterians felt strong emotional swayings and impulses that they were ashamed of not being able to control. Even the Episcopalians were drawn into it.

While that excellent man, and determined Anglican, the Reverend Frank Murdoch, distrusted the whole revival movement, he could not decently refuse counsel and religious comfort and absolution to those of his parish who insisted on coming and confessing their errors to him. Indeed, it was wickedly said by some, not of his flock, that one of his vestry meetings had broken up in testimony and tears like nothing so much as a Methodist experience meeting!

Society was shaken. The owners of the whiskey firms sneered, for they had chosen their part and intended to adhere to it, but they could not prevent their employees' going

THE SEAMY SIDE OF SALISBURY

by benches-full to the meetings, where many of them pledged themselves to throw away their very livelihood in the interest of what they were assured was right.

When, late in April, the results of these great meetings were tabulated, all the churches were found to be greatly strengthened, and the weaker ones were fairly doubled in numbers.

After concluding his work, the preacher called a meeting of the business interests as represented in the membership of the churches. He asked, "What is to be done for these people who have thrown away their jobs and are penniless because they are bound to get right with God?"

It was decided to establish a cotton mill, and all the stock was immediately subscribed. The president was a Presbyterian layman who would never allow himself to be proposed for church office, because, as he declared to my father, the handling of money, the very touch of it, however meticulous the honesty of the business was known to be, in his opinion unfitted a man for distinctively religious leadership. Not that he did not see the need for honest business. The other mill official elected was the Reverend Frank Murdoch himself. He had been born with keen business acumen; his executive ability had long craved legitimate outlet. He gave his services freely.

The Salisbury Cotton Mill was one of the advance movements of the industrialization of the South. Everyone connected with it was personally known to both of its executives. It gave employment where none had been before, and it prospered exceedingly. It is the fashion to decry moving to town to work in the mills; and as such mills came to be operated by outsiders for all that the traffic would stand, some of the instances will bear out the criticism. But who that knew the condition of the one-horse farmer could say he had stepped into a narrower life when he moved into a mill village?

The "great revival" put the churches of Salisbury in command of the town for a time, making it as decent outwardly as small towns ever are, although no one for decades after the War would have described it so.

Did this reformation last? Does anything last in this world? Why, in every generation, do we all have to go back to the kindergarten? Could not the plant have been so well cultivated that it would have given a perennial crop? How strangely mixed are values in this world; passing strange how mixed are people's motives in estimating what is worthy. Not many angels grow in any small town, and there are few to be found in old Salisbury.

Moreover, there had been a great big devil living in the back yard of the place.

The whole living, the entire pay roll of our town had been soaked in whiskey since the beginning of time, but, as you know, people have to make a living somehow. When the revival came and attempted to pull this demon out by the tail, of course it was impossible to lift it out with but one jerk. And, of course, there was a man behind it!

When looking for the bold bad man who was thus corrupting society—and usually there is such an one—what was he found to resemble? Was he a brutish fellow, one who "feared not God neither regarded man?"

His name was Lanier. He was kinsman to a well known southern poet. He was college-bred, and in appearance a small, pale Napoleonic person. He was full of charity for his poor neighbor, giving away more in proportion from the profits of his disintegrating traffic than most thrifty pillars in churches consented to spare from their legitimate gains. Although he never gave to anyone who begged, he knew his poor. In a snowy time, he would send around

THE SEAMY SIDE OF SALISBURY

loads of wood and put meat and corn meal on the wagon. He was unmarried and lived an almost monastic life in a bare room over one of his stores. He had relatives, however, a sister and a brother, and these with their families he kept in the lap of luxury. He was their meal ticket, their especial Providence; but when doing all this for them, he knew well how greedy and ungrateful they were.

James Lanier had an imaginative and copious liberty in profane swearing which was in the nature of a literary gift. The very sacrilege of it was enough to make a man turn pale and scuttle out of hearing. Tales were told about his cursings.

Once the iceman presented the overdue bill owed by Lanier's "family." It was extravagant. Before artificial ice was common, when every pound had to be shipped into town in freight cars and was very expensive, these people had been making ice cream, a dessert not lightly to be undertaken in the eighties. They had been making it every day, and, in short, the bill for ice *was* a bill! When Mr. Lanier saw it he "cussed" about it in his most artistic and florid style. The driver of the ice wagon, who knew how to cuss a little for himself, straightened up and made answer, first giving a general broadside and then applying his remarks in particular. Mr. Lanier listened, and then asked in a quiet, anxious tone, "How much do they pay you for driving that ice wagon?" The man told him. He said,

"Throw up the job. I'll pay you twice that to do my cussing for me." A story is told of how lightning once struck Lanier's tobacco factory, and he came raging out like an angry midge. He jumped upon a box in the yard and shook his fist upwards at the streaming heavens, cursing God and shrieking "Strike me, strike me!" The Negro hands all ran away in a body, scurrying through the pouring rain—but next day they were all back. The sky was clear, and Mr. Lanier was a good paymaster.

How, then, may be classified Salisbury's typical bad man? He died in his bed, lonely, laconic, pathetic. His large fortune melted away, as do all accumulations made by ministering to a vice, being re-absorbed by the society from which it was amassed.

After the great revival had been over some time, the Woman's Christian Temperance Union became enthusiastic and decided to try to pray the saloons out of Salisbury entirely. At any time they might choose, they would bear down, twenty or thirty strong, upon one of the big drinking places opposite the courthouse on Main Street. There they would kneel and pray for, or rather against, the owner, the barkeeper, the loafers, the drinkers, and all sometimes by name. Then they would get up, brush the sawdust from their black alpaca skirts and go on to the next. I have never been of the stern stuff of which reformers are made. I am not tight-twisted enough for that. One day, however, I went along with them, wishing to see with my own eyes what a place popularly called a "gin palace" was like, and knowing no better way of finding out. While they were praying, I ducked my head sidewise and peered out. I saw the polished and well furnished bar, but except for that, the place was dull and dirty, sordid, sticky, and pervaded by a horrible sickish-sour smell. I could perceive nothing attractive, no allurement, unless a man was eager to lose himself, willing to be trapped in a cheap, nasty-looking haunt.

A few years later, one of the big saloons on Main Street spread a painted sign over its door, which said, "All Nations Welcome but Carrie."

XXVI

A YANKEE COURTSHIP

IF LIFE IS like a ball of yarn, then memory is like a tangled skein of threads, out of which, first one and then another may be separated, but there will always be other strands to come away with them. Many plies and windings are to be unraveled before all is reeled into continuity. Dates are uncertain, unless nailed down on a definite fact. All things combine to make an old wife's memory the most tantalizing tangle, and all this is but a long way of saying that these stories have not been consecutive. Life after my mother's death settled early into a jogging gait. The seasons changed, but the same people were seen week by week. About these I could ramble on at great length, have done all I dare of it already!

There came a certain Sunday—was it not in the autumn?—when the old brick church, with the cupola for a steeple, where I usually worshiped with Father, was not opened for services. In such cases the Doctor enjoyed attending some other house of worship, and distributed his visits among all denominations. Upon this morning, we walked down a different street and turned toward the Methodist headquarters. Before reaching the church, we had to pass a familiar door, where two young men stood conversing with the family as they were leaving the porch steps. One of these was Tom Bruner, who lived now in Raleigh and was employed by the state in advertising its resources to attract settlers. The old state was merely imitative in this attempt, for nobody in it really wanted outsiders to settle here, or liked them if they did come. Father greeted our former neighbor as he passed. The man with him was a stranger, and strangers were none too common in Salisbury. So while I spoke to my old acquaintance, I observed his companion as minutely as possible without seeming to stare.

In my small-town fashion I was critical of him. I thought him too distinctively dandified. When he removed his hat as I passed, he showed glossy hair, parted in the middle—a somewhat effeminate note according to my ideas. The impression of spic-and-span-ness was further accentuated by his coloring, by the pink and white of his girlish complexion, by the visible blue of his eyes under a fair forehead, and by the warm chestnut of his hair. For a virile person this was too high coloring. He ought not to look like that, I thought as I took note of him.

Father and daughter entered the church almost immediately, where, because of the general esteem felt for my father, the cheerful Methodist brethren came handshaking about him and welcomed him to a conspicuous seat right in front of the pulpit. They were about to hear their new preacher for the first time, and this will definitely fix the date in the late autumn, after Conference, after the Bishop had shuffled and redealt the preachers all around to the churches. This new preacher was young, eloquent, and, as it was rumored, unmarried. He spread himself like a green bay tree before his new charge, and, observing the second strange young man in one day, I forgot the first. To complicate all, the new preacher had been coached. He called on Father for the closing prayer, out of deference to his piety. Father had thought well of his sermon. He felt thankful to the Lord, and said so.

Old Mrs. Rufty, who loved to shout, was in church that day, and was anxious to give an exhibition. She had spoken a number of preliminary "Amens," but many of the older folk had done so as effectively as she. As Father prayed, good Mrs. Rufty recognized her call. She began to shout vigorously in the rearward of the church, and my father, who, being a Presbyterian, did not approve of such (to him) unseemly behavior in the House of God, concluded his thanksgiving with a snap. Going home, he was too cross to be spoken to, while I was shaking with inward laughter. In this way, the whole impression made on my mind by the handsome stranger was overlaid. That afternoon I accompanied Father when he drove into the country to visit his charity patients according to his custom. On returning, I found two cards under the front door. One was Tom Bruner's, the other bore the name I write whenever I sign my own.

Late in the ensuing spring, I had another of those pleasant journeys Father encouraged as often as once a year. My elder brother was now pastor of a church in an eastern town. I visited them for a fortnight, then continued farther into the low-lying tidewater to visit the home of my old Nash and Kollock chum, blonde May. The quiet town where May lived slumbered beside a broad, lazy river, whose current was stopped twice a day by the inflow of a slow tide. The approach to the town was over a float-bridge resting on the surface of the water. Great trees of Cape jessamine flanked the front gate of each dwelling; the gardens were full of clove pinks and gay annuals. Nobody took anything urgently in that town. There were many little parties, much soft flattery given to a visiting girl. The May weather was as warm and enervating as a poultice. The glassy river reflected a blinding sunshine, and the soft air intensified its brooding calm.

Worth recording, because it is an old custom, was the way that we had of pleasure driving very early in the morning. At six, or even earlier, a girl would rise and open the door to her beau, and the two would eat a cold lunch left ready. Then they would mount a high buggy, with no canopy over it, and enjoy a long drive in the dewy morning, while streaks and streamers of mist lifted from the green desolation of the swamps beside the way. Bay-flowers, tiny spicy-scented magnolias, perfumed the air. It was windless, sickish, tepid, a bit of subtropical experience; subtropical like the steaming climate, the luxuriant useless vegetation. At half past seven they would come in and the man be invited to the family breakfast of hominy-grits, fish, hot biscuits, coffee. He would then go about his leisurely business, while the girls would relax to their day's loafing, gossip, and afternoon siestas. This social early rising sounds strange to a generation which would rather sit up the whole night in quest of pleasure than rise ten minutes early to find it. A week or two of this existence was pleasant, although longer would have bored me to desperation.

My next stopping place was to be the University, where I was invited to attend commencement; but in Raleigh was to be found the one and only dry-goods store in the state where really dependable finery might be bought, and girls liked to say that their things came from "Tucker's." After the fashion of the day, I wore white dresses made of mull (soft white cotton), or of linen. These I made myself, but I must buy the slippers, the broad satin sash-ribbons, and the fan, needed to make a complete outfit. Tom Bruner had invited me to stop to visit his home, as he and his wife lived in Raleigh. I accepted the invitation for two days, to have a chance of buying my pretty things at Tucker's.

I arrived late in the afternoon. My hosts lived well out on the western edge of Raleigh, where it was still almost country. Near their home was the newly established agricultural experiment station, a sightly, pleasant place, standing on a rise of ground. This spring the lawn was thick and fine, made of crab-grass well clipped and rolled; the mild hills looked lovely to eyes tired of the insipid flatness of the East, where the horizon fitted down tight upon the land like a great inverted bowl. Here, for the first, could be seen blue distance.

After supper that evening, the three of us sat on the porch in the soft dusk, and a young man, not recognizable in the twilight, came from the house next door to join us. I heard the name I had read once on the visiting card. He was a native of "Up-state" New York, so I learned, a member of the first class to graduate at Cornell, or at any other college, in scientific agriculture. He had been imported by our state to find out what was the matter with farming in this part of the United States—quite a large demand to make of such a rosy-cheeked young fellow, who, although very dignified and apparently older than most recent graduates, must so lately have left college. We sat, the four of us, upon the dim porch and chatted and watched clouds gather thick and fluffy, while a business-like little wind drove them over. By nine o'clock it had begun to sprinkle and to spatter; it was raining determinedly at bedtime, and the next morning it was flooding.

Here is a date, now, of which I am certain, for just at this point the story synchronizes with well known events. It was May the thirtieth, in a year that was marked by a great disaster, and the storm which was preparing the Johnstown flood was the one which was gathering while we young folk sat on the porch and watched its progress. Nothing could be done all the next day save sit in the house and watch great sheets of water pour down so continuously as to shut out all prospect whatever. In this deluge, no one could see a dozen yards before him. In the middle of the forenoon came the young man from next door, saying he was stormbound; so the four of us spent the day together. In the afternoon of the third day, a weak and watery sun came out to survey the drowned prospect. Next morning, I went into Raleigh, bought my slippers, my fan and ribbons, and in the afternoon, took the train for the University—all of which is a story in confirmation of that old adage about the ill wind indeed, and that other, about the time to make hay.

What a pretty story I could tell about what we did in Chapel Hill that commencement, about the small talk, the merriment, the grove permeated with happy nonsense and laughter, as if it were a thicket flashing with sudden wings. I wore my new white dresses, my ribbon bows and sashes. The young men wrote autographs all over my pretty fan. I was not, however, an overwhelming success. The real heartbreakers never wore glasses. But it all did very well. It was too soon over, and afterwards I must go home again.

It was not till the leafy stillness of August that anything more happened. Then I was surprised by a letter from the man from New York State. He was coming to Salisbury on business. He asked if when he came he might renew the pleasant acquaintance of the spring. He had been recently selected as professor of Agriculture in the new "Farmer's College" at Raleigh, and said he expected to remain in the state, perhaps permanently. I laid the letter down and bit my lips. I did not need to be told that here was fate beginning to stalk me in earnest.

When I told the family about the letter, my sister was really disagreeable about it. She was still a Rebel unreconstructed, hated Yankees, and had little tolerance for men from New York. Normal southerners at that time might perhaps manage to treat "Yankees" with outward politeness in common intercourse—even that way they could barely tolerate them—but to have one of them paying his respects to the daughter of the family, to have him actually come to visit her, marking her out by his attentions, was indeed very annoying; a thing to be prevented by any method short of coercion. My sister remembered my independence of spirit. She knew nothing could be sharply forbidden, no ultimatum given, or the family would meet defeat. She did, however, have a great influence with Father (she was his daughter before I was), and she derided the friendship with this man as much as she dared. The brothers were more or less with

A YANKEE COURTSHIP

her in this. Men were never so determined "secesh" as women, but my father looked on, feeling pained about it all. He did not care to contemplate losing his daughter. He felt as they bade him feel. He did not take my side, although he was not drawn into the discussion.

When in course of time my friend came to see me, it was only me that he saw. Nobody save myself came into the parlour to meet him, and he must have perceived the meaning of that. After such a cool reception, never alluded to between us, it was not possible that he should come very often; besides, he had to make a good long railway journey on every visit, but several times that year we two young people spent long quiet seances getting acquainted. We did not approach sentimental subjects, for neither one cared for small talk; we exchanged ideas on equal footing. I found him a man of excellent principles, a thorough student of what he desired to understand; and because he had attended one of the very few colleges which at that time had tried the doubtful experiment of coeducation, he expressed a respect for the powers of women which from the first warmed my heart to him on that especial account. He did not call us either "females" or womanish, but said plainly that women's minds were actually equal to men's so that they learned quite as easily and made better grades, because a college man did not try his hardest in competing with women, and that was the result of his prejudices—it did not make his ability greater than the woman's.

I knew that this man was not coming so far, coming so repeatedly, and coming under such frigid conditions without some definite object. I knew this all the better because he had said so little, and had made no protestations. Here was a real decision I must make regarding him, and that in advance, and without too much delay. It was not fair to let him come to the point and then discover that after all there was no point to his coming. I must think it out, while I could be level-headed about it! All the qualities perceptible in his accent and bearing, different from what I was accustomed to, were perpetually being called to attention by my family. They made me conscious of the very conspicuously brilliant complexion, the somewhat stiff manners, which indeed had had no encouragement to unbend and become easy. Their silent hostility, and surface criticism must have had its influence. And yet I had become definitely sure of his clean young-manhood, of his idealism, of his honesty.

In the very beginning of his visits, goaded by my sister, I had freely declared that there were three men I never intended to marry—a Yankee, a Methodist, and a Republican. This man was all three; so why should she and Father worry? But now he had been coming for a year. It was easy to guess his object. Without any unseemly self-commendation on his part, it was easy to see that he knew himself to be the catch of all the eligible young men of his own home corner. I noted that fact for reference and decided that I could punish him for it, not vindictively, but in a purely missionary spirit. He must not be allowed to be too sure of anything. And as I continued to temporize, the family, as families do, injected themselves into the uncertainty and took a vigorous part in helping me make up my mind.

There was quite an unpleasantness. "This Yankee," said my older sister, and my brothers, "must not continue to come to see Hope. She cannot marry him, and it is undesirable to have him so much in evidence. He may drive off other possibilities."

Why must I not marry him? What possibilities? I demanded, blushing to think that so far the man had said no word of wanting to marry anybody! This plain showdown broke up in high dudgeon on both sides, although all Father did was merely to look sorrowful.

When in doubt, we all consulted Aunt Margaret Mitchell, who lived in Statesville, and I went to spend a week with her.

A YANKEE COURTSHIP

In outward appearance she was the most uncompromising of old maids, but in her youth she must have had a broken love affair intense enough to warm her heart during all the rest of her life, for she was truly a sympathetic person. Besides, she belonged to my mother's generation. She knew Yankees did not always have horns and tails. I did not talk over affairs openly with Aunt Margaret; somehow it seemed immodest, although I might just as well have done so. I put hypothetical cases, and absorbed the friendly atmosphere, and in that week I thought matters over to the extent of getting my own mind made up. There was a young doctor of the town whom I had known some time, and whom I shrewdly suspected my own family of regarding favorably in connection with his liking for me. He began a week of attentions which helped me, although he was unaware how useful he was to another man. He was so sentimental and silly that I grew disgusted with him and found out what I did not want. So lying awake all night the last of my week at Aunt Margaret's I thought out all my condition.

All the usefulness, all the employment I could claim was that of housekeeper for Father. At this I might manage to keep reasonably busy if I made the most of my task, but the concrete fact was, and I could see it, that I was not indispensable for that, or for anything else. I was a superfluous female. I was without adequate preparation to become a teacher, which at that time was the only employment recognized for women outside the home. I had wanted to be a bookkeeper, but Father had vetoed that. Women were not being used in business in our conservative old state, not as yet. Suppose that anything should happen to Father, who had already attained the age of seventy, well beyond the usual age limit of usefulness of the average hard-worked practitioner. Then I had nothing to expect but dependent maidenhood—that, or marriage while I was fresh on the market. This was not merely my own point of view, as I justified myself in what I meant to do; it was cold fact. It was what nearly every girl was forced to face if she was sincere with herself, to ignore if she was sentimental. It arose from conditions which are now happily passing away. If these changes bring difficult problems with them, as changes do, let no one on that account forget the finalities of a former time, which have been reviewed and which are now done away with forever. The pioneer woman was absolutely indispensable in our land when it was new, but by this time the frontier had reached the Pacific coast, and the question was no longer busy hands, but clear minds, and understanding hearts. Women were looking about them, to find that their importance had diminished because their old employments had been taken away from them.

I thought that I was being cool and judicial when at this time I reviewed my life, remembered my high ambitions, and saw their meager fulfilment. I could perceive that there was but one profession open to me, the ancient and honorable profession of matrimony. . . . I resolved to marry this man from outside, this man who had been so strongly attracted to me that he would brave disagreeable slights in coming to visit me. I deliberately decided to lead this man on, and, after I had kept him on the anxious seat long enough to bolster up my own feelings of importance, to accept him. I knew, as every mother's daughter knows if she consults her mother wit, that I must be careful, not too precipitate, nor sell out too cheaply. But this was the very best thing I could do.

And so, after the week with Aunt Margaret, I went home and told my sister and my father in a sufficiently saucy and cocksure fashion, that while I never intended to marry any man whose moral character and reputation was not above suspicion, and while I never should marry any man not able to support me as well as I had been accustomed to, I did intend to marry this Joseph Chamberlain when he asked me.

That I would give them time to prove that they, and not I myself knew the truth about him; and after they had failed, as inevitably they must fail, to prove him unworthy, the affair would be my affair, the marriage my business. I was going to be twenty-one pretty soon anyhow, and my own mistress.

After I had administered this facer to my family, things quieted down. They said no more to me, but they wrote letters and wrote them. As they told me nothing of the answers, I knew they had found nothing they wished to tell. Their reasoned opposition made me gravitate the closer to my lover, and loyalty to him grew in my heart. When in due course he did ask me, and I did accept him, I fell in love with him after we were engaged, and all the more truly and sincerely because of what I supposed to be my cool-headedness, which may have been less cool than I supposed it to be.

Sometimes in reflective moments I faced the momentous issue which I had settled for myself—and shuddered. Sometimes I wakened in a cold sweat, as I thought of being so irrevocably bound, and would recall the fact that it was not yet too late to unbind myself. But I did not want to be unbound. If indeed I did not want it, then I was bound by the strongest fetters, and I would let it go that way!

One thing was most gratifying to me—the engagement ring he sent me. It was pure as a dewdrop and very large, although not vulgarly so. I could well be proud of that ring, of the good taste and the generosity of it, and of its superiority to those worn by any of my friends about that time. But my engagement was a trying time; my family was still very hostile, there were so many questions possible, and so few answers that I meant to give.

The accepted intimacy, the warming of natural feeling, the thrill—all these things are going to be left out of this account. All were present, increasingly present, but I choose to tell here only that part of my love story which I might share with anyone. Love letters are all alike; all lovers tell the same old story: and so I will let this narrative go on to those things that are different, and tell them.

John Boyden, the sneering, the profane, had been born in what he loved to call the Commonwealth of Massachusetts. He was a cantankerous man, both by reputation and actual character. The reason he was so open to public insult might be found in his real convictions, or in his pure obstinacy, which made him refuse to join the political stampede away from all "Radicalism," a change which was obligatory for every southerner after Reconstruction misdoings. Even strong conservatives, the remains of the old Whig dynasty, were quickly turned, for they could not endure the carpet-bagger-Negro regime. John Boyden did not sink his old allegiances on any account. He said he did not mind being in the right with two or three; so his fellow citizens set about making him mind!

In his crotchety way, John was very fond of my father. Sometimes he would sit a long evening telling him the most atrocious anecdotes about all the pillars of Salisbury society. Now and again the good Doctor would say, "John, now aren't you ashamed of yourself!" and John would grin the Mephistophelian grin of the successful satirist and tell another story.

When my Yankee began coming regularly to see me, he was likely to arrive upon a train which came in at seven in the evening, the train which John Boyden invariably met to receive his northern newspaper. He would take note of the stranger, and although the visits were not generally much noticed, he perceived the regularity of them. One night he sidled confidentially up to him and spoke to him.

"Say, young fellow, what are you up to, anyhow?" he asked with his knowing leer. "Some girl, I'll swear, and I'll bet I know her!" My friend was taken aback; then, feeling that he had far better have such an astute old fellow on his side than against him, he answered quite simply:

"Yes, it is a young lady, and yes, I am sure you must know her. You do not know me, but neither do you know anything bad of me. You must be fair, and until you do, you must promise not to spoil my chances." Then he went on and told the reason of his coming and the manner of his reception at my home, sufficiently to call out that element which John Boyden used for sympathy. He promised to spoil no sport, and he kept his word; but for some time before I was actually engaged to Joseph Chamberlain, and invariably afterwards, Mr. Boyden seemed to be passing by me in a continuous procession. If I went up town, he met me; if I entered a store, he was standing outside when I emerged. At first he would bow gravely, then suddenly grin that diabolical, leering grin of his. As far as I could see him, I could see him grinning. I thought it accidental at first; then I noticed the regularity of it; and at last, before the wedding day was set, I could not help blushing as far as I could see the old wretch, although I am not a particularly blushful person. John Boyden's teasing, his enjoyment of knowing more than other people knew, was another feature of those last difficult months at home.

With his characteristic kindness, Father decided to give me as good an outfit as he could afford. A small legacy coming to him just then, he turned it over to me to buy wedding things. I made a good many of the clothes myself, I tucked and trimmed underthings in the dozens then thought indispensable. Miss Mollie Wren was engaged to make my three best dresses. I was to have a black silk, very heavy and stiff, the costly material for which was the gift of Aunt Margaret. At that time such a dress was the foundation, the cornerstone of any proper wedding outfit. I had a traveling suit of heavy brown ladies' cloth, with hat and shoes to match. This was made tight in the body, high in the collar, long and close-fitting in the skirt, and it was as confining as a closed coffin, and a far more fervid envelope. Finally there was an evening dress of yellow China crepe, ruffled at the bottom like the tube of a great daffodil, and trailing on the floor. It was low-necked and had no sleeves, so that I did not dare try it on for Father to see, because he would have been shocked and would have thought it indelicate. The wedding was to be only a marriage in church, with no festivity and no "reception." When the ceremony was over, we would proceed directly from the church door to the train. The groom's only brother was coming to be best man; my niece would be the bridesmaid.

On the wedding day, late in the afternoon, I stood all alone, all ready dressed for the marriage which would take place about half-past six. I looked about the familiar living room, not for the last time, but for the last time it would be home. All but my niece had preceded me to the church. There was not a soul within hearing. I was pale, trembling a little over the parting from all I had ever known, but not crying. I was aware how momentous all this was for me. My bridegroom came in suddenly (and it is said that he had to open the front door for himself, but no matter, he came in), and he understood without a word from me. With an expression of infinite tenderness on his handsome face, he came to me, took me in his arms, told me how much this day meant to him, and how steadfastly he was resolved never to give me cause to regret it.

Then the four of us were collected and were driven away in that familiar livery rig which was called the "wedding carriage" and maintained exclusively for such occasions. We went slowly down the street, past the homes of friends. Miss Alice Brown had made them carry her out to the porch in a reclining chair so that she could see me go by on the way to be married. She waved me farewell, and so did a great huddle of the Negro servants of the neighborhood, calling to "Miss Hopie" and loudly wishing her a great deal of good luck, bending double from the hips with loud, friendly

A YANKEE COURTSHIP

guffaws of laughter. Munroe and Charlotte were not among these. They were already seated in the front row of the gallery in the Methodist Church.

It was here, oddly enough, that the ceremony was to take place, for the progressive party in the Presbyterian congregation had finally prevailed, and a new, large, and extremely hideous church had been planned to take the place of that dignified old building of pillared brick which had been the church home of my mother. The new was not yet founded, but the old had been entirely torn away to make room for it; so in the Methodist Church, hard by the spot where I had first beheld my husband, I was married to him. Afterward we went to the station to take that familiar train to the North and fare out into the world together.

Here was one of the earliest of those marriages which, by the bridging of what we southerners used to love to call the "bloody chasm," have gone far to make the United States once more homogeneous, or, to be exact in our phrasing, more evenly heterogeneous. Here was a man descended from the steady habits and sober sanctions of New England by way of Western New York State, who was choosing his wife from among rebellious southern folk. Here was a woman, half New England by way of the South, who would have nobody but one of her section's dearest enemies. Here were their two families in the background steadfastly disapproving, standing severally aghast at their willfulness! It cannot be conceived what would ever become of a country where the young should be as willing as the old to stew forever in their own juice. These young people were evenly matched. The girl had no money, a fact she was afterwards given cause to remember, but she had everything else that goes into a good marriage. She had health, common sense, reasonably good looks, and a serene temper. Add to this a love for her husband, warm but not too exacting. The husband was a good match for her in every excellence.

When they began after a while, as people will, to talk genealogy, they discovered that a first ancestor of one of them had settled near Boston in the very early colonial period, and that he was a member of the church of which the ancestor of the other was pastor. They found that all the first crop of young Americans of the one family had been baptized and catechized by the minister-ancestor, along with his own olive branches. So these two must have had a few drops of neighbor blood to call to each other, when they met casually on that rainy evening when it was soon going to be the week of the Johnstown Flood.

This story has happened more than once, but I do not think it is ever an entirely prosaic tale.

XXVII

NEW YORK STATE HONEYMOON

THE CITY of refuge for all the newly married seeking their own unadulterated society was Washington, for all those who came from south of it. Always they went there because Niagara Falls was not so accessible; always they desired some slight excuse of sight-seeing, such as Washington afforded, but refused to be too greatly occupied with it, their duty being to become acquainted with each other, and solitude being best obtained among a crowd of strangers. After escaping Salisbury's rice and congratulations my new husband and I had nothing to do but board the evening train for Washington. Joseph knew an old but comfortable hotel, and we found a cool apartment on the shady side of it. Washington in late June was rather empty, very fervid; the asphalt burned like an oven, the cicadas, hot and cheerful, were tuning up early in the day in the trees of every avenue. Heat waves quivered around the bronze statues placed at the crossings of the diverging streets where the spokes of the wheel of the avenues intersected the regular checkerboard pattern of the city.

And it was so hot! It was my first experience of a great city in torrid weather. It was sickening, when stepping outdoors, to feel the furnace breath of the pavement rise to scorch our faces. Inside the shadow of the buildings it was endurable; the going about was the real difficulty; for then only horse cars were used in transportation, and sunlit superheated pavement had to be traversed on foot to reach these;

while would-be passengers must stand broiling like gridiron saints to wait their coming.

Like most girls embarking on the greatest adventure of their lives, I had begun my journey tired out. After a couple of languid days in Washington, I begged to go on, hoping for cooler weather. We went next to Philadelphia, where there was mercifully little one ought to go and look at, save Independence Hall.

When riding on the streetcars during our day in Philadelphia, I asked Husband Joseph whether the old Quaker costume with its muslin cap, plain, covered bonnet, and dove-gray clothing was any longer to be seen there. He answered that at least on the street it had been entirely discontinued. Just as the words left his lips, there entered three women who might have stepped out of an engraving of Elizabeth Fry and her daughters, for they were handsomely dressed in the exact regulation costume. The flowing amplitude of their gray draperies, the rosy cheerfulness of their quiet faces, were worth a long journey to see and remember.

New York was the third midsummer city to be rapidly dismissed, but it was not then the magnificent, far-seen, dream city of today. Its towers and cliffs plumed with jets of steam, its grandiose sky-line, had not been conceived. It was all brick and brownstone, frankly an ugly, huge place, but this time we went straight through. New England, which was our farthest goal, would be cooler and more endurable, and leaving New York to be revisited a few weeks later, we set out next morning for the East.

Almost at once there came a change in the character of the country. Often I had been told of the charm of the New England landscape, and I found an aspect of things full of a strange suggestion of my having been familiar with it all in some former state of existence. The sky of distant porcelain blue, the delicate green of the near fields, the small rounded contours of the distances, and the great elms here and there, drooping like fountains of slender branches beside a little meadow brook, came to my consciousness like a half-remembered tune. The limpid, silver-flowing Connecticut was a dream river to one whose rivers had hitherto flowed only with liquid mud. The first day in New England was a showery, summery one, and when we reached New Haven we alighted to spend the most of it there.

This was a town where my grandmother had once lived, and it was from New London, very near, that she was married, early in the nineteenth century, to leave New England for the South, to begin a new home in far-away North Carolina, in the University village. When she became a part of society there, when she came to share the opinions of her southern friends, she was held to be a renegade by her stern puritan kinsfolk back home. There were letters, written by these relatives before the Civil War, in which they had dealt plainly with her regarding these matters, had even dared to condole with her hard lot, in having to *pretend*, in order to keep on living in that benighted parallel. Her mother pitied her because she had "the care and direction of more servants and poorer ones than any one woman could ever decently manage."

I probably had relatives in New Haven, but we did not go a-cousining there. The southern branch of the family was too proud, the northern too opinionated for the present. I desired especially to see the old brick college where Grandfather had studied and been a tutor, and accordingly we sauntered around the Yard at Yale, then in its summer solitude. When the time drew near for us to be expected, we took the train for a city in the western part of that old commonwealth of Massachusetts—that state so proud, so cool, so intellectual and at the same time so passionate. Something in my nature rose to meet and greet the state of mind which, comprehended in the word New England, had at that time, far more than now, a great deal to do with American thinking. We read their books and reflected on their maxims. The convinced little southerner, as I believed myself to be, had early absorbed the literature of their all too short period of inflorescence, and had been taught the story and legend which these people compiled of their own ideals and experiences. If you read at all as an American it could not be avoided. And so I found that I could apprehend the spirit and savor the established and wonted atmosphere of these conservative towns. I could notice how different they must be from the society in which I had grown up. In that time, New England had not been overrun with foreigners. It was still its sober, staid, definite self.

My husband's relatives whom we young folk were invited to visit on our wedding journey, were not New England born, but they were gladly conforming to the ways of life there. The snug upholstered look of their rooms, the prim exactitude of their housekeeping methods, so different from the bare spaces and homelier ways I had known, the trimness of their fine-grown lawn where a daily effort was expended to make each blade of grass grow exactly as it was bidden—these interested me greatly. It was so regulated and so restricted. I believed New England people must grow like that, careful, self-directed, self-disciplined, but very little envisaging the problems of other parts of our great community which they hymned in terms of New England and adorned with the "woods and templed hills" never seen save in their own especial environment.

By their thorough education and real culture, both of which I abjectly admired at that time, they must be ages ahead of what the poor mid-south had ever attained, or was perhaps ever likely to attain. But even then I seized an idea from their poet-philosopher who said,

"Yet not for all his faith can see
Would I that cowlèd churchman be."

In New England I respected, I admired, but my feeling had the impatience in it which comes when a citizen of some stark new land goes back to visit an older country. He cannot for his life endure the weight of so much set custom. He may love the air of it for a little while, but he knows that living there very long would be apt to smother his personal significance.

The kinsfolk were more than kind. They took pains with the little outsider and showed the real country as well as that continuous city which lay then, as now, almost unbroken along the Connecticut Valley. They had a carriage and team of good horses which made this possible. Among them I found that those serious, questioning qualities which had made me a sort of speckled bird at home, were normal and usual. I liked it all, and rested, relaxing in the cool pure air.

Soon we were ready to return to New York which we had passed through hurriedly at first. In that city then, we saw the usual sights, although there was not much to enjoy in the way of theaters, because the summer solstice was upon them. Except in Washington, I had never seen a really fine painting, and in Washington I had been too tired and too warm to care. Now the days were too short for what I wanted to see in the Metropolitan. We were already overdue at Joseph's father's home in the western end of "Up-State" New York. Joseph's sister joined us from her visit in New England, and the three of us bought tickets for a long day on the train.

My husband had told me that his people were prosperous farmers, but as I never had seen any, I was entirely at a loss as to what sort of people I was going to meet. His sister was as well dressed as any girl. Members of his family often went to Florida in winter, that I knew, and I did not think it very farmerish of them! Purposely, and with the prudishness of old southern custom, as well as with a cautious reserve of my own, I had avoided meeting any of the far-away family of my intended, although I might have managed to do so on one of their trips. I suspected they were going to misunderstand me; I knew they were sure to criticize me, although I did not blame them. I had believed they would be more apt to make the best of their bargain "sight unseen," as the boys swap jackknives. No lover could ever describe his sweetheart so that her real picture would come to the eyes of his hostile mother, resenting every rhapsodical comment: the real girl would be the same question mark a new daughter always is. It is impossible to describe even your father and mother and make them convincing. I have tried and I know!

Here was the next adventure, chancy and thrilling, and I gathered my courage for something as important as life itself. From New York City to the western end of the state is several hundred miles, and in the whole distance I filled my eyes with the joy of green fields, the manifest fertility, the pleasantness of the landscape, which was hilly without grandeur. Even at this time, because of the propensity of each successive generation of our people to seek new land and keep moving to find it, and because each established family sent out sons into new fields, these rural counties of New York State had already passed the pinnacle of prosperity. The best of its young blood was already occupied in building up the West, where fortunes were planted more easily and grew faster; and it was the elders and stay-at-homes who were carrying on. The foreign invasion was still in the future. Solid, simple farm homes stood trim and well kept, with apple orchards, with huge hip-roofed barns stuffed with hay. Placid cows could be seen, sleek farm horses, and there were meadows and fields of grain—the ideal and type of country living. None of the cities was so large that it was spoiled as a pleasant home for children; all was peace and plenty, a picture which it cheered my heart to contemplate. Farther west, the hills grew higher, although always round and smoothly moulded. In remote geologic past, western New York had been ground down under the sheet of glacial ice which scoured away all the peaks and ridges from its hills and strewed the dust of them in the valleys. These great hills, like crouching, round-backed monsters, had valleys like paths winding between them. Streams were limpid, soil fertile, and at every turn an intimate near-by prospect came to view—a picture composed of those elements which make us feel safe and established in our own country, pleasant farmsteads, shade trees, water, and green fields. All this was true more than forty years ago; now, after the shift of population westward, and the scattering of the old American stocks, it would not be so perfect as a description.

In late afternoon we stopped at a little square station dwarfed to a dry-goods box by the size of the hills close on either hand. It was only a tiny hamlet, and the family met us and drove us the two miles up one of the valley roads to the Chamberlain farm. The vehicle was what they called a democrat wagon, a high road-wagon with springs, but no canopy, with seats across, and drawn by two horses. The Chamberlain homestead, built before the Civil War, was in the classical style favored all through that part of the country. It had low gables and, along the porch, short fluted columns. The mouldings were very heavy, and seemed to weigh the house down, and set it into the landscape with an air of stability, nestling low against the sheltering hill behind it to the north. Two tall fir trees stood by the path, and the fenced dooryard was ringed around with a row of hard maples.

These excellent farms of western New York were already being wasted of their fertility to compete with the great prairies, a thing which has been greedily done from Maine southwards, with no thought of those who should come after. In that summer nearly fifty years ago, the place I saw, looked like a bit of home paradise. The middle of the road was unpaved and dusty, but grass and flowers grew and pressed in to the wheel track, so that the highway was bordered by a strip of meadow. There were walls laid up of loose stones, with apple trees hanging over them, as it is in New England; but, unlike New England, this countryside had spaciousness. Ranges of round hills could be seen in any direction, and the square fields upon their high slopes looked as if some immeasurable giant had thrown his patched cloak down on the landscape, letting its folds billow in falling.

Behind its bodygard of maples, the homestead stood in its enclosure, shaped like a corpulent letter L, with the lower bar facing the road, and the upright part gable-wise to it, and full two stories high. The two-story part, which had a separate entrance, contained the parlour and the rooms of Joseph's grandmother, who was spending her age there. Upstairs, by one of the most beautiful small stairways I ever saw, were guest room and other bedrooms. Directly off the front porch of the lower ell opened the family sitting room. In this part were several bedrooms, a large dining room, a kitchen, and, in the rear, all those woodsheds and outbuildings which northern books of children's stories had rendered familiar.

It was all homelike and patriarchal. The furniture of the home was solid walnut, very substantial, but warted and knobbed with the carving and post finials thought so handsome during that period of poor taste immediately after the Civil War. This huge house was warmed in winter with wood stoves having "drums" on the second floor, and it was said that water had never been known to freeze either in the house or in the great cellar. Across the road, filling up all the prospect from the front, were the huge red barns. Over the ell, in the half-story rooms, the hired men had their quarters. It was very spacious, very compact, a unit of much industry.

My coming must have been an important event in the family, for I was the bride of the eldest son. Joseph's mother must naturally have resented her son's selection of a wife out of an alien society, rather than courting one of the home girls who would have been glad to be kind to him, knew the ways of the country, and would not have to be eternally decorated with a great question mark. Besides, I had not one penny to rub against another. Mothers a-many before and since have felt similar qualms, but if this one had only known it, I came from New England origin much like their own. My grandfather had fared southwards to take up his professorship, the same identical year that Joseph's grandfather, of the same christian name, had shouldered his knapsack and stepped sturdily out toward the West in the dead of winter, when all streams would be bridged for him by the ice.

My new family wished, as I know now, not to be ill-disposed to me, but were afraid to let me become aware of my importance. They looked at me, but did not seem able to say much. Joseph's mother was a large fair-skinned woman, handsome, capable, moving with decision, and having a critical blue glance which pierced through and through. She was a little embarrassed in manner, for she usually allowed herself the plainest of running commentary on anything that concerned her, and this time she wished to reserve judgment. When we young people arrived in the late afternoon, the father had not yet come back from a neighboring town; so my husband called me to walk with him along the road over which he would come. Soon we heard the wagon rumble over the hill; we stepped out and hailed him, and he reined in. Upon the driver's seat sat a stocky man, not so short as compact, and heavy-built. He had the same rosy cheeks Joseph had inherited, which gave his young face such a model-schoolboy look. His beard was cut exactly like General Sherman's or General Grant's, and his eyes were deep-set, with a grim expression, but somehow I did not feel afraid of him. He reached down a hand and half pulled, half lifted me over the high wagon wheel to a place beside him. "Joe" followed, striding across the wheel from the hub.

I looked at him and said, "Here I am, your new daughter." He gave me a sidewise glance very keen, a trick he had, and suddenly burst out laughing and kissed me heartily, so that I felt at ease with him at once. Somehow I felt him my friend. He began joking Joe about the reddish color of his trim mustache and asking me why I allowed him to raise such a one, and laughing we drove in on the barn floor, where Joe helped his father take out the team.

Beside the father and mother, there lived at this home Aunt Mary, the father's sister, a plump, stylishly dressed maiden of fifty, and the mother's mother, tall, snowy-haired, and quite imposing, as well as sweet and kindly. Joseph's sister, a lovely girl with violet eyes and the perfect family complexion, had come with us from New York, and the brother was away. After a day or two, however, an endless procession of relatives and friends from the neighboring town began to come calling on "Joey's wife," as they called the southern daughter-in-law.

Finding myself in surroundings so unfamiliar, I understood that I must not resent the attitude of suspended judgment, and the carefully feigned disinterest in all my former works and ways which was maintained by my husband's mother. I understood a good deal of it, by recalling my own family's reactions. I refused to hold it against her. What I could do was to find out all that I could about my husband's enormous family connection, and as people like to talk about themselves, this I succeeded in doing. I tried to behave discreetly, listen impersonally, ask the interested questions that bring detailed answers, and as they became more and more candid with me, I could piece out a good deal of the family history, like a new book of stories to me, which I wished to remember. The different relatives lost consciousness of my alien origin, and used little reserve in discussing their prejudices and preconceptions before me. Pretty outspoken, not at all complimentary, they were, in their opinions of my part of the country and its people, but, I reflected, not more disparaging than were my own people concerning the regions north. Chamberlain prejudices were like all such local beliefs, held because they had been repeatedly asserted, not because they had been reasoned out. The collection I made of them ran something like this.

"All southerners are lazy," principally because they did not work with their own hands and insist upon waiting upon themselves, but had Negro servants; and this I might acknowledge to be in part true, but again, they were "lazy because they were born so," and how could that be when they came of much the same mixture of racial stocks which had settled this country?

"Democrats are fond of whiskey, every single one of them," and when I remembered the dripping-wet political condition of the old home town, I could almost believe it. But up here, "The Irish are to blame for it," and back home there were no Irish to direct things to their minds, but politics got engineered in just the same direction, that is, to suit inside control! The difference seemed to be that here were two live parties in active struggle, and while this did not clear the air, it did stir and enliven its currents. For the rest, they repeated the same old assertions about Negroes (about whom they really cared nothing whatever!), with a smug gusto. "Southerners," said they, "never would get ahead financially," and this was true because "they will not pay the price of early rising, hard work, or strict economy, but want it all to come too easily." This was getting somewhat personal, and I felt it leveled rather obviously at my own head; so I kept still and looked innocent. I was not going to lose my temper, not yet. I recalled how the one note which had jarred in my early acquaintance with my husband had been hearing him plainly state how he hoped to get ahead in the world, how he intended as soon as possible to be making money. Perhaps we were simpletons, but in my experience I had never heard money-making set first in importance in such matter-of-fact fashion. Such subjects were politely disregarded in my own family. The people I knew might, if the possibility of making a fortune came before them, become as eager about it as he, but they would not say so beforehand.

I had been fond of criticizing my old town, as youngsters do; I did not believe they knew all things there which it was proper for people to do and think. He might be right after all—perhaps it would be better if everyone strove for independence, honestly won, before he did anything else. Poverty was not a virtue, though it seemed as if, to console ourselves for it, we chose to think so!

Now here was the other side of it. All in the way of honest enthusiasm, as a technician might discuss his methods, or intelligent bees rejoice over the harvest of honey they had hived, everybody was talking of making money, saving it, keeping it, but not a word of what they meant to do with it. I found it just the same when later I met Joseph's friends, and with some of them initiated lifelong friendships. There was one characteristic, not universal, but common to five-sixths of them, and this was their quality of convinced materialism.

I could hear my mother's voice saying to me, "It isn't money, we have to have that; it's the too great love of money which is the root of all evil."

I was beginning to estimate the necessity for some accumulation in my own country, for money well expended was the key to progress down South, and well I knew it, even though my home training had bred in me a prejudice against openly confessing the fact. I found the subject very puzzling.

It was Aunt Mary, Father Chamberlain's sister, who told me her parable of the Money Tree.

"We Chamberlains have growing on this farm," said she, "a money tree, and it is a handy thing always to go out and gather the fruit when you will. I tell my friends I will be glad to share it with them; I will give anyone a slip so that they may grow it for themselves. At the same time, I always warn them that if they fail on a single morning, even once, to water it before five o'clock, it will inevitably die. There's no other way to keep it alive, and so most people decide they do not want to bother with it on these conditions."

Servants were far from plentiful in this part of the United States. In the towns people of means kept Irish maids, and here and there on the farms some prosperous family had a "hired help," who sat at table with the rest, very much as if they had a tame duchess to do their cooking, must pay her accordingly, and treat her with all the consideration due her rank. My mother-in-law was a psychologist as well as an excellent manager. She had imported a stout German girl from Pennsylvania, who was a model of faithful industry. She did not overpay her and thus demoralize the labor market, but she did treat her as an important person, an indispensable member of the family. She consulted her and held her loyalty. The amount of work this woman could dispose of in one day was a marvel to me with my standards of accomplishment; but besides this, each and every woman of the family could step in beside her, if need arose, and work at any household task which was in progress. There was no talk of this one's business, or that one's proper work. Every household industry was a common interest, and Mother Chamberlain, like Solomon's famous housewife, looked well to the ways of her establishment. I, who liked doing things, found this admirable.

But the women of this family obviously did not enjoy in the least their ability to turn off work. They might tell how they had striven, but they took no joy in the striving. The summer had brought more visitors to the farm, and Mother Chamberlain had to keep urgently busy herself, while at the same time directing everything, and keeping in motion the varied industries of her establishment. She had equally to attend in person to the making of the butter. It was before the days of separators. A great dog did the churning by means of a geared treadmill. Then Mrs. Chamberlain would wash, salt, and pack tub after tub of butter, shipping it to regular customers and obtaining for it because of its excellence and reputation the highest price of the market. Haying and harvest had been going on all summer, with hungry hired men to be fed, and after this wonderful woman had followed all her other businesses, like her ancient prototype in Solomon's time she found opportunity to make garments for her family. Since the days of farm machinery had come to lighten the load of the mowing and reaping from the shoulders of the men, the farm woman had far the heavier share of the work. Father Chamberlain could sit and read his paper when he came in from the barn, but his wife must always be alert and masterful, awake to the instant need of things, with work in her hands for the few moments of sitting down. It all seemed to be an overwhelming burden to her, rather than the exciting game it might have been.

When I first came, I had taken from my trunk a pile of soiled and crumpled underthings, which I thoughtlessly "put in the wash," as I would have done at home. The German woman did them beautifully, but as I at once perceived it was an imposition upon her, burdened as she was. I begged Friend Husband to pay Lizzie for the work, but he said he would make her a substantial present in my behalf when we left, and talked to me about being more careful not to make so much extra work in the house. After that I was careful, doing the smaller articles, and finding that not half the changes of clothing were needed in that cool climate which would have been absolutely necessary in a southern summer.

My acquaintanceship with my husband's family grew more intimate, and quite accurately I appraised their opinions of me. My mother-in-law's cool impersonality was hard to penetrate. I did not feel that I could ever win her approval. It is strange how unreasoningly the opposition rises between mother-in-law and daughter-in-law, when they do need each other to make life successful, but it was thus, no doubt, with Mother Eve and Mrs. Cain.

One day toward the end of this summer, Mother Chamberlain said to me behind her hand,

"My dear, I hope you are not going to be in a hurry to supply this family with any babies right away."

"We have to take what is sent us, do we not?" I replied showing my astonishment.

"You southern women are imprudent, so I have heard, but you must see the need of giving Joe time to get his feet set on the ladder."

"Down South, everybody expects to have ten." I answered with spirit, "and I think that's just a nice size for a family!"

"No wonder, then, that you are all so poor," pursued my mother-in-law, meditatively. "Now I think you ought to be a little careful, considering that you brought no money with you, not to hamper your husband with too much family."

"Let him help it if he wants to," I cried, fairly aroused. "I'm not the one to say how many Chamberlains there'll be twenty years from now." And I swelled with indignation. This was indeed insufferable, but Mother Chamberlain did not seem to perceive that she had made me angry, nor to know that she herself had been too outspoken. She had merely said what she had meant to say and held her peace until the next time she felt like expressing her mind. There seemed no point in being sulky when nobody took the least notice whether you were sulky or not. I told Joe about this passage at arms, and he said, "Mother has worked so hard all her life that she knows all the trouble it means to raise a family. She was telling you what she thought it was for your good to know, even if she did it a little bluntly. She is a woman who can teach you a good many things."

I sniffed to myself after this and resolved to be careful how I tried to teach people things, in any such fashion! But if ever I gave any opinion about any practical matter in their hearing, they did not acknowledge that I knew anything at all.

One day I expressed a definite opinion about some matter of cookery. They all smiled around as one would smile indulgently at some prattling child. Mother Chamberlain asked if we kept a cook at our house. When I said, "Always," they all smiled round again to intimate that I did not know anything about cooking. I had set about preparing bed linen for going to housekeeping, and in making my sheets and pillowcases (for they had to be made at home in those days), I came into collision with my mother-in-law, who criticized my methods. I quoted my own mother's way of sewing them. Then Joseph's mother said, "You must be a pretty conceited girl, aren't you, Sis?"

"Nobody ever told me so before," I replied.

"Well, you really are, because you think you know so many things you know nothing about."

This was pretty blunt, and for a moment I did not know what answer to make. I flushed angrily and looked straight at my mother-in-law, but made no reply. It took all my self-control to do this, and I began to tell myself over again, that these were fundamentally kind people, able people, people merely doubtful about a case which seemed to them filled with future difficulty for the future of their eldest son.

Next the women of the family began a fashion of haranguing each other at length about the exact methods of accomplishing various household tasks. All this was, of course, leveled at my head, but I found a way to enjoy even this. At night I would lie awake thinking out foolish questions which might be interpolated in these lectures to convince them fully that I was either crazy or idiotic, and which might satisfy them that there was no use trying to teach me household methods or anything else. At the same time I pretended to be quite terrified of the big oil lamp in my bedroom. We had in fact used gas, and I knew little of oil lamps, but now I besought my husband to come up and light it for me, when I went to bed before he did. When he did this without protest, I next insisted on his buttoning up my high kid boots for me. He was very much in love with me, quite infatuated just then, but he balked at this.

"I do not mind," he said. "I would be glad to do it for you, but what would Mother say?"

By that I knew she had been talking to him, which was what I wished to find out.

The result of this silly game was serious, and it was all a mistake. In a long subsequent life of being serviceable to my husband's family, whom I came truly to regard and respect, I never overcame in them the impression of incapacity which in fun I had at first carefully built up. What I really accomplished was not credited to me, although I have never been one to shrink from complicated tasks. I think I was never considered by them quite regular, quite possessed of the real solid variety of common sense.

In August Joseph and I went ourselves on a round of visits. We felt like really sedate old married folk as we watched the newly-weds perform at Niagara Falls. We visited Cornell, Joe's Alma Mater, set high upon its hill, overlooking one of the lovely Finger Lakes. We met many of his friends, and I had to acknowledge that he had a great many and that they were interesting people, some of them important figures in the University community. Our last dissipation of this summer of intense experience, was a house party "down the Lake."

Near the Chamberlain farm, not a score of miles over the hills, lay one of those emerald lakes which dot the northwestern quarter of New York State. It was twenty miles or more long, lined throughout the loop of its shores with summer cottages bearing fanciful names. The hills sloped steeply back for several hundred feet, and from their base to the lake there was only a narrow beach occupied by these houses, and behind the houses, enough space only for a roadway encircling the whole. These hills with their precipitous sides and their sudden lift were one unbroken vineyard around the whole circuit of the lake. Here and there wine cellars were excavated into the cliff, buildings of stone with labyrinthine caves behind them, running under the hill, where champagne, as well as other still-wines, were blended and bottled. The entire country was given up to this industry.

Late in the summer the Chamberlain young people were invited to join a party which had taken a cottage halfway down this lake. Again came a new experience. My husband's sister, her fiancé, and a number of their intimate set were packed together in a cottage of the flimsiest description, perched over the water. We took our meals at the hotel near by, and they did their dancing in the evenings. All day we would be outdoors and on the water. In the evenings all constraint vanished; we sat on our porch and joked and sang and rollicked—a joyous party, full of the most spontaneous nonsense. Northern people had seemed to me stiffer in manner and colder in social contacts than they ought to be, but when this party lost their self-consciousness entirely and relaxed in wholesome fun, they seemed to me more delightfully jolly than any young folk I had ever known. The fortnight flew by like a day, and has been a lifelong pleasure to remember.

It was here that I learned about the wine. None was ever served anywhere, and although the whole country was in the business of making it, I was told this was a strictly prohibition county. The owner of a wine cellar would offer a glass to a visitor to drink, but would sell not less than a ten-gallon cask to one customer. I was taken through one of the largest of these wine cellars and given any number of vintages to taste. It was said that visitors did not become troublesome by coming often to these cellars, because it seems that wine was never a favorite intoxicating agent, and neither strong enough nor quick enough to please Americans. There was, however, excessive wine-drinking among the employees of these cellars, most of whom were from foreign wine-growing countries. These men soaked in it all the while and were seldom sober. Most of the champagne was transshipped to France to be relabeled there and returned to bring a higher price. But all we tasted of the flowing river was what our acquaintance, who was part owner of the wine cellar, gave us.

Never in all my long life as a member of the Chamberlain family have I personally experienced the winter slowing up of all kinds of work, nor enjoyed the pleasure folk used to find in the easy going about in sleighs. In one corner of the great barn were stored the various sleighs and "bobs" and the "cutters" they used in winter. Upon the wall behind them hung the well oiled harnesses with rows of bells attached. The size of the stoves in the homestead stood witness to the cold weather that was coming. Summer was but the embroidered border on the white winter garment of the year. And now in the last of August it was already growing cool. Mornings were snappy. A fire was made up for the grandmother each morning in her sitting room, and the family gathered before it there. The first of September came, and Joe and I must be flitting south. We wished to be in time to settle ourselves. We had no place to live selected, and could hear of none by any correspondence.

I packed my belongings, and at the last my mother-in-law turned very kind in a blunt way. She gave me many useful things for my house-plenishing, she came and helped me pack, and was pleased to approve of the way I did it.

My father-in-law I understood, so I thought, very well. He was a man who tried to be gruff, but did not succeed in convincing me, at least. He was my friend; no one could doubt his perfect sincerity. He had been a Forty-niner. It was delightful to hear him tell of his walk across the plains. He had brought gold back with him, nobody knew how much, but enough to give him a good start. His crotchets were his own, he was like nobody else, and he was what people call a real personality. Respected by his whole circle of associates, he too had his friends who were interesting as well as able. But there is no time to tell all.

My mother-in-law was a person who said to you exactly what came into her mind, and you must accept it. I hoped not to have to see too much of her, and yet I speculated about her and cared for her good opinion more than I acknowledged. I hoped to keep my husband from home for a while so that she could not remind him of my inadequacies. I also repented of my foolish joking, for this family could not take a humorous view of things. Life was "full of seriousness" for them.

And so the honeymoon summer was over, and we started southward. So far I had found my life with Joseph very good.

XXVIII

SOUTHWARDS, TOWARD HOME

As we were rolling southwards, I was thinking about it all, how well on the whole everything had turned out. I was happily married, with all my heart I affirmed that. I loved my Joseph. He was not perfect; he did care very intensely for money; he was crotchety about some things, but all men were that. He loved me and was kind to me, and if there was ever a subject about which I chose to be silent, he was never anxious to raise it. He was on the whole a reasonable person. At first I had been too eager to note his faults. I believed my own to be more evident; yet he did not seem to concern himself about them. He took them as part of my personality, in the way I meant hereafter to consider his. I could understand him far more intelligently, now that I had seen the manner of his upbringing. I had found a brand new set of conditions and persons and events about which to become interested. I did not care to have his people spell me too correctly, but how much I intended to speculate about them!

Taking the sleeper at Washington City, we slept until the next morning, when the motion of our car ceased and it was left behind on a siding. We dressed leisurely, in the familiar tepid atmosphere, and looked out upon the untidy edges of Raleigh. It was a sunny September morning; the sky was several shades bluer than anything I had seen in New England or New York. The open wounds of the land, the red clay banks and roadside ditches showed beyond the ragged weeds of the railroad yard. Tangles of passion-flower, masses of morning-glory vines drenched in heavy dew, draped the path beside the railroad embankment. Presently a darky came shambling along, and the picture was complete. I was at home, and home was the same as ever, humid, disorderly, but somehow soft and kindly to be returning to, and the whole tempo of life could now be slowed to a more leisurely measure.

Came the yard engine and jerked us violently down to the station. We had no settled place to live, because houses were so scarce in Raleigh, but until we could look about us we had a temporary haven. Joe had made fast friends with a charming old couple, Dr. and Mrs. Martin, who, though well-to-do people who did not have to take the trouble, had written him to bring me to their house, to board for the house-hunting interval. So we drove out westward that morning, past Saint Mary's School, along Hillsboro Road, one-half of whose unpaved red clay was torn up and piled at the side of a grading. How beautifully red my native soil looked that morning, dark from a recent rain! The Negro hack driver bragged about the "gra'big street cars" soon going to run out to the College, "wid wide tracks to run on, same's a real train track." And then we turned into a gate leading apparently nowhere. The Martins lived at the very back of a park of some acres. They were expecting us that morning. So we went in, to a new life, and I felt it good.